THE OAKWOOD PRESS

Trams and Buses of Poole

by
C.G. Roberts MCIT, MILT
and
B.L. Jackson

THE OAKWOOD PRESS

© Oakwood Press, C.G. Roberts & B.L. Jackson 2001

British Library Cataloguing in Publication Data
A Record for this book is available from the British Library
ISBN 0 85361 572 1

Typeset by Oakwood Graphics.
Repro by Ford Graphics, Ringwood, Hants.
Printed by Inkon Printers Ltd, Yateley, Hants.

Poole & District car No. 4 awaits departure from the loop in Upper High Street with a County Gates-bound tram. The obstruction to the driver's vision by the reversed staircase is clearly demonstrated, the ladies seated on the upper deck have their parasols up to protect them from the summer sun in this quintessential Edwardian scene.
Andrew Hawkes Collection

Title page: Photographed standing spare in Kingland Crescent bus station is Bristol K6A No. 1177 (TD 885) (HLJ 34) new in December 1948 and delivered direct to London Transport where it ran from Barking garage until March 1950. The five bay construction ECW L27/28R body was typical of the period, three destination boxes being fitted, as shown in the photograph the one over the platform was subsequently painted over. No. 1177 was withdrawn from service in August 1965. Today only the buildings in the background remain as a reminder of the old bus station. *Photobus/Turner*

Front cover, top: A scale model, built by Roy Wright, of Poole & District tramcar No. 6 showing the company's livery. *R.A. Wright*

Front cover, bottom: No. 1295 (KRU 961) a 1951 Bristol KSW6B with an ECW L27/28R body, renumbered in 1971 as 1358. Withdrawn the following year and acquired by the late Jim Maddison for preservation. *D.M. Habgood*

Published by The Oakwood Press (Usk), P.O. Box 13, Usk, Mon., NP15 1YS.
E-mail: oakwood-press@dial.pipex.com
Website: www.oakwood-press.dial.pipex.com

Contents

County Gates, much mentioned in the history of local trams and buses, contemporary saloon cars of the period wait at the traffic lights in this pre-war scene. A Hants & Dorset Leyland double-deck is just about to cross out of Bournemouth into Poole, Westbourne Congregational church has now been demolished and other works have today completely changed the scene.
Ian Andrews Collection

Introduction

The year 2001 sees the centenary of the introduction of trams in the Borough of Poole and this book sets out a history of road passenger transport in the town and its links with neighbouring Bournemouth.

The development of both tram and bus services in Poole is inextricably involved with those of Bournemouth. Less than 200 years ago Bournemouth did not exist, the two principal towns in the area being Christchurch to the east, and Poole to the west. Between the two lay a stretch of land known as 'The Liberty of Westover', with Wallis Down to the north and Canford Heath to the west, the area consisting of heath land with a few scattered hamlets.

In 1836 Sir George Gervis commenced to develop a seaside village around the mouth of the Bourne stream, thus Bournemouth was born. It rapidly became a modern development of the Victorian era, the Bournemouth Commissioners being formed in 1856 to administer it, with jurisdiction over a one mile radius from a point where the Pavilion Theatre now stands. By 1860 the population was 1,700, and a municipal borough was formed in 1890 when over 37,600 persons lived in the expanded township. It became a County Borough in 1900 with a population of nearly 60,000. By the outbreak of World War II the ever-expanding borough was home to almost 144,500 people.

Bournemouth and Poole are as different as chalk and cheese, the former a modern Victorian and Edwardian development, and the latter is an old established seaport, which has developed enormously in the past 50 years. There had been both Roman and Saxon settlements on the site, although no mention of Poole appears in the Doomesday Book. By 1148 there was a recorded settlement, when the seamen and traders of Wareham decided to move to the site, owing to the silting up of the River Frome. In 1248 the Borough was incorporated, and by 1568 it had a population of 1,573.

From the reign of Elizabeth I until the mid-19th century Poole had a lucrative trade with America and Newfoundland, and later the clay and timber trades created additional business together with other coastal traffic. Unfortunately, until recent years the lack of deep water in the harbour had restricted the size of visiting vessels.

Old Poole, with its Queen Anne and Georgian houses, was mainly situated seaward of the railway crossings of the 1870s, Longfleet and Parkstone being separate communities. By the late 19th century, as at neighbouring Bournemouth, rapid expansion had taken place, with the development of available land in the Parkstone and Branksome areas, Branksome becoming part of the Borough of Poole in 1905. In 1930 there had been plans for the Ford Motor Company to establish a factory at Hamworthy, but Dagenham became the preferred site. Following the war many factories opened in the Poole area, a process that has continued up to the present day, resulting in large industrial estates on the outskirts of the town.

Apart from stage-coaches, the earliest passenger transport in Poole was the railway. On 1st June, 1847 the Southampton & Dorchester Railway opened from a junction with the Southampton & London Railway at Northam, the new line running via Blechynden (today's Southampton Central station), Millbrook, Redbridge, Totton, Lyndhurst Road, Beaulieu Road, Brockenhurst, Christchurch Road (later renamed Holmsley), Ringwood, Wimborne and Broadstone, with a branch to Hamworthy (later known as Hamworthy Goods) to serve the adjacent town of Poole across the harbour bridge. Within a short while the line became part of the London & South Western Railway (LSWR).

A further link in the railway system was the opening of the LSWR line between Broadstone and a new station in Poole on 2nd December, 1872, this being extended to Bournemouth West via Parkstone and Branksome on 15th June, 1874. This allowed the through running of Somerset & Dorset trains, in later years including many in the summer months from the Midlands and North bringing holidaymakers to the area. With further railway development Poole and Bournemouth West were linked directly to Brockenhurst via Bournemouth, Boscombe, Pokesdown, Christchurch, Hinton Admiral, New Milton and Sway from March 1888. The opening of the Holes Bay Curve in June 1893 between Poole and Hamworthy Junction completed the final link in a direct Weymouth-Waterloo line via Poole and Bournemouth, after which the Hamworthy Junction to Brockenhurst line via Wimborne and Ringwood declined into a secondary route.

There is evidence of a Poole to Bournemouth horse bus service operating in 1856, and it is also known that at one time there was a horse bus service between Christchurch and Poole, but little more is known of horse bus services in Poole itself.

A regular bus service operated from the Bath Hotel, Bournemouth (re-named Royal Bath Hotel in 1880) to Poole station - this being one of two stations which were regarded as being the nearest to the then new resort of Bournemouth. An old edition of *Bright's Guide* to Bournemouth explains that there was a horse bus service from Bournemouth to the London Hotel, Poole to connect with trains. A regular operator on this route was Mr Francis Graham (grandfather of Mr W.W. Graham, the founder of Hants & Dorset Motor Services Ltd) who was later to abandon this route to concentrate on operating between Bournemouth and Christchurch Road, which was the other station regarded as being a railhead for passengers travelling to and from Bournemouth.

An early provider of horse buses in the Bournemouth area was Mr T. Elliott (founder of Royal Blue Express Services). At this stage it should be mentioned that 'Royal Blue' and Hants & Dorset were later to form part of the National Bus Company (NBC). Royal Blue Express Services was later to form part of National Travel (South West) Ltd and following further re-organisation in NBC, came under the wing of Hants & Dorset from May 1981, and later still 'Royal Blue' became part of the now defunct 'Shamrock & Rambler'. Sadly, 'Royal Blue' and Hants & Dorset have disappeared as the result of various re-organisations within the bus industry.

It is against this background that the local transport system developed. When the first trams travelled between Poole and County Gates in April 1901 the motor vehicle was very much in its infancy. Looked upon as something of a novelty, and certainly unreliable, it was no match for the electric tram, then by far the superior method of moving people within a town. It was also at that time a matter of civic pride for every respectable town to have a tramway system, be it either municipally or privately operated.

Poole was the only town in Dorset to take the steps to instigate a system, although Weymouth gave the matter consideration for a number of years before the scheme was abandoned following the arrival of the Great Western Railway motor buses.

Six Poole & District trams lined up in Ashley Road in July 1904. The occasion being the St John's Church Sunday school outing to Poole Park. *Ian Andrews Collection*

As at many other towns the Poole trams became entwined in Town Hall politics, and within a short while it became the 'Withered Arm' of the Bournemouth system. Ironically the first public motorbuses (motorised wagonettes) had commenced to run in the eastern suburbs of Poole during 1899, two years before the tram. It took World War I and the perfection of the motor vehicle to make it a worthy substitute for the tram, and within a few years it was taking over with a vengeance!

Whereas Bournemouth switched from tram to trolleybus, Poole did not, the motor buses of Hants & Dorset taking over and rapidly expanding their operations. The story of the company's expansion from small beginnings has already been well recorded, but they were handicapped in most principal towns they served, such as Bournemouth, Southampton, Winchester, and Gosport, where municipal and other operators deprived them the operation of the lucrative town services. At Poole they were (with the exception of one route) the sole town service operator; indeed for many years Poole was the only Dorset depot in the Hants & Dorset empire. Today, trading as the reformed Wilts & Dorset, it has become their principal depot. The old Wilts & Dorset never had a depot in the county until Blandford opened in 1940!

Since de-regulation the bus industry has seen many changes, some too complex to describe fully in this book. When the first tram ran between Poole and County Gates, the country was still mourning the recent death of Queen Victoria, and much has changed in that hundred years. Bus services reached their peak about 50 years ago, and have since declined as private motoring became within the reach of many. However, the development of the Poole and Bournemouth conurbation was greatly assisted by the tram and motor bus, the subjects of this book.

Chapter One

Early Tramway Proposals

The development of tramways in Poole was closely bound up with those of Bournemouth and Christchurch as will be seen.

The first proposal for the establishment of tramways in Poole was made when Mr W. Mate presided over a meeting at The London Hotel, Poole in November 1881 in support of a scheme for a route from Bournemouth East station to Poole via Bournemouth, which a firm of London engineers was submitting to the local authorities of Bournemouth and Poole. Nothing came of this scheme, nor did a further scheme initiated some four years later and for which the date of starting construction was postponed again and again, and after a long period the promoters withdrew their deposit which they had lodged with the Board of Trade. It should be added that at this time the authorities at Bournemouth were against the introduction of tramways in that town.

The anti-tram attitude of the Bournemouth Commissioners (then the local authority for Bournemouth) was particularly evident in the case of the Poole & Bournemouth Tramways Order 1890. This Order was confirmed by The Tramways Order Confirmation No. 2 Act 1890, which authorised the promoters - Messrs J.W. & J.E. Haynes (William and Josiah Edward Haynes) of 81 Gracechurch Street, London to construct the following tramways.

Tramway 1. Poole station (Towngate Street - with a short extension into the railway goods yard) along Parkstone Road, North Road, 'proposed New Road' (Springfield Road), and Constitution Hill Road West to Sea View Hotel. There was also to be a short siding in Sea View Road, and a triangular junction at Sea View Hotel;
Tramway 2. Sea View Hotel, along Ashley Road and Poole Road to County Gates;
Tramway 3. County Gates to (Bournemouth) top of Poole Hill.

The Bournemouth Commissioners lodged an objection (dated 14th January, 1890) containing 22 clauses. Various extensions of time were sought and granted, the last being at a meeting of Poole Town Council on 26th October, 1894 when it was agreed that the time for commencement of construction be extended for a period of 12 months from 4th August, 1894 provided a sufficient guarantee was given that work would be commenced on 1st February, 1895 and started from the Poole end of the line. The tramway from County Gates to the top of Poole Hill could not be constructed without the consent of Bournemouth Council. These lines were never built mainly due to the objections of Bournemouth Council. Mention should be made of an application by Messrs Harrison and Robinson on behalf of the promoters to a Poole Council meeting on 28th July, 1890 for sanction for a branch line from the main line to Poole Head (this location being the seaward end of Shore Road at Sandbanks). The Council decided to withhold their permission until such time as the main line had been completed.

The British Electric Traction Group came into existence to construct a countrywide system of electric tramways, commencing an energetic propaganda campaign on the subject. It was the brainchild of a naturalised Englishman, Emile Garcke born in Germany during 1856, who in 1883 became the Secretary of the Brush Electrical Engineering Company. By the end of 1895 he had formulated plans to achieve his aim, the British Electric Traction Company (BET) being registered on 26th October, 1896. By the turn of the century almost 40 tramway undertakings were either operational or under construction within the group, progress having been assisted by the Light Railway Act of 1896.

Public opinion was very much divided as to the desirability of tramways. Bournemouth Town Council was still against the idea and Dorset County Council would not consent to tramways being constructed in Poole, Bournemouth or Christchurch - odd, as only Poole was then in Dorset!

The following tramway schemes were being considered by Poole Council in 1897:

New General Traction Co. - Poole, Bournemouth, Boscombe, Pokesdown, Southbourne, Tuckton Bridge to Christchurch with branch lines;
British Electric Traction Co. - Poole, Parkstone, Westbourne, Bournemouth, Boscombe, Pokesdown, Iford, Christchurch with a probable extension to Purewell; and
Bournemouth, Poole & District Light Railways (Electric) - Poole to Christchurch with a branch from Constitution Hill (Sea View Hotel) to Branksome (Pottery Junction).

Draft Orders were prepared by the promoters mentioned above, although one of these was described as General Electric Traction Co. (presumably New General Traction Co.), but only two were pursued, and these were:

a) British Electric Traction Co. - Christchurch, Bournemouth & Poole Light Railways Order 1898: Railways 1/2/2A/2B/3/3A/3B/4/6/7/8 related to proposed lines in Bournemouth and Christchurch.
Railway 4A Bournemouth Square - Triangle (west end, junc. with Poole Hill) via Avenue Road;
Railway 4B Bournemouth Square - Triangle (west end, junc. with Poole Hill via Commercial Road;
Railway 5 - Triangle (junc. with Poole Hill) to Poole (junc. High Street and Towngate Street) via Poole Road, Lower Parkstone, Parkstone Road;
Railway 5A - Junction with Railway 5 at Poole High Street along Towngate Street to level crossing at Towngate Street, Poole;
Railway 5B - Junction with Railway 5 at Poole High Street along High Street to level crossing in High Street.
b) Bournemouth, Poole & District Light Railways (Electric) Co. Ltd Order 1898:
Railway 1 - Poole (High Street junc. with Mount Street) to (Bournemouth) top of Poole Hill (junc. with Commercial Road) via Parkstone Road, Lower Parkstone, Branksome, Poole Road;
Railway 2 - Constitution Hill (Sea View Hotel) to Branksome (Pottery Junction) via Ashley Road (Upper Parkstone);
Railway 3 - Top of Poole Hill (junc. with Commercial Road) via south side of the Triangle and Commercial Road to Bournemouth Square;
Railway 4 - Top of Poole Hill (junc. with Commercial Road) to Square via Commercial Road direct;
Railways 5/6/7/8/9 were proposed lines in Bournemouth.

The Light Railway Commissioners held a local inquiry in February 1898 and these schemes were rejected mainly due to the objections of Bournemouth Council and residents along the proposed routes. One report stated that Poole objected to the Bournemouth, Poole & District Light Railways (Electric) proposal on the grounds that the tramway would carry people from Branksome, then an independent local authority, to Bournemouth. However, the promoters were not deterred and announced that they intended to apply for powers for modified schemes.

Modified schemes were submitted to the Light Railway Commissioners in May 1898 and all were to be electrically powered with a gauge of 3 feet 6 inches. The BET promoted two schemes: The Christchurch, Bournemouth & Winton Light Railway - which as its title implies was for lines in those areas - and The Poole & District Light Railways which was for the following lines:

Railway 1 - Poole Quay (junc. Poole High Street with Salisbury Street) - Poole High Street (junc. with Towngate Street - west end);

1A - From junction with Railway 1B at Poole High Street (junc. with Towngate Street) to level crossing in Towngate Street (with spur to Poole Station);

1B - From end on junction with Railway 1 (Poole High Street) to junction with Railway 1A at Poole High Street (junc. with Towngate Street - east end);

2 - From Poole High Street (junc. Towngate Street - east end) to Park Gates East via Parkstone Road;

3 - Park Gates East - Branksome (Poole Road, Pottery Junction) via Commercial Road, Lower Parkstone, Bournemouth Road;

4 - Park Gates East - Branksome (Pottery Junction) via North Road, Upper Parkstone, Ashley Road;

5 - Branksome (Pottery Junction) - County Gates via Poole Road;

6 - County Gates - (Bournemouth) top of Poole Hill (Pembroke Hotel) via Poole Road.

It should be noted that Railways 1 and 1B were shown on the Deposited Plans but not in the Draft Order. Bournemouth, Poole & District Light Railways (Electric) proposed the following:

Railway 1 - Poole (High Street junc. with Mount Street) - Park Gates East via High Street, Parkstone Road;

2 - Park Gates East - Branksome (Pottery Junction, Poole Road) via Commercial Road, Lower Parkstone, Bournemouth Road;

3 - Park Gates East - Branksome (Pottery Junction) via North Road, Upper Parkstone, Ashley Road;

4 - Branksome (Pottery Junction) - Bournemouth (Triangle, north side) via Poole Road, Queen's Road, Suffolk Road.

The Light Railway Commissioners held a second Inquiry in June 1898 at Bournemouth, where The Christchurch, Bournemouth & Winton Light Railway and Bournemouth Poole & District Light Railways (Electric) schemes were rejected. It should be noted that although the last named scheme had been examined by the Inquiry, the promoters had decided not to proceed with their application so far as it related to lines within the Borough of Bournemouth. However, the Poole & District scheme was approved in part. The Light Railway Commissioners' attitude at this time was that they could see no reason why part

of the area outside the Borough of Bournemouth should be deprived of the
benefit of tramways. Bournemouth still maintained its objection to tramways so
far as these latest schemes were concerned. In July 1898 the Light Railway
Commissioners informed the promoters that they were not prepared to
overrule the objections of Bournemouth (as stated by them at the February
Inquiry) and that it would be useless for the promoters to proceed with that part
of their applications which related to lines within the Borough of Bournemouth.

Construction and Opening

Following the Light Railway Commissioners' Inquiry, the BET prepared a
Draft Order for two routes consisting of Railways 1A, 2, 3, 4 and 5 of the May
1898 application; i.e. Poole Station to County Gates via Parkstone Road, Park
Gates East, North Road, Upper Parkstone; and Park Gates East to Branksome
(Pottery Junction) via Lower Parkstone. In July 1899, the Board of Trade
announced their intention of granting the Order of the Light Railway
Commissioners, and the Order (The Poole & District Light Railways Order
1899) was finally made on 17th August, 1899 authorising the construction of a
line from Poole Station to County Gates via Upper Parkstone, but not the line
via Lower Parkstone. The BET formed a company, namely The Poole & District
Electric Traction Co. Ltd which was registered on 5th April, 1899, with a capital
of £100,000. The Directors were E. Garcke, J.S. Raworth, C.S. Drummond, F.
Chanter, Wm Murphy, and E.F. Vesey Knox. The offices of the company were
at Donington House, Norfolk Street, London, WC and the first Board meeting
was held on the 9th May, Mr E. Hopwood being appointed Secretary.

Materials for the construction of the line had arrived by late April 1900, rails
and heaps of stone 'setts' being placed alongside the roads in various places
ready for the work to commence. As construction had been delayed the Board
of Trade granted an extension of time until 17th May. Work actually started on
Monday 7th May along the Parkstone Road, outside the middle entrance to
Poole Park, 25 to 30 men working under the direction of the resident engineer,
Mr W.J. Gale. It was hoped that the labour force would shortly be increased to
150 men as the work progressed.

Negotiations were proceeding to purchase land from the Retreat Estate for
the construction of a depot in Ashley Road, Upper Parkstone, and by May 1900
the capital subscribed was 407 ordinary shares at £10 each. Later in the summer
Mr F.W. Chanter had been requested by the Board to act as Engineer on behalf
of the company during the construction of the permanent way. On 11th
November *Tramway & Railway World* reported that good progress had been
made during the past few months with the tramway construction, and the
roadway would be paved with Australian hardwood. By November, Mr T.
Bawden-Provis had become Secretary, and delay in the delivery of paving setts
had been alleviated as satisfactory shipping arrangements had been made for
immediate delivery. It was reported that 3 miles 7.6 chains of line had been
completed and just over three furlongs were under construction, and the
overhead equipment was also being proceeded with, whilst plans for the tram

shed were being prepared. It was also reported that progress had been greatly impeded during the past month owing to the exceptionally wet weather. But all the turnouts had been laid, and only a few short lengths of single track remained to be completed, and it was hoped that the trams would be delivered about the middle of December. The financial situation improved, as £22,070 had been subscribed up to the end of the year.

Surviving records clearly show that tools and other equipment were transferred between BET companies. During construction various quantities of permanent way and overhead fittings, and a 250 gallon two-wheeled water cart were transferred from the Dudley & Wolverhampton system. Merthyr sent 40 shovels and 10 wheelbarrows, and a considerable amount of tools arrived from the Kinver Light Railway.

Likewise, on completion of the work, various tools were sent to the Bideford & Westward Ho! Light Railway, and the Merthyr system, the latter also receiving 7,680 assorted wood blocks, the cost of which was £85 4s. 4d.including railway cartage.

Mr E.H. Mottram, traffic superintendent, and Mr E.L. Ingram, power superintendent, commenced their duties on 1st January, 1901, it being reported that the permanent way except for the entrance to the depot at Retreat was complete. A short length of tarmacadam which remained to be completed was then being laid. The car shed was also in course of erection.

With construction well advanced by the end of January 1901, the arrival in mid-February of three or four of the tram cars at Poole railway station created much interest. They were reported as being stored there on the 21st of the month. Seven trams had been delivered by the following month, and trial trips were conducted over the system on Sunday and Monday 17th and 18th of March. All was then ready for the Board of Trade inspection by Major Pringle on Wednesday 20th March. Having travelled the entire length of the line and carried out a thorough inspection of the general arrangements he passed the line fit for opening.

However, there appears to have been a slight difference of opinion between the tramway company and the council over the completed work. The council sub-committee appointed to meet the Inspector on the occasion of the inspection pointed out several objections that the council had made to the manner in which the tramway was laid, the Inspector promising to give attention to these objections. The sight and sound of trams soon became familiar to residents living near the line as they began running empty for crew training purposes.

It was proposed to open the line for public use on Good Friday, however the anticipated Board of Trade certificate failed to arrive until the Saturday morning, thus Dorset's first and only tram system opened rather hurriedly on Saturday 6th April, 1901. There was no ceremony to mark the occasion such was the rush to commence the service, and in consequence the local press report was rather subdued:

During the course of the morning the first tram left the terminus near the Poole railway station, full of passengers. There was no public ceremony connected with the opening

Poole & District car No. 11 posed for the camera in Parkstone Road alongside Poole Park during a trial run before the opening of the system in April 1901. The bowler-hatted gentleman at the controls appears to be Mr C. H. Mottram the Poole & District Traction Company Manager.

R.A. Wright Collection

Poole & District car No. 2 stands in the loop in Upper High Street awaiting departure for County Gates. The buildings to the left of the tram have been replaced by Keel House.

B.L. Jackson Collection

The conductor of Poole & District car No. 2 poses for the camera at County Gates before departing for Poole. Note the trellis gates closed at the driver's end to prevent passengers boarding and alighting on the off side.

R.A. Wright Collection

A superb view of Poole & District car No. 4 in Ashley Road, Parkstone. Clearly showing the detail of the Milnes body and the Brill 21E truck. Notice small detail such as the intricate lining of the corners of the lower panels, to the right of the conductor, the 'wheel and magnet' symbol, platform detail with sliding doors into the lower saloon, and the driver standing in characteristic pose with his right hand on the controller, and left hand on the brake. *C.G. Roberts*

of the service, but it nevertheless marks an important epoch in local history, and shows the development of the district, which between Poole and Bournemouth has grown with such marvellous rapidity.

In consequence as we are informed, on having to provide an additional brake to the cars which are used between Constitution Hill and Poole, because of the steepness of the gradient, the company was somewhat handicapped. They could only fix one car with the additional brake, and whilst five or six were running between the County Gates and Heatherlands, only one car could be utilised for the journey from there on to Poole. Passengers when they arrived at Heatherlands had to be transferred to the other car, and needless to say this proved very inconvenient, but the delay will soon be rectified.

The trams ran on Sunday and a large number of persons availed themselves of the opportunity to travel on the electric cars. The traffic over the Easter holidays was very considerable, and the Directors of the Company have no reason to complain of the patronage bestowed.

The original advertised service stated:

The trams will start at 6.20 am from each end of the system, and the journey time will take about 25 minutes. There will be a 25 minute service for work people until 7.8 am from Poole, and 6.56 am from the County Gates terminus, after that time a twelve minute service will be maintained throughout the day. The last car at night will leave County Gates at 10.30 pm except on Wednesdays and Saturdays, when the last car will depart at 11.20 pm. On Sundays there will be a service of trams from Poole to County Gates at 9.56 am and continuing at intervals of twenty-four minutes until 1.56 pm. For the remainder of the day, there will be a twelve minute service until 10.8 pm.

Even before the tramway opened the proposed Sunday service brought forth protests, a petition signed by the clergy and many townspeople being presented to the Council.

We the undersigned beg to call your attention to the proposal of the Electric Tramway Company to run their cars on the Lord's day. This in our opinion will entail unnecessary labour for the men, and will add one more to the temptation already presented to the youth of our town for facilitating the desecration of the Sabbath and will thus involve great moral loss to them and the public generally. On these grounds we earnestly petition you to use your powerful influence to discountenance the intentions of the company in this respect.

At a council meeting Councillor Hawkes asked under what powers or agreement the Electric Tramway Company were enabled to run so frequent a service of Sunday trams. The Town Clerk replied that he had examined the order granted to the Poole & District Light Railway Company, and he could find nothing in it which prevented the Tramway Company from running cars on Sundays. In fact, by implication, the order gave it express power to do so.

Sunday problems aside, the trams were proving very popular and far more flexible than travelling by train between Poole, Parkstone, and Branksome. Local traders were also pleased with the service, some offering inducements to customers. A local press advert made the following offer:

CHEAP RETURN TICKETS FOR THE TRAMS - on paying a visit to the branch establishment of J.E. Tydeman, at 2 Ashley Terrace, Upper Parkstone, customers

Poole & District car No. 5 with an attentive audience stands in the loop in Upper High Street, the trolley pole appears to have left the wire and shot 'skywards'! The original junction with Kingland Road is visible alongside King's cycle shop on the right. *Below,* tram No. 17 runs out of the lower end of the passing loop towards the Poole terminus whilst on the left tram No. 5 departs towards County Gates.   *(Both) R.A. Wright Collection*

spending 10s. and upwards receive their return tram fare. A well selected stock of boots and shoes, Men's and Boy's clothing to select from.

To celebrate the success of the venture the Directors entertained a representative body of the local authorities to dinner on 22nd May at the Grand Hotel, Bournemouth, to celebrate the opening of the Poole & District Light Railway, and the inauguration of the work in connection with the Christchurch and Bournemouth Tramways. The *Monthly Gazette* - a confidential paper issued to the officers of the BET and associated companies - reported in May that the results of traffic were very satisfactory, with seven trams in operation, details of the staff employed at the time being given as clerks, 2; foreman/inspectors, 2; drivers, conductors and brakesmen, 24; fitters, carpenters, 3; car washers and labourers, 2; linesman, 1. Total 34. By June the fleet had been expanded to 11 cars, 10 being required to operate the service, and the staff increased to 51.

Owing to the nature of the beast it was not long before a tram was involved in an accident, a matter that was to draw attention from the press. On 13th June a collision took place at Brown Bottom Corner (near the Sloop Inn) between a Poole-bound tram and a landau containing four ladies heading towards Bournemouth, the ladies being thrown out onto the road. The accident immediately brought forth demands for road improvements!

Financial matters were to occupy the remainder of the year. The overseers of the parishes of Parkstone, Branksome, and Longfleet assessed the company at the rate of £306 per mile of track, but the Secretary showed cause before them, and it was reduced to £120 per mile of track. Five more trams were ordered, this time from Brush of Loughborough. At the November Board meeting of the BET a Prospectus for the issue of 2,793 ordinary shares of £10 each of the Poole company at the price of £11 per share was submitted and the Board decided to apply for 1,500 such shares.

By the end of the year 1,558,784 passengers had been carried over the system, although inclement weather had affected receipts towards the end of the year, the returns had exceeded expectations. The total revenue from the opening on 6th April, 1901 to 31st December, 1901 amounted to £10,738 14s. 5d., and the total expenditure £5,116 0s. 9d., leaving a net profit of £5,622 13s. 8d. After charging £1,439 5s. 5d. for interest on advances the sum of £4,183 8s. 3d. was available, which was disposed of as follows.

	£	s.	d.
Depreciation and Reserve Fund.	1,000	0	0
(This amount added to the premium on 2,793 shares issued in November 1901, now amounts to £3,253 13s. 2d.)			
Dividend at the rate of 6%, per annum, in terms of prospectus	1,396	7	10
to be carried forward	1,787	0	5
Total	4,183	8	3

Poole & District car No. 7 has just passed Pottery Junction heading towards Poole. At the time this photograph was taken the Lower Parkstone line had not been constructed, it later joined the existing line from the right-hand middle of this photograph. In the background the road rises to cross the railway at Branksome station. Today this section of road consists of several roundabouts, and the Bourne Valley Pottery is now the site of a trading estate.   *C.G. Roberts*

Poole & District car No. 6 on the right about to pass another car thought to be No. 7 on Constitution Hill in the loop near the junction of St Peter's Road.   *R.A. Wright Collection*

In February 1902 Poole Council passed a resolution in favour of the Poole & District Light Railway extension order. Despite the overtones of plans for extensions and a threatened take-over by Bournemouth Corporation the financial health of the company was good. During 1902 2,121,328 passengers were carried and the vehicles travelled 330,194 miles. The total revenue for the year ending 31st December was £13,601 13s. 3d. and the total expenditure, including £258 17s. 8d. for loan interest, was £9,429 7s. 2d. leaving a net profit of £4,172 6s. 1d. With £1,787 0s. 5d. brought forward from the last account this made £5,959 6s. 6d. available for distribution. This amount was applied as follows: depreciation and reserve fund £1,000 (bringing the fund up to £4,253 13s. 2d.); dividend at the rate of 8 per cent, per annum £4,000; carried forward £959 6s. 6d. A glance at the BET Gazette reveals that R.P. Simpson had become Secretary, and the company was moving into the modern world with the installation of a telephone (Parkstone 15), its telegraphic address for telegrams being 'Tramways Parkstone'.

Receipts improved during 1903, 2,428,212 passengers being carried with a total income of £15,661 14s. 6d. Total expenditure amounted to £9,993 0s. 1d. leaving a profit of £5,668 14s. 5d. to which was added £959 6s. 6d. brought forward from last year's account, making a total of £6,628 0s. 11d. available for distribution, which was applied as follows: depreciation and reserve fund £1,000 (bringing this fund up to £5,253 13s. 2d.); dividend at the rate of 10 per cent per annum, £5,000; £628 0s. 1d. carried forward to the next account.

During the latter part of 1903 R.P. Simpson relinquished his position as both Secretary of the Poole company and the Auckland Electric Tramways Company, having been appointed a Director of both companies, his position at Poole being taken by A.B. Grindley.

Despite the uncertain future of the company operations in Poole, the August Bank Holiday of 1904 was a record one as regards traffic receipts, the amount taken being £168 15s. 4d. This worked out at 25.47d. per car mile. During the year 2,474,336 passengers travelled, although there was no significant increase in the total yearly revenue, the receipts amounting to £15,673 18s. Expenses including £461 3s. 3d. for loan interest amounted to £10,791 19s. 7d., leaving a profit of £4,881 18s. 5d. to which had been added £628 0s. 11d. brought forward from the last account to make a total of £5,509 19s. 4d. available for distribution. A dividend at the rate of 10 per cent for the year absorbed £5,000 and the balance of £509 19s. 4d. had been carried forward.

The Chairman reported at the Annual General meeting that 'although the traffic receipts are a little in excess of those for the preceding year, they have carried 46,124 more passengers, but whilst more passengers travelled over short distances there was a marked falling off of the numbers who travelled the whole distance between Poole and Bournemouth' (at that time the terminus being County Gates). The decline in patronage was blamed on the fact that visitors to Bournemouth had been fewer than usual, and that Bournemouth Corporation Tramways had been offering additional routes to visitors who travel by tramcar for pleasure. This statement was supported by the number of lower fare tickets sold compared with the previous year.

Year	1d. fare	2d. fare	3d. fare	Total
1903	1,519,798	516,278	392,136	2,428,212
1904	1,576,120	529,267	368,949	2,474,336

Poole & District car No. 8 has just arrived in the loop outside the 'Dolphin' public house. The gentleman riding his cycle keeping well clear, in days past tramlines were the curse of cyclists, no doubt King's cycle depot made a lucrative living repairing bent cycle wheels for of those unfortunate enough to come a cropper on the tramlines! *R.A Wright*

Poole & District car No. 9 leaves the loop in Upper High Street on the final single line section to the Poole terminus in Towngate Street. In this scene the driver is wearing a 'straw boater' this was summer issue to tram crews, although the stifling high collar jacket was still *de rigueur*. To the right a horse and cart are turning out of Kingland Road. *Andrew Hawkes Collection*

The final year of the Poole company commenced with the annual dinner of the employees, which took place at Branksome on 5th January, 1905. It started at midnight to allow late shift staff to attend. Amongst the 60 people present was the Mayor of Poole, who gave the toast 'The Poole & District Traction Company Ltd', adding that all felt inclined to weep because the subject of the toast was about to die (*see Chapter Two*).

Councillor James said that but for the company, Bournemouth would not yet possess trams, the Mayor then presented Mr Mottram, the General Manager, with a clock on behalf of the employees. In his reply Mottram stated that the trams had run over 400,000 miles, and had not cost the company £10 for accidents.

Mr Mottram had proved to be a popular, well respected manager with the Poole undertaking, having received three previous testimonials from the employees and also from Poole Borough Council and Branksome District Council testifying to the excellent way the lines had been worked. In 1902 he won the first BET prize for an essay on the organisation of traffic in a competition open to its managers and engineers.

Poole & District car No. 10 and crew pose at County Gates before returning to Poole, although the side destination board reads 'Bournemouth' the actual terminus was at that time a few feet short of the boundary. Other details include the trolley mast being off set to the near side of the upper deck, the brackets above the fleet number on the front dash are to support the oil headlight, and the absence of a ticket punch to compliment the cash bag worn by the conductor, the Poole company using a hand-held pistol punch. *R.A. Wright Collection*

Local children pose for the cameraman as Poole & District trams pass at the loop situated in Parkstone Road, Poole. *Andrew Hawkes Collection*

Poole & District car No. 11 departing from Upper High Street, Poole, towards Parkstone Road. In the background is the old toll house at the junction of Wimborne Road which curves away to the left behind the tram, the Longfleet Cigar Store, foreground, is now the site of Keel House. *Andrew Hawkes Collection*

Chapter Two

Other Schemes and the Take-over

In November 1899 The Poole & District Electric Traction Co. Ltd gave notice of its intention to promote a Bill in Parliament to authorise it to construct certain tramways within and outside the Borough of Bournemouth. The original title of this Bill was 'The Christchurch, Bournemouth & Winton Tramways' and powers were sought for lines in the areas suggested by the title. Bournemouth Council, already noted for its anti-tramway attitude, had a change of mind and applied to the Board of Trade for a Provisional Order under the Tramways Act 1870 to construct tramways in the Borough.

The schemes were competitive, were mutually opposed, and were brought before the same Select Committee of Parliament. The Committee gave the Corporation its Order, which contained a clause providing for the company to have running powers over the corporation's tramways running through the Borough from east to west; and also passed the company's Bill in which was inserted a clause giving the corporation running powers over the tramways authorised in the Bill (which became the Christchurch & Bournemouth Tramways Act 1900), and the Poole & District line from County Gates to Poole via Upper Parkstone. It also provided that the company's power to construct its tramway from Lansdowne to the Bournemouth Borough Boundary (Pokesdown) should be suspended until 1st August, 1902, and if before that date the corporation should build its line from Lansdowne to Pokesdown, the company's powers for the line would cease. The Christchurch & Bournemouth Tramways Act 1900 authorised Poole & District to build lines from Bournemouth (Lansdowne) to Purewell Cross via Boscombe and Iford and, Bournemouth (Lansdowne) to Southbourne (Carbery Avenue) via Boscombe and Fisherman's Walk.

The company's Act and the Act (Tramways Order Confirmation (No. 5) Act 1900) confirming the Corporation Order both received the Royal Assent. Bournemouth Corporation applied for further tramway powers which were granted in the Bournemouth Corporation Act 1901 which received the Royal Assent on 9th August, 1901. Under the terms of this further legislation Poole & District were granted additional running powers from Poole Hill to Bournemouth Square via Triangle, and Bournemouth Square to Moordown.

On 5th March, 1902 the Poole & District's Chairman and Engineer called on the Bournemouth Town Clerk and said that they were advised that the Corporation's powers had lapsed because it had not made a 'substantial commencement of works' by 6th August, 1901. They asked for an undertaking that the corporation would not proceed with the laying of tramways in the roads until they had come to an agreement with the company as to the disposal of its line from Lansdowne to Pokesdown, which they suggested the corporation should complete and hand over to the company on terms to be agreed upon. The Town Clerk - acting on the instructions of Bournemouth's Tramways & Parliamentary Committee Chairman - declined to consider, upon

Ashley Road depot, tramcars form a backdrop to this photograph of the Poole & District Electric Traction Company staff shortly before the take-over by Bournemouth Corporation. Seated centre in the second row is Mr C.H. Mottram the manager. Built on land purchased from the Retreat estate, the public house next door took the name 'The Retreat'. Today a Safeway supermarket occupies the site of the depot.   *R.A. Wright Collection*

A Poole & District car heads along Ashley Road, Parkstone, towards County Gates. The bank on the left is situated on the corner of Albert Road, the Wilts & Dorset Bank was taken over by Lloyds during 1913, in 1983 Hants & Dorset was replaced by Wilts & Dorset, it is said that the original Wilts & Dorset Motor Services took the name to perpetuate the former banking company. The offset trolley mast on the tram is clearly shown to the right-hand side of the upper deck.   *R.A. Wright Collection*

which the company issued a writ commencing an action, and served it, together with motion for an injunction.

First of all the company took the case to the Court of Chancery in London, where Mr Justice Swinfen-Eady held that the corporation, in letting its contracts, and in many other ways incurring expenditure which obliged it to carry out the tramways scheme, had sufficiently complied with the Tramways Act 1870 as regards the commencement within 12 months. Its powers had not lapsed by reason of that Act, inasmuch as there was time to carry out the works through to completion within the two years specified. The company, however, appealed to the Court of Appeal, consisting of Lord Justices Vaughan, Williams, Romer and Stirling who reversed the decision on 15th July, 1902. Bournemouth Corporation made preparations for a determined legal struggle over the matter, but this great fight never came off as arrangements were instead made for the purchase of the company. The Bournemouth Corporation Tramways Act 1903 empowered the corporation to maintain and operate the tramways authorised under the Bournemouth Corporation Tramways Act 1900 and to take over the Poole & District Electric Traction Co. Ltd. Following arbitration proceedings which commenced on 27th May, 1903 and were not concluded until December 1904, agreement was reached whereby Bournemouth Corporation purchased the company at a value of £112,000, which included the rights of the BET in the Bournemouth area, the financial potential of the period of the lease of the Poole system, with Poole Corporation purchasing the track between County Gates and Poole and leasing the same to Bournemouth for 30 years. The Bournemouth Corporation Act 1904 included the transfer of powers from Poole & District to Bournemouth Corporation, which were contained in the Christchurch & Bournemouth Tramways Acts 1900 and 1903, although the terms were not finally agreed upon till early in 1905.

Until that time the Poole & District line ended at County Gates with just a passing loop, and the Bournemouth Corporation system from the Square, which had opened on 18th December, 1902, ended likewise. This resulted in passengers between the two towns having to make two separate journeys, a gap of about 100 yds existing between the systems until April 1905 when a length of line was constructed joining the two.

Following all the disagreements concerning the take-over of the Poole tramways, it comes as little surprise that even at the final hour there was a little drama.

On 20th May Bournemouth Corporation wrote asking whether the company would accept the purchase money without waiting for the terms of the Conveyances to be agreed. The company granted the request, and were willing to complete on 30th June being a convenient day for making up the accounts.

The draft Conveyances submitted by Bournemouth Corporation were approved, subject to several material alterations, to which the corporation agreed without question, and on Thursday, 8th June the Secretary of the company received a letter from the Town Clerk of Bournemouth stating that he would attend the office of the company to complete the purchase of the undertaking. However, when they arrived and tendered the purchase money the Secretary refused to complete owing to want of a proper and reasonable length of notice.

Above: Local passions were raised over the issue of the take-over by Bournemouth Corporation of the Poole trams. This cartoon appeared in the *Bournemouth Graphic* on 9th June, 1904, claiming that the Poole system would be a drain on Bournemouth.

Ian Andrews Collection

Right: Former Poole & District car No. 2 renumbered as Bournemouth Corporation No. 56 receiving attention inside the corporation depot at Southcote Road, Bournemouth. Although the staircase has been altered and electric headlight fitted, the car is still in Poole & District livery. In the foreground are wheel sets, bogies, and the other paraphernalia associated with tram car maintenance.

V. Jeffrey Collection

On the following day a writ was served by the corporation upon the company for specific performance, and claiming receipt as from the 8th. The Board of the Poole company met the following Tuesday and agreed to receive the purchase money in London on the morning of the 15th June and to complete and hand over the undertaking at midnight of the same day.

The Town Clerk and his London Agent attended with the purchase money on the morning of the 15th, and after some difficulties being raised owing to further alterations being required by the Solicitor of the company in the draft Conveyances, the purchase was at length completed without prejudice to subsequent settlement of the terms of the Conveyances or to any claim either party might have against the other.

When midnight arrived the Chairman of the Bournemouth Tramways Committee, the Borough Engineer, the Town Clerk, the Bournemouth Manager (Mr Barber) and three corporation clerks put in an appearance, and the undertaking was formally handed over to the Town Clerk by the Secretary. Questions as to stock and to what portions of land were to be handed over and other matters were subsequently gone into and discussed at length.

The corporation took over existing employees on the weekly wages list for the term of one fortnight, giving each one liberty to apply to be continued in their services for a further period should they so desire. Mr Di Marco, chief clerk, was taken over for a period of one month on the same understanding.

The ticket stock-taking could not be commenced before midnight as the last car did not arrive until that time, but with the aid of the three clerks brought by the corporation it was completed at about 2 am. Thus at the stroke of a pen the British Electric Traction Company's involvement in the Poole & District Tramways had come to an end, although certain unfinished business remained to be concluded.

Bournemouth Takes Control

Although through running was now possible there were certain operational difficulties to overcome, in Bournemouth the conduit system of current collection was employed in an area circumscribed by the top of Richmond Hill, The Lansdowne, and St Michael's Church at the top of Poole Hill. As the Poole cars were not fitted with plough equipment, Bournemouth cars had to be transferred before through running could commence. Within a few days Bournemouth cars towed many of the Poole cars over the conduit section to Southcote Road depot where they were modified to Bournemouth specification, although plough gear was never fitted.

Through running commenced on Monday 3rd July, 1905 via Upper Parkstone when a procession of four Bournemouth bogie cars headed by No. 1 'The State Car' departed from Southcote Road depot. On board were the mayor of Bournemouth, Alderman J. Elmes Beale, members of the Council, other civic dignities and officials. At County Gates members of Branksome Urban District Council joined the cars, the convoy then proceeding to the Poole terminus, from where they returned to Park Gates East where the Mayor of Poole Councillor F.H.W. Gwatkin welcome the guests before tea was served in the Park. This was

Bournemouth Corporation trams forming part of the ceremonial procession from Bournemouth at the Poole terminus on 3rd July, 1905. This event marked the commencement of through running to Bournemouth. The trolley poles have already been turned for the return journey, note the elaborate decoration of the cars, greenery on the upper deck and bunting fixed around the lower saloon, the tramway staff all in their full uniforms despite it being a summer's day pose for the camera proud to have been involved in the event.

Andrew Hawkes Collection

followed by the usual speeches before the procession departed for Bournemouth at 6 pm.

Despite the press headlines, 'Commencement Of Through Working', 'Bournemouth and Poole Wedded', 'Celebration Of The Happy Union', there was soon dissension over the fares charged and other matters. At the July Poole Council meeting, Alderman Wheatley, Chairman of the Tramway Committee said there had been several complaints now that Bournemouth had control.

The principal complaint was respecting the slowness of the trams, and he must personally admit that they were very slow indeed in comparison with the old service. Another matter, which ought to receive attention, was the inconsistency of the new fares. In the negotiations for the transfer it was arranged that the fare between Poole station and Bournemouth Square should be 4d. But he found only through tickets were being granted on the Bournemouth cars, and if a person journeyed on the old Poole cars they had to pay the 3d. to the County Gates and 2d. from there to Bournemouth Square. He considered that this was against the spirit of their agreement with Bournemouth and tickets ought to be granted on all cars whether the passengers had to change or not. He moved that these matters be brought to the notice of Bournemouth Corporation.

Councilor Martin complained of 'The slowness of the traffic causing great inconvenience and the matter if the fares resulted in people for Bournemouth waiting for the Bournemouth cars which were consequently crowded, while the Poole cars went through nearly empty'. Alderman Curtis thought the Bournemouth Tramways Committee ought to have their fares in order by this time. There was also an increase in workmen's fares causing a correspondent in the *East Dorset Herald* to pen an adaptation of Tennyson's well known poem, the first verse of which ran:

> Half a 'D', half a 'D',
> Half a 'D' onward!
> Rushing the workmen's fares.
> Who was it blundered!
> Forward the 'Tram Brigade',
> 'Charge them,' the Chairman said,
> So the Committee made
> 'Ds' by the hundred!

There followed by another six verses, clearly a demonstration of the two old sayings, 'Better the Devil you Know' and 'New brooms sweep clean'.

At Bournemouth construction of the Christchurch extension had been proceeding. This opened on 17th October, 1905, allowing a through route between Poole in Dorset through the County Borough of Bournemouth to Christchurch in Hampshire, a distance of 11 miles. This at the time (London excepted) was the longest tram route in the South of England. The opening ceremony, consisting of eight decorated cars, proceeded to Christchurch from Bournemouth Square and returned there. Although the Mayor and other officials of Poole and Branksome UDC attended, the fact that the procession failed to travel over the Poole system, thus truly proclaiming the through service, must have been a snub to many Poole residents.

Former Poole & District car No. 2 as Bournemouth Corporation No. 56 outside Southcote Road depot after repainting into corporation livery. The original reversed stairs have been replaced by spiral staircases along with other alterations carried out on Milnes cars 1-4 to bring them up to Bournemouth standards. *Below,* former Poole car No. 5, as Bournemouth Corporation No. 59, stands outside Southcote Road depot shortly after the take-over. This photograph clearly shows the massive oil headlight carried by Poole cars, and the trolley mast set off centre. Still in Poole livery a 'Richmond Hill' sticker on the dash panel denotes the car was being employed on Bournemouth local services. Cars Nos. 5-11 constructed by the Electric Railway & Tramway Carriage Works, Preston, had short upper decks with no canopy extensions over the driving positions, this being altered by Bournemouth Corporation who extended the upper deck to form canopies. *(Both) V. Jeffery Collection*

Although a through route, there were many short workings along its length, some regular, others to suit traffic needs. It is difficult to compare tram and train, as most tram passengers used the many intermediate stops the railway could not provide. However for any travelling the greater distance the time taken by the train, although not so frequent, was shorter. Poole station to Christchurch was 9¼ miles compared with the tram's 11, the train taking 36 minutes stopping at five intermediate stations, whilst the average tram jouney took 72 minutes. A train from Bournemouth West to Christchurch with three intermediate stops took 22 minutes.

Unfinished business

Application had been made by Poole & District to the Light Railway Commissioners for an order to construct 1¾ miles of route in November 1901 and this was approved at an inquiry held on 10th March, 1902. The proposal was submitted to the Board of Trade on 29th September, 1902 and was finally approved as the Poole & District Light Railway (Extension) Order 1903, and this authorised construction of the Lower Parkstone line from Branksome (Pottery Junction) to Park Gates East.

Even in the tramway world the wheels could grind very slowly. Ironically this line was eventually constructed by Poole Corporation for the use of Bournemouth Corporation trams! The Poole Council meeting of January 1906 discussed the proposed Lower Parkstone line in great detail, as decisions had to be taken concerning construction. The consulting engineer for the project was Mr Lacey who was the Bournemouth Corporation Borough Engineer and Surveyor. The legend 'F.W. Lacey, Tramway Engineer' was carried on the side of Bournemouth trams.

Mr Lacey furnished his estimate for the cost of the proposed new line, amounting to £26,167 16s. 3d. The estimate of the cost per mile for a single track was £6,132 and for the double line £15,889. The cost of the new line for the single length would be £7,795 and for the double line £9,593 making a total of £17,388. To this had to be added £7,330 for the electrical work, £500 for road widening, and £150 for tramway shelters, bringing the total cost to £25,368. A later decision that wood blocks should be substituted for granite setts increased the estimate by £ 1,228, making a grand total of £26,496. Mr Lacey pointed out there could be 'extras', and he mentioned as an instance that using wood blocks would cause Poole Council additional expense in road repairs. This was considered by the committee and approved, so as to provide for wood blocks and granite setts outside the rails of the width of 15 in. and 8 in. respectively. The committee recommended that the Town Clerk be instructed to forward the plans and estimate to Bournemouth Corporation for approval in accordance with the terms of the agreement of 5th May, 1903, and to apply to the Board of Trade for permission to borrow the sum of £26,497 14s. 4d. for the purposes of the works, and that tenders be invited for the construction.

Tenders were received from W.T. Glover & Co. Ltd, George Holloway, J. Moran & Sons Ltd, British Electric Equipment Company Ltd, William Griffiths

& Co., J.G. White & Co. Ltd, Smith & Company, Dick, Kerr & Co. Ltd, George Law, and the British Electrical Engineering Co. Ltd. As work had not yet commenced, the Town Clerk reported that the Board of Trade had extended the time for completing the Parkstone Extension Light Railway for a further period of 12 months. and had also sanctioned the borrowing of the sum of £20,068 for a period of 30 years to construct the line.

Bournemouth Corporation did not think it necessary to pave the full width of 18 inches outside the rails as requested by the Poole Corporation, but they were willing to agree to such paving with wood blocks wherever the full width of the road was to be paved by Poole Corporation in the same manner. Also the Bournemouth Town Clerk had written to Poole Council requesting they provide two new, and lengthen two existing, passing loops, in order to run the summer traffic, and called upon Poole to provide these in accordance with the terms of the agreements. The tramway committee recommended that the same be approved, subject to the passing place at the junction of Ringwood Road and Parkstone Road also being extended. The Town Clerk was instructed to apply to the Board of Trade for permission to borrow the sum of £3,565 5s. 5d. for the purpose of such works.

The contract for the construction of the new line was awarded to the Brush Electrical Company of Loughborough at a tendered price of £26,497 14s. 4d. Work proceeded apace under the supervision of F.W. Lacey, who had also to deal with the complaints of the tradesmen and residents of Commercial Road, Parkstone, concerning inconvenience caused during construction, and negotiations to acquire a strip of land near Messrs Baylay & Sons shop, for road widening. Attention was also drawn to the obstruction of the footpath in Ashley Road during the alteration to the loops.

Bournemouth Corporation wished to increase the speed of the tramcars from 12 mph to 14 mph, and even 18 mph on various portions of their system. On Friday 2nd March, 1906 Major J.W. Pringle of the Board of Trade travelled over various routes, the result being that in the December a new set of Regulations and Bylaws were issued by the Board of Trade for the Poole & District system:

> The Board of Trade, under and by virtue of the powers conferred upon them in this behalf, do hereby make the following regulations for securing to the public reasonable protection against danger in the exercise of the powers conferred by the Poole and District Light Railway Order 1899 (confirmed by the Board of Trade on the 7th day of August 1899), the Poole and District Light Railway (Extension Order, 1903 (confirmed by the Board of Trade on the 5th day of February, 1903), and the Bournemouth Corporation Tramways Act, 1903, with respect to the use of electrical power (overhead trolley system) on all or any of the railways which were authorised by the said Orders and on which the use of such power has been authorised (hereinafter called 'the railways').

> And the Board of Trade do also hereby make the following byelaws with regard to all or any of such railways worked on the overhead 'trolley system'.

> The Order of the Board of Trade in this behalf, dated the 9th day of May, 1906, is hereby rescinded.

Regulations

I.   Every motor carriage, used on the railways shall comply with the following requirements, that is to say -

(a) It shall be fitted, if and when required by the Board of Trade, with an apparatus to indicate to the driver the speed at which it is running.

(b) The wheels shall be fitted with brake blocks, which can be applied by a screw or by other means, and there shall be in addition an adequate electric brake and a slipper brake or other track brake approved by the Board of Trade for use on the railways.

(c) It shall be conspicuously numbered inside and outside.

(d) It shall be fitted with a suitable lifeguard, and with a special bell to be sounded as a warning when necessary.

(e) It shall be so constructed as to enable the driver to command the fullest possible view of the road.

II.   No trailer carriage shall be used on the railways except in the case of the removal of a disabled carriage.

III.   Every carriage used on the railways shall be so constructed as to provide for the safety of passengers, and for their safe entrance to, exit from, and accommodation in such carriage.

IV.   Every carriage on the railways shall, during the period between one hour after sunset and one hour before sunrise or during fog, carry a lamp so constructed and placed as to exhibit a white light visible within a reasonable distance to the front, and every such carriage shall carry a lamp so constructed and placed as to exhibit a red light visible within a reasonable distance to the rear.

V.   The speed at which the carriages shall he driven or propelled along the railways shall not exceed the rate of -

Sixteen miles an hour -

(a) In Poole Road between County Gates and The Pottery.

(b) In Poole and Bournemouth Road between Mansfield Road and Poole Road.

Twelve miles an hour -

(a) In High Street (Longfleet).

(b) In Parkstone Road.

(c) In Ashley Road.

(d) In Poole and Bournemouth Road between Parkstone Road and Mansfield Road.

Four miles an hour -

(a) Through facing points, whether fixed or movable.

(b) From the junction of Ashley Road with Constitution Hill to the junction of a new road (close to the 4-furlong mark on the deposited plans) with St Peter's Road.

(c) The curve between Poole and Bournemouth Road and Parkstone Road.

(d) The curve between Poole and Bournemouth Road and Poole Road.

At all other places, on all curves with radii less than 100 feet, and on falling gradients steeper than 1 in 20, the speed shall not exceed the rate of eight miles an hour.

VI.   The slipper brake shall be applied to every carriage in descending Constitution Hill.

VII.   The electrical pressure or difference of potential between the overhead conductors used in connexion with the working of the railways and the earth, or between any two such conductors, shall in no case exceed 550 volts. The electrical energy supplied through feeders shall not be generated at or transformed to a pressure higher than 650 volts, except. with the written consent of the Board of Trade, and subject to such regulations and conditions as they may prescribe.

VIII.   The overhead conductors used in connexion with the working of the railways shall be securely attached to supports, the intervals between which shall not, except with the approval of the Board of Trade, exceed 120 feet, and they shall be in no part at a less height from the surface of the street than 17 feet.

IX.   The overhead conductors shall be divided up into sections not exceeding (except with the special approval of the Board of Trade) one-half of a mile in length, between every two of which shall be inserted an emergency switch so enclosed as to be inaccessible to pedestrians.

X.   Each separate insulator on the overhead conductors shall be tested not less frequently than once in a month, and any insulator found to be defective shall at once be removed and an efficient insulator substituted.

XI.   All electrical conductors fixed upon the carriages in connexion with the trolley wheel shall be formed of flexible cables protected by India-rubber insulation of the highest quality, and additionally protected wherever they are adjacent to any metal so as to avoid risk of the metal becoming charged.

XII.   The trolley standard of every double-decked carriage shall be electrically connected to the wheels of the carriage in such manner as either to prevent the possibility of this standard becoming electrically charged from any defect in the electrical conductors contained within it or in the event of the standard becoming electrically charged to give a continuous warning signal to the driver or conductor. No passenger shall be allowed to travel on the top deck of a carriage as long as there is risk of electric shock.

XIII.   An emergency cut-off switch shall he provided and fixed so as to be conveniently reached by the (driver in case of any failure of action of the controller switch).

XIV.   If and whenever telegraph or telephone wires, unprotected with a permanent insulating covering, cross above, or are liable to fall upon, or to be blown on to, the overhead conductors of the railways, efficient guard wires shall be erected and maintained at all such places.

XV.   Where any accident by explosion or fire, or any other accident of such kind as to have caused or to he likely to have caused loss of life or personal injury, has occurred in connexion with the electric working of the railways, immediate notice thereof shall be given to the Board of Trade.

Penalty

Note   The Poole Corporation or any company or person using electrical power on the railways contrary to any of the above regulations is, for every such offence, subject to a penalty not exceeding £10; and also in the case of a continuing offence, to a further penalty not exceeding £5 for every day during which such offence continues after conviction thereof.

Byelaws

I.   The entrance to and exit from the carriages shall be by the hindermost or conductor's platform except at a terminus when the carriages are stationary.

II.   The carriages shall be brought to a standstill whenever it is necessary to avoid impending danger, and immediately before reaching the following points: -
(a) The junction of Ashley Road with Constitution Hill, on the inward journey.
(b) The junction of North Road with Poole and Bournemouth Road, on the inward journey.
(c) In Poole and Bournemouth Road -
(1) At Mansfield Road.
(2) At Ashley Cross.

(d) The junction of Poole and Bournemouth Road and Parkstone Road.

(e) The junction of Poole and Bournemouth Road and Poole Road.

III   A printed copy of these regulations and byelaws shall be kept in a conspicuous position inside of each carriage in use on the railways.

Penalty

Note Any person offending against or committing a breach of any of these byelaws is liable to a penalty not exceeding forty shillings.

The provisions of the Summary Jurisdiction Acts, with respect to the recovery of penalties, are applicable to the penalties for the breach of these regulations or byelaws.

Signed by order of the Board of Trade, this 6th day of December, 1906.

Herbert Jekyll,

assistant Secretary, Board of Trade.

By the end of July 1906 work on the new line was complete. The contractor then reminded the Council that, upon the certificate being issued by the Board of Trade, he would be entitled to receive 90 per cent of the value of the work completed.

The inspection was carried out by Major E. Druitt on the morning of Friday 3rd August. He was accompanied by representatives of Messrs Brush and Messrs Callender (the latter having carried out the cable work), and also present were officers from Bournemouth Corporation Tramways (BCT). Following the inspection, which took just over an hour, the line was opened to public traffic, without ceremony. It was fortunate the opening was not marred by tragedy, as shortly beforehand a workman on a tower wagon came into contact with the live overhead wire. Thrown from the tower, he landed in the road, luckily suffering only mild concussion and severe bruising. Thus the last section of line opened in Poole came into use.

Poole & District had also applied for a line over a circular route from Poole station (junction with existing tramway) to Poole station via High Street, The Quay, East Quay Road, Baiter Street, South Street and Mount Street to rejoin the existing tramway, the route having been approved (following modification) by Poole Council on 11th November, 1902, ironically at the same meeting that they approved the take-over by Bournemouth of the Poole & District undertaking. Needless to say, this line which was to have been promoted in the 1903 Parliamentary Session was never constructed. The reader should note that the Poole station referred to here is that which was located on the west side of Towngate Street and immediately adjacent to that street and which was closed *circa* 1968.

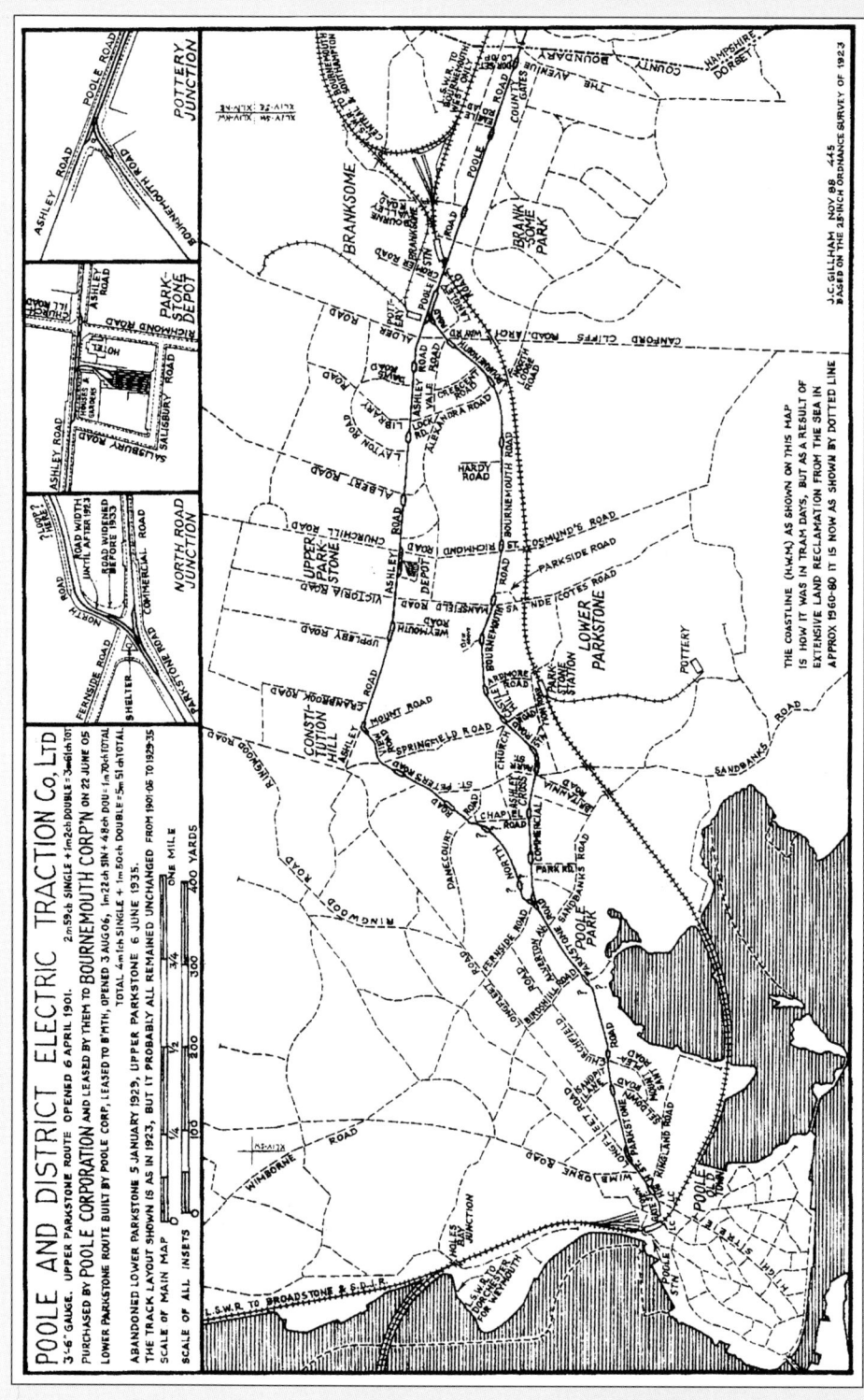

POOLE AND DISTRICT ELECTRIC TRACTION Co., LTD

3'-6" GAUGE. UPPER PARKSTONE ROUTE OPENED 6 APRIL 1901.

PURCHASED BY POOLE CORPORATION AND LEASED BY THEM TO BOURNEMOUTH CORP'N ON 22 JUNE 05

LOWER PARKSTONE ROUTE BUILT BY POOLE CORP., LEASED TO B'M'TH, OPENED 3 AUG 06.

ABANDONED LOWER PARKSTONE 5 JANUARY 1929, UPPER PARKSTONE 6 JUNE 1935.

THE TRACK LAYOUT SHOWN IS AS IN 1923, BUT IT PROBABLY ALL REMAINED UNCHANGED FROM 1901-06 TO 1929-35.

2 m.59 ch. SINGLE + 1 m.26 ch. DOUBLE = 3 m.85 ch. TOT

1 m.22 ch. SIN + 48 ch. DOU = 1 m.70 ch. TOTAL

TOTAL 4 m.1 ch. SINGLE + 1 m.50 ch. DOUBLE = 5 m.51 ch. TOTAL

SCALE OF MAIN MAP

SCALE OF ALL INSETS

J.C. GILLHAM NOV 88   445
BASED ON THE 25 INCH ORDNANCE SURVEY OF 1923

THE COASTLINE (H.W.M.) AS SHOWN ON THIS MAP IS HOW IT WAS IN TRAM DAYS, BUT AS A RESULT OF EXTENSIVE LAND RECLAMATION FROM THE SEA IN APPROX 1960-80 IT IS NOW AS SHOWN BY DOTTED LINE

Chapter Three

Track & Overhead

Whilst the motor bus is familiar to most people, the conventional tramcar is now almost a distant memory, and therefore it is not out of place to give the reader an outline of its operation. Trams had more in common with a railway than a road vehicle, and tramways themselves were governed by Acts of Parliament, the various Light Railway Acts, and subject to Board of Trade inspection (after 1919 the Ministry of Transport).

The lack of reference to a Board of Trade report denies us many construction details of the Poole tramway, in particular the track. To judge from statements made at the Poole-Bournemouth arbitration proceedings it was of a low standard that would not have been accepted by the Board of Trade several years later.

Whereas on a railway when the line crosses or is laid along a road the inside guard rail consists of a second rail laid inside the running rail, on a tramway the rail was rolled as one section, known as flat bottomed grooved girder rail. Regulations laid down that the groove did not exceed a width of 1⅛ inches on the straight and 1¼ inches on curves. Generally, trackwork was laid in chairs on longitudinal baulks with cross ties to maintain the gauge, otherwise cross sleepers were used, both being laid on a good concrete foundation under which would be a bed of well packed stone. The road level was made up either of macadam, wooden or granite blocks. Where railway track was accessible, tramlines were partly buried making regular maintenance difficult. Although extra long fishplates were used at joints often supported underneath with special clips and sections of inverted rail, 'dropped joints' were common and could not be relied upon for electrical continuity. As the rails carried the return current, bonding with heavy copper wire using the Thermit welding process was employed.

Poole like most other systems operated at a line voltage of 550/600 volts DC, the electricity for the Poole-County Gates system being supplied by the Bournemouth & District Electricity Supply Company from their Bourne Valley Generating station, with an original agreement to supply it at 1¹⁵⁄₁₆d. per unit with a minimum of 300 units per annum. The contract for the overhead equipment was let to Messrs Macartney, McElroy & Co., and underground cable and feeder supplies to Callenders Cables Ltd. The overhead conductor consisted of hard drawn copper wire, being divided into half-mile sections where a short insulated section created an electrical break, this safety device being a statutory requirement. The supply to each section was provided via underground cables to roadside distribution boxes which in turn supplied the overhead line via the nearest traction pole. These poles were of tubular steel construction and were usually spaced 110-120 ft apart on straight sections and less on curves where additional pull-off wires were employed to meet the required curvature of the overhead. Regulations insured that the wire was 20ft above ground level except in special circumstances. The wire was either

County Gates looking towards Poole, the junction on the left is the Avenue. Today the modern traffic system has completely changed the alignment and the scene, the lodge and trees on the left is today the site of Frizzell House. The bottom photograph looks down the Avenue towards Branksome Chine, the scene of early motor bus services in the area, to the left is a Bournemouth tram, to the right the lodge. The crests of Bournemouth and Poole add to the purpose of this delightful period postcard.   *(Both) Andrew Hawkes Collection*

COUNTY GATES. (WITH CRESTS).

clamped or soldered to 'ears' which in turn were attached either to the cross arm or span wire, the necessary porcelain insulators being inserted to ensure insulation of the live wire from the traction pole.

Being a single-track system with passing loops, the majority of traction poles were placed to one side of the road with span arms to give the necessary alignment between track and overhead wire, except for a short section at the Poole end where poles both sides of the road supported the overhead by the use of span wires. The poles themselves, as Victorian and Edwardian tradition decreed, had filigree scrollwork in the angle where the span arm and pole joined. The base of the poles were of ornamental design with the 'Magnet & Wheel' symbol of the British Electric Traction Company cast in relief, as were the panels of the road-side distribution boxes.

Just as pointwork was required for diverging trackwork, the same applied to the overhead, the overhead point being usually referred to as a 'frog'. In the case of Poole where a single wire became double at passing loops a simple expedient was employed. The movable blade of the frog was lightly sprung with a bias for the forward direction, thereby guiding the trolley head onto the left-hand wire as the car approached the loop. On departing the loop the trolley head displaced the sprung blade as it passed through, the blade then returning to the forward position. The actual point of contact between the overhead wire and the trolley pole at a pressure of between 20-25lb. was made by a steel or gunmetal grooved wheel usually about 4 in. diameter, set in a carrier that allowed it to swivel and keep alignment with the wire. (The replaceable carbon slipper inserts later used on most trolleybus systems, causing less wear to the overhead wire, were developed after the days of the Poole and Bournemouth trams).

The entire Poole system was single track with passing loops, 18 between the Poole terminus and County Gates via Upper Parkstone, and a further 12 loops on the Lower Parkstone line. A majority of these were only sufficient for trams to pass, the Depot loop, and Library Road loop in Ashley Road were longer, whilst although double track from just west of Pottery Junction to Branksome station, it could only be described as an extended loop, as was the short section from Park Gates East into North Road. With few exceptions tramways were without the signalling employed on railways. Adherence to the timetable and a strict code of conduct between drivers had to be exercised to avoid two cars meeting on a single section.

The Trams

Like the motor bus the tram can be divided into two parts - the chassis (known as the truck) and the body. The latter was craftsman built from the finest hard woods available, particularly in the construction of the framework, to which steel sheet panels were attached as an outside covering. Whilst the interior was lined with wood and usually of varnished finish, the exterior was painted to a very high standard. In the case of Poole this was in a livery of Cambridge Blue and White, with the BET 'Magnet and Wheel' insignia displayed on the lower side panels.

A stack of new tram rails await laying, although not from the Poole system, the grooved rail is
clearly shown in this end profile.   *D.D. Gladwin*

Bournemouth Corporation car No. 18 has just arrived at the Poole terminus in Towngate Street,
beyond the tram is the railway level crossing. The building on the right is the 'Ansty Arms'
public house. Today the west side of the Dolphin Centre complex occupies this site. No. 18 was
in the first batch of Milnes trams delivered to Bournemouth in 1902. *Andrew Hawkes Collection*

The truck was the framework on which the springs, axles, motors, gearing and brake assembly were mounted. Until the turn of the century the majority of trucks had been imported from America either complete or in kit form. Brush had just commenced building trucks of their own design, the type 'A' truck was of 6ft wheelbase and of rather lightweight design, many having to have their springing modified in later life.

Compared with modern electrical equipment the tramcar was reasonably simple. The current reached the car via the overhead wire and trolley standard, first passing through circuit breakers (known as 'canopy switches'). These would cut off the current in the event of an electrical fault or overload and also allowed the current to be cut off within the car for any reason.

The current then passed to the controllers situated on the platforms at both ends of the car, a system of interlocking allowing only one controller to be used at a time. The purpose of the controller was to regulate the amount of current supplied to the motors thus controlling the speed of the car. This was achieved by sets of contacts on a revolving spindle operated by the handle, firstly with both motors connected in series with the maximum resistances in circuit and then as the handle was moved clockwise the resistances were decreased until at the halfway point, at which the motors were switched to parallel with the resistances re-introduced. As the handle moved further around the resistances again decreased until full power was reached with just the motors in parallel. The two optimum positions for the controllers to save power and wear on the resistances was with the two motors in series, or full power, both without resistances.

The controller also operated the rheostatic braking, when the car was going downhill or moving forward without power applied the motors acted as dynamos, the output of which by turning the controller handle anti-clockwise engaged other contacts and varied the amount of current dissipated into the starting resistances, the load or EMF put across the motor acting as a retarding force thus slowing the speed of the car. Additionally, where fitted, magnetic track brakes were wired into these circuits.

The original Poole & District fleet consisted of only 17 cars, all single truck cars (four-wheelers). However they were not without interest. G.F. Milnes constructed cars 1-4 which were mounted on Brill 21E type trucks. The bodies had five windows each side with fanlights mounted above and they were the only cars of that type constructed by Milnes. The staircases were reversed and the rails around the upper deck were low, only 3 ft high, the entire car being 27 ft long. Seating on the lower deck consisted of an upholstered longitudinal bench seat on each side facing inwards, each one seating 11 passengers. Upper deck seating consisted of the conventional 'garden seat' benches arranged in sets of two with single seats to suit the position of the staircases and the trolley standard.

Cars 5-11 were constructed by the Electric Railway and Tramway Carriage Works, Preston, who had been sub-contracted the work by Dick, Kerr. The Poole cars were part of a large order placed at the time with Kerr to supply cars to the BET group. Three windows were fitted along each side with fanlights above but the canopy and top deck did not extend over the lower deck at either end. This was altered later by Bournemouth Corporation, although the direct 90 degree staircases were retained.

Cars 12-17 were delivered during the latter part of 1901 and early 1902 and were constructed by the Brush Electrical Engineering Company of Loughborough, but owing to the forthcoming arrangements between Bournemouth Corporation and the BET further cars for this order were diverted to the South Staffs system.

The bodies had four windows each side with fanlights above, and full length canopies. The truck was of the Brush A type, that company also supplying the electrical equipment although - as with all Poole trams - BTH electric motors were employed.

When new, all Poole cars were equipped with both oil headlights and signal lights, although interior and top deck lights were electric. The provision of the former was designed to warn of the tram's presence when the trolley pole was removed from the wire or the electrical power interrupted. The trolley standards were mounted off centre on the upper deck, being on the south side, or left-hand side when viewed looking towards Poole. Following the Bournemouth take-over the standards were placed in the centre.

Braking was by the standard BET mechanical track brake, which applied wooden brake blocks to the surface of the rail. This was operated by a horizontal lever mounted on a vertical post on the platforms of the car, and was assisted by the conventional rheostatic brake and a screw-down handbrake.

Following the take over of the system by Bournemouth Corporation, the Poole cars were equipped with electric headlights, roller blind destination indicators, and carried their new BCT numbers, although repainting into the Bournemouth livery took a little time. The cars were not equipped with ploughs so they could not work through the Bournemouth Square area, thus restricting their usefulness, but many worked the routes to the north of Bournemouth until the plough section was abandoned in May 1911, although their lack of power and brake force made them second class compared with their Bournemouth counterparts. This no doubt resulted in many of them being placed in store at Moordown Tram Depot during part of World War I, following which some were overhauled and returned to service whilst others, although retaining their passenger accommodation, were mainly employed as works cars. All were withdrawn when new cars were purchased between 1921-1926. In August 1924 it was reported that only six old Poole trams remained in Moordown depot. One Poole car alone survived, No. 55 (ex-Poole No. 1), converted into a rail grinder in 1921 and retained until the closure of the system.

Bournemouth trams took over the through services between Poole and Bournemouth, and later Christchurch. Being a 'trunk route' the newest and best cars were usually employed, their maroon and primrose yellow livery setting the tone for the high standard for which Bournemouth trams became renowned.

Without wishing to proceed too far into the history of the Bournemouth cars, a brief description will suffice. The entire fleet of 114 cars except No.1 were double-deck open-top cars, Nos. 21-48 were four-wheelers and the remainder bogie cars. Whereas the four-wheelers had an average length of 27 ft 6 in. the bogie cars ranged from 35 ft 6 in. to 36 ft 6 in., and were 6 ft 4 in. wide over the body. The headroom in the lower deck of all the Poole and Bournemouth cars was 6 ft 7 in., a luxury never possible in a double-deck bus!

The bogie cars were mounted on Brill 22M Maximum-Traction bogies of 4 ft wheelbase, set at 16 ft centres. All Bournemouth cars were equipped with Westinghouse magnetic track brakes from the end of March 1903, this system being further improved following the fatal accident of May 1908, when mechanical operation was added to the system, allowing it also to be applied by hand. This arrangement was special to Bournemouth.

It is interesting to note that, with the exception of the former Poole cars, no Bournemouth trams were withdrawn prior to the closure of the system, a credit to the maintenance standards of the tramways department.

Poole & District Tram Car Fleet

No.	Built	Builder	Truck	Electrical Equipment	Motors	Seats L T	BCT No.	Notes
1	1901	G.F. Milnes	Brill 21E	BTH 18	BTH GE58	22 26	55	A B
2	1901	G.F. Milnes	Brill 21E	BTH 18	BTH GE58	22 26	56	A
3	1901	G.F. Milnes	Brill 21E	BTH 18	BTH GE58	22 26	57	A
4	1901	G.F. Milnes	Brill 21E	BTH 18	BTH GE58	22 26	58	A
5	1901	Dick, Kerr	Brill 21E	Dick, Kerr	BTH GE58	22 21	59	C
6	1901	Dick, Kerr	Brill 21E	Dick, Kerr	BTH GE58	22 21	60	C
7	1901	Dick, Kerr	Brill 21E	Dick, Kerr	BTH GE58	22 21	61	C
8	1901	Dick, Kerr	Brill 21E	Dick, Kerr	BTH GE58	22 21	62	C
9	1901	Dick, Kerr	Brill 21E	Dick, Kerr	BTH GE58	22 21	63	C
10	1901	Dick, Kerr	Brill 21E	Dick, Kerr	BTH GE58	22 21	64	C
11	1901	Dick, Kerr	Brill 21E	Dick, Kerr	BTH GE58	22 21	65	C
12	1901	Brush	Brush A	Brush	BTH GE58	22 26	66	A
13	1901	Brush	Brush A	Brush	BTH GE58	22 26	67	A
14	1901	Brush	Brush A	Brush	BTH GE58	22 26	68	A
15	1901	Brush	Brush A	Brush	BTH GE58	22 26	69	A
16	1901	Brush	Brush A	Brush	BTH GE58	22 26	70	A
17	1901	Brush	Brush A	Brush	BTH GE58	22 26	82	A D

Notes
A Reversed stairs replaced by BCT with spiral staircases.
B Became railgrinder, to Llandudno & Colwyn Bay as railgrinder No. 23A. Withdrawn 24th March, 1956.
C Canopy fitted over end platforms by BCT.
D No. 71 until 1908.

Bournemouth Corporation Tram Car Fleet

No.	Built	Builder	Truck	Electrical Equipment	Motors	Seats L T
1	1902	G.F. Milnes	Brill 22E	Westinghouse	WH49B	30
2-20	1902	G.F. Milnes	Brill 22E	Westinghouse	WH49B	30 32
21-48	1902	G.F. Milnes	Peckham	Westinghouse	WH49B	20 22
49-54	1904	G.F. Milnes	Brill 22E	Westinghouse	WH49B	30 32
71-81	1907	Brush	Brill 22E	Westinghouse	BTH GE58	30 32
83-92	1904	UEC	Brill 22E	Westinghouse	WH49B	30 32
93-112	1914	Brush	Brill 22E	BTH B49CC	BTH249	30 38
113-132	1924/6	Brush	Peckham	Metrovick	MV104	30 38

Staff

Employment on the tramway in the early days was a much sought-after position. Like the railways, it was secure with prospects of promotion and wages were as good - if not better than for many others plus a chance of overtime to further increase earnings.

Little is known of the pay structure of Poole & District, but upon take-over the staff were informed they could apply for re-employment on the terms given to Bournemouth Corporation employees. As a general rule, municipal conditions of employment were superior to others.

At that time the weekly wage was calculated on a 10-hour day, 60-hour week, Mondays to Saturdays. A conductor received 5*d.* per hour for his first year of service, then 5½*d.* per hour giving a weekly wage of 27*s.* 6*d.*, whilst a driver commenced at 5½*d.* per hour rising to 6*d.*, a weekly wage of 30*s.* Hours worked over 60 were paid on a pro-rata basis and 10 hours pay was awarded for an eight hour Sunday shift. During 1906 a conductor's basic wage was increased by 1*s.* to 28*s.* 6*d.* per week.

A bonus scheme was introduced during 1910, under which each man was awarded a 1*s.* per quarter for freedom from accidents, complaints, or breaches of rules, men obtaining four consecutive awards received an additional payment of 4*s.* The following year a bonus scheme for the highest receipts on each route over a three-month period was introduced, the results of which were reported by the General Manager as most satisfactory. A bonus of 1½ per cent of the profit from the tramway was distributed to staff in 1915, but wartime difficulties and subsequent increased expenditure quickly terminated this scheme.

Following World War I the pay structure altered as various agreements between management and trade unions started to take effect. In March 1919 the basic working week was reduced to 48 hours, and by 1924 a driver's weekly wage was 59*s.* 6*d.*, and a conductor's 55*s.* 6*d*, by the time the trams ceased running a driver earned 62*s.* and a conductor 58*s.*

Life was not easy for tram crews. Prior to the fitting of windscreens the driver, standing on an open platform, was exposed to all winds and weathers, relying on the protective clothing of the period to keep him warm and dry. The conductor fared little better. Fare collection on the upper deck was difficult on rainy days as everything - including the tickets - got wet, and there were passengers' umbrellas to negotiate. Added to the requirement to have a large amount of tact and patience in dealing with the general public, conductors had to give the stopping and starting signal to their drivers by means of whistles, although on later cars there was a bell cord in the lower saloon. One-ring meant stop, two-rings proceed, and three was an emergency, whistles still being used when conductors were on the upper deck. At each terminus there was the ceremony of flipping over the backs of the reversible top deck seats so the passengers on the next journey would be facing the direction of travel, and the trolley pole had to be 'swung round' as the trolley head always had to be in the trailing position - not an easy task in the dark with the meagre street lighting of the period.

Fare Collection

The collection of fares was also difficult during the hours of darkness, especially on the top deck where there was only one light at each end to assist with this important job. The subject of tickets is a complex one, so to give the reader an insight into the working only a brief outline of ticket systems in general, and the peculiarities of Poole-issued tickets, will be explained.

In this modern age the bland paper ticket issued on a Poole bus has little interest except to the inspector who might board the vehicle and check to ensure the correct fare has been paid for the journey taken, the passenger has not over-ridden, or any other fraudulent action taken place. But thanks to the electronic age all details required for audit purposes are recorded within the machine for later downloading into a computer

Until the introduction of the 'Setright' machine there was no satisfactory mechanical method of accounting, so the numbered packs of tickets in a variety of colours were the only way the operator could account for revenue. Basically a conductor paid in cash to the difference of the serial numbers issued by the ticket office at the commencement of duty and those returned at the end of duty, for example if 211 1d. tickets had been issued, the conductor had to pay in 17s. 7d. for that fare value alone. As these tickets had a value even before issue, if they fell in the hands of some unscrupulous person it left the conductor with a debt!

The tickets were in numbered bundles, stapled at the base, each bundle of different fare denominations being held under a spring clip on a wooden ticket rack, a short rack usually sufficed for short town routes, (on long routes sometimes two large racks were required). To issue a ticket the conductor would pull the top ticket from the bundle of the required fare from the rack in an upward direction, it tearing away from the staple and slide out from under the spring. He would then insert the ticket into the ticket punch at the correct cancelling point, and depress the trigger to punch a hole in the ticket. At the same time he would collect the fare, give change, and manage to stand up on a moving, swaying tram or bus. To say the conductor had his hands full would have been an understatement!

The punching of a hole in the ticket denoted not only that it had been issued, but, the position of the hole combined with the serial number made a simple check for the inspector or other person to determine the validity of the ticket. The hole was punched in the fare stage number (or name in the case of a geographical ticket) at the point the passenger had boarded, this combined with the value of the ticket determined the distance for which the ticket was valid and at what point the passenger should have left the vehicle

The ticket punch itself, although a simple looking device, was extremely complex. An internal register recorded the number of tickets punched, and the thumb lever which worked the punch could not be depressed unless a ticket was placed in the ticket slot, this being machined to fine tolerances only allowing the thickness of one ticket at a time to be inserted. The punchings from the tickets were collected in the base of the machine, and if required a 'confetti' audit could be carried out in the event of a discrepancy. The punch could only be opened with a special key held by the cash office staff, in fact any tampering with the punch would cause it to lock up solid!

Despite the complexities of the bell punch system, albeit not always supplied by the Bell Punch Company, it served many tram and bus operators for over 50 years. Many older readers will remember with affection the deft movements of the conductor, who made it look so simple, many a boy imitating him with his toy conductor's set that could be purchased from most toy shops!

The passage of time has denied us many details of the tickets originally used by the Poole & District Tramways. It is recorded that four values of ticket were in use. Although the bell punch was in use by the time the Poole tramways opened, it was not used in the early years. Instead, the conductor used a hand held pistol punch to cancel the tickets, which were not held in a ticket rack, but just in bundles secured by elastic bands, requiring the hapless conductor to be more ambidextrous than ever!

Following the take-over by Bournemouth Corporation the standard Bell Punch system was introduced, and the tickets held in the traditional ticket rack. With through running to Bournemouth and the extension to Christchurch the range of tickets increased. The tickets were of the geographical type with the fare stage names printed on the ticket, a style that continued for many years, although later stage numbers appeared. The colour scheme also remained substantially unaltered, indeed it carried on into Ultimate machine days, 'Bournemouth Corporation Tramways' being printed on the tickets, whilst motor bus tickets had 'Bournemouth Corporation Motor Buses' printed on them. Towards the end of trams, all tickets had 'Bournemouth Corporation Transport Services' printed on them, this resulted in the overprinting of 'T' and 'B' to ensure a correct audit of the respective forms of transport.

Bournemouth Corporation Tram Ticket Colour Scheme

Fare value		Colour
s.	d.	
1	2	Pink (Tuckton Bridge Toll)
	1	Buff
	1	White/green, issued to school children before introduction of school buses
	1½	Pink (originally Lilac)
	2	White
	2½	Sage (originally bright green)
	3	Orange red
	3½	Salmon
	4	Light blue
	5	Yellow
	6	Grey (not issued until the 1920s)
	7	Lilac (issued towards end of World War I)
Parcel		White/red
Dog		Mauve

Valediction

Following the closure of the Bournemouth system nine Bournemouth cars and rail grinder No. 55 were sold to the Llandudno & Colwyn Bay Electric Railway, where repainted in a green and cream livery they gave good service, their Llandudno fleet numbers being:

Bournemouth	Llandudno	Bournemouth	Llandudno	Bournemouth	Llandudno
55	23	103	10	115	7
85	6	108	9	116	8
95	11	114	15	121	14
				128	12

The Bournemouth cars survived until the closure of the Llandudno system on 24th March, 1956, No. 8 acting as the official last car. This 21 year reprieve for the Bournemouth trams was over and only No. 6 survived, later being put on display - in Llandudno livery - at the British Transport Museum, Clapham. Upon the museum's closure the tram returned to Bournemouth, and following restoration to its former Bournemouth glory and taking its old No. 85 it was stored at Mallard Road depot. Today it is on display in the Electricity Museum at Christchurch.

Of the other trams that once ran through the streets of Poole and Bournemouth only bodies recovered from the countryside remain. The body of 88 is with the Ashton Manor Road Transport Museum, Birmingham, whilst 126 was rescued from a farm at East Coker (Yeovil) to be restored by the Llandudno & Colwyn Bay Electric Railway Society as Llandudno No. 7. The body of No. 53 is currently undergoing restoration near Wareham, and the Bournemouth Passenger Transport Association (BPTA) have saved the bodies of 13, 42, and 101, whilst the body of 72 (the tram involved in the 1908 accident) has become a donor to help restore the others. The body of No. 106 forms the major part of No. 16 on the 2 ft 9 in. gauge Seaton Electric Tramway, where fixtures and fittings of other former Bournemouth cars are incorporated into several of the miniature trams.

Very little remains to remind us of Poole's trams, apart from photographs and a few tickets, the only large items being the framework of the body of car No. 6 rescued from a farm near Fordingbridge which awaits restoration by the BPTA, and a roadside distribution box, now standing outside Poole Museum.

A view in Poole Road, Branksome looking towards Branksome station, from the loop at Eagle Road. Bournemouth Corporation car No. 112 proceeds towards Parkstone, whilst car No. 116 draws out of the loop, heading towards Bournemouth. Car No. 112 was in the batch purchased in 1921 and No. 116 of the last batch purchased in 1926. No. 116 passed to the Llandudno & Colwyn Bay Electric Railway in 1936, and as No. 8 performed the closing rites of that system on 24th March, 1956.   *R.A. Wright Collection*

Bournemouth Corporation car No. 108 stopped at Albert Road, Upper Parkstone. A passing motorist obliged to wait as passengers board in the road clearly demonstrates one of the disadvantages of the tram over the motor bus which could pull into the kerb. No. 108 a Brush-built bogie car of 1921, passed to the Llandudno & Colwyn Bay in 1936 and as No. 9 survived until March 1956.   *Yellow Buses*

The last survivor of the Poole & District fleet was No. 1, becoming No. 55 under Bournemouth Corporation. Converted into a rail grinder during 1921, later as the sole surviving former Poole car she passed to Llandudno & Colwyn Bay Electric Tramways in 1936 where as works car No. 23A she survived until the closure of the system in March 1956. Photographed at Llandudno depot on 11th July, 1955.   *R.S. Carpenter Collection*

Chapter Four

Progress and Problems

A letter from H.W. Dibben, Deputy Chairman of the Branksome Park, Sandbanks & Parkstone, Tramways Extension Association, was read at a meeting of Bournemouth Council held on 6th December, 1904. Enclosed with the letter was a petition (termed a 'Memorial') of 156 signatures in favour of extending the tramways. The letter and petition were also addressed to Poole Council and the Council of the Urban District of Branksome. The lines mentioned were 'Westbourne Arcade, Westbourne, Branksome Park, Canford Cliffs to Poole Harbour and Sandbanks, and in the opposite direction to the centre of Parkstone, effecting there a junction with the authorised main line of the Poole and Bournemouth tramway system'. The matter was referred to Bournemouth's Tramways Committee, where it was discussed on 22nd September, 1905 following the receipt of a letter from Poole Council. This letter sought Bournemouth's views on the proposed extensions, and asked whether Bournemouth would be willing to work the proposed routes, and if so, on what terms. In December 1905 the Bournemouth Town Clerk received a copy of an application (intended for the Light Railway Commissioners) from Messrs Proffitt and Scott (Parliamentary Agents) for an Order authorising a light railway. Both Poole and Bournemouth Councils and the residents of Branksome Park objected to the proposals. The objectors considered that these tramways were unnecessary as they served a sparsely populated area, Poole in particular was against the construction of a 'permanent structure' (whether by means of a conveyor bridge or otherwise) over Poole Harbour, and needless to say 75 per cent of the residents of Branksome Park (then a very exclusive area) were opposed to this scheme. The application - 'Branksome Park and Swanage Light Railway - November 1905' was for the following routes which would have connected into the existing tramway system:

Railways 1, 2 and 3	County Gates - Sandbanks Ferry via Lindsay Road, Burton Road, Western Road, Eaton Road, Tower Road, Western Road, Haven Road, Shore Road and Sandbanks Road;
Railway 4	Studland side of Poole Harbour to Swanage;
Railways 4A, 5 & 5A	were local lines in Swanage; and
Railways 6, 6A, 6B & 7	Poole (Commercial Road) - Sandbanks Ferry via Salterns Road, Sandbanks Road to junction with Lilliput Road thence via reserved track on the seaward side of the present road to the junction of Evening Hill with Shore Road, along Shore Road and Sandbanks Road.

The promoters of this scheme were Lord Alington, Sir J.M. Burt and Mr T. B. Scott. The scheme was for 13¼ miles of 3 ft 6 in. gauge electric line, the cars to be carried above the water between Sandbanks and Shell Bay suspended on cables by a form of Transporter bridge. The estimated cost of the scheme was £138,457. It was rejected at a Light Railway Commissioners local Inquiry held on 26th March, 1906, thus Swanage was denied the tram and Poole Harbour a landmark enjoyed by Middlesbrough and Newport!

Bournemouth car No. 48 heads towards Poole along Commercial Road, Lower Parkstone, note the double track of the passing loop. The main road to Bournemouth curves to the left. Parkstone Park is behind the tram, whilst Station Road leading to Parkstone station bears off to the right. In the lower photograph the photographer has turned around looking towards Poole. The tram is passing Ashley Cross, today the shops on the left have been replaced by a car park and widened road. The shops on the right remain, as does the Central Hotel on the corner of Parr Street.   *R.A. Wright Collection/Andrew Hawkes Collection*

Fairly soon after Bournemouth had acquired Poole & District, difficulties appeared in relations with Poole over some aspects of the tramway. The matter of tram shelters again arose during the year. In December 1905 a letter from the Town Clerk of Poole to Bournemouth Corporation referred to the agreement of 17th November, 1902 between the Poole & District Electric Traction Company and Poole Corporation, under which the company were under obligation to erect a shelter at Brown Bottom Corner, and to the Poole & District Light Railway Order of 1899, under which the Poole Corporation had the right to call upon the company to provide and maintain a waiting room in a situation to be approved by the council. It also stated that the obligation to carry out these works had now devolved upon the Bournemouth Corporation and called upon them to erect the shelter at Brown Bottom Corner, and a waiting room at the Towngate Street terminus of the railway. Bournemouth Council replied that they did not consider the shelters necessary and, as lessees, were not prepared to provide them.

In early 1906 there was correspondence with the Board of Trade over the matter of workmen's fares. It was pointed out that there was no provision relating to such fares in the Poole & District Order, but in spite of this Bournemouth Corporation introduced workmen's fares in Poole.

Although not directly connected with the Poole system, the fatal accident caused by a runaway tram on 7th May, 1908 involved the death and injury of Poole and Parkstone residents. Car No. 72 departed from the Poole terminus at 6.15 pm, and by the time it reached the top of Poole Hill, before descending into Bournemouth Square, 40 passengers had boarded. A fault in the magnetic brake system caused the driver to lose control, and gathering speed the tram left the rails at the final bend and plunged over the embankment into the garden of 'Fairlight Glen' resulting in the deaths of seven passengers and many others injured.

Meanwhile the final obsequies of the Poole & District Electric Traction Company were being enacted at Electrical Federation Offices, Kingsway, London, when the liquidators' report was presented to the shareholders at a general meeting of the company on 11th October, 1909. Liquidation of the company had commenced in July 1905 but, owing to delay caused by litigation with Bournemouth Corporation, it had been impossible to convene the final meeting.

The total proceeds from the realisation of the assets amounted to £137,880 15s. 11d. and the disbursements to £136,600 5s. 6d., which latter amount included, with the final distribution of £3 3s. 0d. per share, a total return to the shareholders of £19 3s. 0d. in respect of each £10 share of the company held by them. The balance amounting to £1,280 10s. 5d. had been retained by the Board of Trade; £30 10s. 5d. to meet outstanding Dividend Warrants, and £1,250 reserved as remuneration for the Liquidators, including office accommodation and services provided by The British Electric Traction Company during the four years over which the liquidation had extended and a contingency claim of £158 18s. 10d. for legal costs. Resolutions were submitted at the Meeting to authorise the payment of £1,250 to the Liquidators, and to authorise the Liquidators to hand the books and papers of the company to the British Electric Traction Company to be dealt with as that company might decide.

Bournemouth car No. 42 stands at the Poole terminus before departing with a short working to Boscombe. The up train passing over the level crossing in the background is to be noted, as are the two overhead wires tied off to the traction poles either side of the road, to alleviate a frog at the bottom end of the final loop 'down' and 'up' wires were provided over the final length. Viewed from a different angle, below, Bournemouth car No. 54 awaits to depart for Boscombe, Fisherman's Walk. The wooden fencing to the left of the tram in 1915 became the site of the long awaited passenger shelter. The imposing frontage of the Station Hotel lies beyond the level crossing.   *(Both) R.A. Wright Collection*

Towards the end of the year there were complaints regarding the state of the tramway (Bournemouth's response being that this was taken into account when fixing the price paid for Poole & District), and that there were fewer trams through Lower Parkstone than originally agreed, some 'Upper Road' cars turning at Constitution Hill, - to which Bournemouth replied that services met demand. A letter dated 23rd November, 1909 suggested that the two Authorities should come to a better understanding, that the Poole to Bournemouth service might be better via Lower Parkstone, and that a 'thinner' service be provided between Constitution Hill and Poole - evidently there were problems in interpreting the agreement over levels of service. There appears to have been a slowness (or even reluctance) on Bournemouth's part to meet Poole, and the upshot was a meeting to be held in 1910 to discuss: (a) October 1899 agreement regarding the Upper Parkstone route; (b) service on 'Lower Road'; (c) stopping places and; (d) waiving of Bye-laws relating to adverts on cars. In a letter of 7th January, 1910, Poole asked for the installation of a waiting room at Poole station 'in accordance with the Poole & District Light Railway Order 1899'. At a meeting with Poole Council on 12th January, 1910 it was agreed that the service from Bournemouth to Poole would be as follows: eight minute service to Poole via Upper Parkstone; 16 minute service to Park Gates East via Lower Parkstone; and a 16 minute service to Albert Road (Upper Parkstone) via 'Upper Road', i.e. departures from Bournemouth Square every four minutes thus: Poole via Upper Parkstone, Park Gates East via Lower Parkstone, Poole via Upper Parkstone, Upper Parkstone (Albert Road) via Upper Parkstone.

The matter of the waiting room was to be examined by the BCT General Manager and the Poole Borough Surveyor.

A recurring problem was the fares charged by Bournemouth Corporation over the Poole route. In November 1910 Poole Town Clerk was instructed to write to the London & South Western Railway with the object of obtaining a cheap return fare between Poole and Branksome. One councillor asked if it was a wise course to ask the railway for cheaper fares, to which the reply was that 'it would make the tram fare come down'.

Finance was a major issue that month. A question of income tax arose in the dispute with Bournemouth Corporation, judgement in the Chancery Division of the High Court finding in favour of Bournemouth Corporation. The Poole authority claimed that they should receive the entire amount of the agreed rent without such deduction, the amount at present in dispute being £604. It was argued that if the case went in favour of Bournemouth the sinking fund would be several thousand pounds short, which meant that Bournemouth Corporation would not have carried out its contract to provide such an annual sum, which would not be sufficient to enable the Corporation to repay the principal and interest on the loan raised for the purchase of the undertaking.

The original track was beginning to show signs of wear. Between November 1910 and January 1911 the section between Park Gates West loop and Park Gates East was renewed, followed by the entire line between the top of Constitution Hill through to County Gates. Details submitted to the Board of Trade stated: 'The existing rails and concrete bed to be taken up. The new rails will be to the British Standard No. 4 section and will be laid on a concrete bed

The junction of Poole High Street and Towngate Street in May–June 1914 during the relaying of the tram track. The horse and cart was still the predominant means of transport, a solitary traction engine stands centre right outside the 'Ansty Arms', to the right the 'Port Mahon Hotel'. Redevelopment has erased every building in this scene.
R.A. Wright Collection

with transverse anchors of old rails. Ordinary fishplated joints will be used, and it is proposed to maintain the existing levels throughout'. It was decided, on the relaying of the Constitution Hill-County Gates section, to lay wooden blocks around the tramline, replacing the macadam previously installed. There was also the question of lengthening the loop outside the Parkstone Tram Depot, fears being raised that this could cause annoyance to worshippers at St John's Church, two councillors speaking of the intolerable nuisance which was caused to members of the Wesleyan Church when the original line had been laid. Alderman Lawford replied that the only remedy would be to stop the running of Sunday trams. During the actual relaying the service was maintained by laying temporary track above the road surface alongside the existing line, the work being carried out in 400 yd sections at a time.

Unlike Bournemouth, Poole always had the luxury of Sunday tram services which continued under Bournemouth Corporation ownership - whereas neighbouring Bournemouth (where the subject had caused much debate over the years) did not commence Sunday running until 9th February, 1913, and then only after lunch, resulting in a situation where trams from Poole ran as far as County Gates only with through working commencing in the afternoon.

The inhabitants of Lower Parkstone were requesting an improved service early in 1914, asking that Bournemouth Corporation provide a 10 minute service from the Poole terminus to the Square and vice versa, and that the trams run through without passengers having to change at Park Gates. The Tramway Committee were willing to arrange for the cars to run through to Poole without passengers having to change, but regretted they were unable to accede to the request for a 10 minute service.

During May and June 1914 the section between Park Gates West loop and the terminus at Poole railway station was relaid, whilst the Park Gates East to the top of Constitution Hill section was relaid between September and December 1915, thus within 14 years the entire Poole system had been relaid. The matter of a passenger shelter at the Poole terminus which had been outstanding since 1905 was also acted upon in December 1915, when a tender from Messrs Walter Macfarlane & Company for £122 10s. was accepted, the work being carried out as soon as possible.

In the early days of World War I the tramways continued as usual, and with the decline in the small amount of private motoring of the period, passenger numbers increased. In 1915 Christmas Day services were withdrawn, and never reinstated on that day. Although there were not the blackout restrictions of World War II, interior lighting was reduced to a 'blue glow', whilst headlights were partly masked. As the war situation deteriorated there were shortages of staff as men joined the services, but not following the general policy of employing women as conductors. The matter having been considered by the Tramways Committee who were 'of the opinion that no advantage would be obtained through the engagement of women conductors', the corporation engaged boys aged between 16-18 years awaiting their call-up. There was a shortage of materials even to carry out essential maintenance, the services being cut as a result, and also to save coal at the power stations. A study of routes was made and traction poles marked at points where drivers should shut off power and allow the tram to freewheel in an effort to save electricity.

Bournemouth Corporation tram No. 30 heads along Bournemouth Road on the Lower Parkstone route with a service terminating at Park Gates East. Photographed near the 'Halfway Hotel' (now 'The Grasshopper') the single track down the centre of the road clearly demonstrates the problems of later years when other road traffic developed.   *Andrew Hawkes Collection*

Bournemouth Corporation car No. 13 heads past Park Gates East with the destination blinds set for Christchurch. In this pre-1920 scene horses and carts are the only other vehicles to be seen.
R.K. Blencowe Collection

During early 1917 there was correspondence between Bournemouth Corporation and the Board of Trade concerning street lights that had been fitted to traction poles in the Poole area by Poole Corporation, who had received sanction to do so from the Board of Trade in late 1913, subject to the provision of triple insulation between the pole and overhead conductor. Bournemouth now informed the Board of Trade that the gas brackets had been attached without the additional insulation, and in one case owing to the fusing of an insulation bolt, the pole became earthed and the gas ignited. Bournemouth Corporation, no doubt becoming concerned about the prospect of exploding traction poles, were pressing the Board of Trade to insist that Poole Corporation carried out the work. However, as Bournemouth were operating the Poole system it had certainly taken them some time to find out the regulations had not been complied with!

In October 1917 members of Poole Council, not for the first time, asked if representations could be made to Bournemouth Corporation to desist stopping trams in the middle of the road and putting out the lights before passengers had changed from one car to another.

An order from the Board of Trade for all tramways to reduce their coal consumption by 15 per cent involved still further reductions in services, including a proposal that the Lower Parkstone line be reduced to a half-hourly shuttle service between Pottery Junction and Park Gates East, only running between 8 am and 8 pm, thus saving 50,000 car miles a year. There was also disagreement between Bournemouth Corporation Tramways Committee and Poole Corporation over proposals to withdraw all Sunday trams, Poole claiming that they were required by workmen engaged in munitions and other war work. By August 1918 Poole Council were complaining about the reduced service, particularly on Sundays. However, it would have been impossible to increase the service without incurring the wrath of the inhabitants of Bournemouth and Christchurch who were also having to endure the same hardships - which were increased when 25 per cent of tram stops were removed for the duration in further attempts at saving fuel.

The problems of the Poole system are best summarised in a report of May 1918 by Mr I.M. Bulfin, the Bournemouth Tramways General Manager.

I find that a very erroneous impression exists in many places, but more especially in the Borough of Poole, as to the yearly financial results of the running of the trams in the Poole area, and in view of this impression, I have considered it essential that the following facts should be known.

The capital cost of the Poole undertaking, as far as Bournemouth is concerned, amounts to some £200,000, which amount does not take into account the necessary future amounts for depreciation and renewals, and this yearly charge on the undertaking amounts to some £12,000. For the financial year ending 31st March, 1918, I find the total car miles run on the Poole system amounted to 396,590, and this represents an amount of 7.26d. per car mile for capital charges alone. The total cost of current supplied for traction purposes on the Poole undertaking by the Bournemouth & Poole Electricity Supply Co. for the year ending 31st March, 1918, amounted to £5,436 11s. 11d., or a cost for power in the Poole area of 3.27d. per car mile. The total working expenses per car mile, exclusive of power costs on the whole undertaking amounts to 6.28d., and in this connection the Poole Tramways obtain the benefit, as the working costs on a large undertaking are very much less per car mile than if the Poole undertaking were run separately. Summarised, the results are,

Park Gates East, very little remains today to identify this site. Bournemouth Corporation car No. 76 awaits to depart for the Poole terminus, a member of the crew can be seen near the shelter approaching the 'Bundy Clock' (The Dumb Inspector) a timing device into which the crews of passing trams had to insert a card to record their arrival time.   *C.G. Roberts Collection*

In this post-1920 view Bournemouth Corporation car No. 104 awaits to depart towards Bournemouth. The shelter has been altered, the road going away to the left originally named Brown Bottom later became Fernside Road. The land to the right of the trams has since 1931 been the site of Poole municipal buildings. The tram shelter was eventually removed to land at Fisherman's Dock, Baiter, until eventually destroyed by vandalism. The 'Sloop' public house is to the right of the tram.   *B.L. Jackson Collection*

Capital charges per car mile	7.26*d.*
Power cost expenses	3.27*d.*
Working costs (exclusive of Power Costs)	6.28*d.*

Or, a total cost per car mile in the Poole area of 16.81d per car mile.

The total takings on the Poole line for the year ending 31st March, 1918, amounted to £25,911 15s., and for the car miles run during the year in the Poole area, namely, 396,590, represents a revenue per car mile of 15.65*d.*, and as the total costs of running per mile amount to 16.81*d.*, there is a deficit of 1.16*d.* per car mile, or on the 396,590 car miles run, a deficit of £1,916 17s., on the year's running, which has to be made good out of the revenue obtained on the remainder of the system.

In considering the position for the present financial year, the results are very much worse, the reduction of car miles by one sixth meaning that the capital charges per car mile are increased to 8.6*d.* The increase in the cost of current by 22½ per cent raises the cost of power to 3.6*d.* per car mile, and the increased bonuses and cost of materials raises the working costs, exclusive of power costs, to 8.72*d.*

Summarised, the total costs for the Poole undertaking for the year ending 31st March, 1919 will be.

Capital cost rer car mile	8.6*d.*
Power cost per car mile	3.6*d.*
Working costs (exclusive of power costs) per car mile	8.72*d.*
Or, a total cost per car mile of	20.92*d.*

I do not anticipate, under present conditions, a greater revenue on the Poole undertaking than that realised last year, namely 15.65*d.*, and on these figures, it will show a deficit of 5.27*d.* per car mile, or on the car miles to be run, namely, 330,492 a deficit of £7,257, on the coming year's running. The slight alteration of fares as suggested on the Poole area would not clear this loss but only ease the amount of deficit that would have to be made good out of the receipts from the Bournemouth area.

For the information of the committee I might state that the total receipts on the Poole undertaking on the last year's running by the company, namely 1905 was £15,538 4s. 3d., and the takings the Poole area for the year ending 31st March, 1918 was £25,911 15s. showing an increase of 66½ per cent in the 12 years of the Corporation's running.

Early Motor Bus Services in Poole

The development of the Canford Cliffs area in the late 19th century by the Canford Cliffs Land Society was the precursor of motor bus services in both Poole and the county of Dorset. The transportation of workmen from both Poole and Bournemouth was carried out by horse-drawn wagonettes, but it was later decided that some form of motorised conveyance would be an improvement, with the public being carried to defray running costs.

In the summer of 1899 the 'Canford Cliffs Motor Omnibus Company' was formed, and an MMC wagonette was purchased and commenced to operate between Bournemouth Square and Canford Cliffs on 23rd September, 1899. The motor bus, albeit in a very crude form, had arrived! A second MMC was purchased shortly after, and a third early in 1900.

History was made with the commencement of this service, the first vehicle and its driver, Walter Le Breton, both having the first Bournemouth licences

The earliest motor buses in the County of Dorset, two of the MMC eight-seat wagonettes operated by the Canford Cliffs Motor Omnibus Company Ltd, stand outside the passenger waiting room. Ironically passengers could be afforded more protection from the weather whilst awaiting their transport, but little once aboard, although top covers could be fitted if advance warning of weather conditions were known.

Ian Andrews Collection

issued for motor bus operation. It was the first public motor bus operation in both Bournemouth and the county of Dorset, and today 102 years later the Bournemouth-Canford Cliffs route as service No. 147 is still in operation, the oldest motor bus routes in the country.

The Coventry-Daimler was amongst the earliest motor vehicles on the road, and was powered only by a 4½ hp two-cylinder engine with a cylinder bore of 90 mm and stroke of 120 mm. The engine was water cooled, but as the radiator had not yet been developed, a large water tank was fitted between the rear frames of the chassis. This system was later replaced by a radiator on the Canford company vehicles.

Electric ignition was also still in development so the 'Hot Tube' system was employed, this being operated by what could best be described as a small petrol blowlamp which heated the platinum tube. Pressure to operate the blowlamp was obtained from the exhaust system. To start the system the blowlamp had to preheated in the time honoured way by creating a small fire!

The drive from the engine to the four-speed gearbox was via a double-faced leather cone clutch, reverse being obtained by shifting the cross shaft to engage the other bevel gear of the differential. The final drive was roller chain from the cross shaft to the rear wheels. The brake system consisted of a foot brake operating a band on a drum fitted to the cross shaft, the handbrake being a simple block application to the tyres of the rear wheels. All four wheels were of the normal carriage type of the period, having wooden spokes and rims onto which solid rubber tyres were fitted, the wheels being the weakest point of the whole design. The chassis frame was constructed basically of wood, reinforced by steel plates, and the rear springs were elliptic as on most carriages of the day. Ackermann steering was employed, controlled through a vertical shaft and tiller, but a steering wheel was fitted to vehicles constructed after 1900. The whole machine was little more than a motorised wagonette, but when first introduced in 1897 it represented the forefront of automobile engineering, and the commencement of motor bus operation in the Bournemouth and Poole area.

The opening of the Bournemouth Corporation tramway between the Square and County Gates, caused problems for the Canford Cliffs Company. Fearing that the wagonettes would take passengers away from the trams, Bournemouth Corporation suspended the licences, the service having to commence outside the Borough boundary at County Gates.

In 1907 the service was extended to Sandbanks, a Vulcan 30/35 hp single-deck vehicle being purchased for the journey. A Leyland 24/30 hp vehicle was added the fleet in May the following year, although for reasons unknown both vehicles had their licences cancelled at the end of 1908. By this time the temperamental MMC wagonettes had reached the end of the road, having become difficult to maintain as the manufacturers had ceased business.

In January 1909 two Milnes-Daimler single-deck buses were purchased from the Glasgow & South Western Railway, each having two bodies; a covered saloon for the winter and a canopied open-sided char-a-banc body for the summer. The latter bodies were considered dangerous, so a local blacksmith, Clements, constructed two bodies with sides up to waist rail level.

George Fox had taken over the company in the early days of World War I, but in March 1915 Bournemouth Corporation, in one of their periodic purges, refused a

Two 1905 Milnes Daimlers were acquired by Canford Cliffs Motor Omnibus Company from the Glasgow & South Western Railway in 1909. Both vehicles were purchased with two Dodson bodies - one for winter, and one for summer use. The 'toastrack'-style summer body on SD 503 is shown above, and below with Dodson B20R bodies for winter use, with George Randall at the wheel, probably in Canford Cliffs just prior to World War I. *(Both) The late George Randall*

The Canford Cliffs Motor Company Milnes Daimlers had their Dodson 'toastrack'-style bodies replaced by safer, more enclosed bodies built by Clements of Westbourne in 1912 for summer use. SD 503 is in a light coloured livery in Canford Cliffs, again with George Randall at the wheel shown above, whilst below George Randall, this time in conductor's uniform, is seen with Milnes Daimler No. SD 504 carrying its 1912-built summer body in a dark livery. *(Both) The late George Randall*

EL 273 one of two De Dion Bouton 18-seat vehicles acquired by Eugene Poulain in April 1905. In a letter to the *Automotor Journal* in the August Mr Poulain was most enthusiastic, stating 'The bus does eight trips a day over 70 miles, and every trip has been exact to the minute. The mechanical part is admirable. Since 15th April when we set out from Paris, the machine has travelled every day, and we have not had a single difficulty, after having covered 6,500 miles'.

B.L. Jackson Collection

FX 776 a 30 hp De Dion Boulton , acquired in 1911, with a body supplied by Poole coach builder Knight, stands outside the Haven Hotel at Sandbanks.   *Ian Andrews Collection*

further licence. Fox continued to operate from Poole where the council had no objection. In August 1918 the business passed to Bournemouth & District Motor Services.

Canford Cliffs Motor Company

Reg No.	Chassis	Type	Built	Acquired	Sold	Notes
EL 59	MMC	WNE	1899	1899	1/09	A
EL 60	MMC	WNE	1899	1899	1/09	A
EL 61	MMC	WNE	1899	1899	1/09	A
SD 503	Milnes-Daimler		1905	1/09	8/18	B
SD 504	Milnes-Daimler		1905	1/09	8/18	B
EL 491	Vulcan	CH	1907	1907		C
EL 547	Leyland		5/08	1908		C

Notes
A   The wagonettes did not receive registration numbers until 17th December, 1903.
B   Both vehicles had a Clements body for Summer use from 1912, and a 21-seat Dodson for Winter use.
C   Registration for vehicle cancelled September 1908.

Previous Owners
SD 503/4 New to Glasgow & South Western Railway. To Martins, Bow, London Autumn 1908.

Disposals
SD 503/4 To Bournemouth & District 8/18. Sold 1919.

Sandbanks at the turn of the century was a very different place than it is today, being nothing more than a sand spit on the north shore of the entrance to Poole Harbour, which had little to offer the visitor. The only building of any importance was the Haven Hotel, its place in history being assured after Marconi set up the World's first wireless station there, transmitting to the Isle of Wight in 1901. The proprietor of the hotel - Frenchman, Eugene Poulain - was far sighted enough to see the advantage of a bus service between his hotel and Poole.

With a capital of £2,000 the 'Poole & Sandbanks Motor Omnibus Company Ltd' was registered in November 1903 (the name was later changed to The Sandbanks Motor Car Company) the business being conducted from an office at 27 Fish Street, Poole. Although a 'motor' omnibus company, the first two vehicles were actually 15 hp 'Lifu' steam buses, the first of which commenced running between Sandbanks and Park Gates East in March 1904, and the second, two months later. These were painted in a livery of crimson lake with black lining and detail work. Built by the Liquid Fuel Engineering Company of East Cowes, Isle of Wight, they were far from successful despite the easy route over which they travelled. It was said they were difficult to maintain, but oil firing of boilers at that time was temperamental and this could well have contributed to their failure, and they were replaced by motor buses.

The first of these arrived in April 1905, a De Dion two ton 18-seat saloon bus, two passengers sitting outside with the driver, and the others in the enclosed saloon. Both of these vehicles were described as painted chrome yellow, lined out in black. Expanding the service from September 1905 six journeys a day to Bournemouth commenced. In 1910 the first of five De Dion char-a-bancs with 28-seat bodies constructed by Poole body builder A. Knight & Co. joined the fleet.

As with the Canford Cliffs company, Poulain had difficulties with Bournemouth Corporation over licensing within the Borough, but Poole

Corporation were only to happy too oblige, and the service was concentrated on Poole. Unfortunately the commencement of World War I soon overtook the business, three of the vehicles being requisitioned by the War Department whilst the remaining two later joined the fleet of Bournemouth & District, which within a short time became Hants & Dorset and became the principal stage carriage operator in the Poole area.

Eugene Poulain

Reg No.	Chassis	Body	Type	Built	Acquired	Sold	Notes
EL 159	Lifu steam bus		SD	1904	3/04		
EL 162	Lifu steam bus		SD	1904	1904		
EL 273	De Dion Bouton 24 hp		B18	1905	1905		
?	De Dion Bouton 24 hp			1905	1905		
FX 776	De Dion Bouton 30 hp	Knight			2/11	7/18	
FX 1080	De Dion Bouton 35 hp	Knight			1/12	11/14	A
FX 1546	De Dion Bouton 35 hp	Knight			3/13	7/18	
FX 1870	De Dion Bouton 35 hp	Knight			9/13	11/14	B
FX 2139	De Dion Bouton 35 hp	Knight			3/14	11/14	C

Notes	Disposals
A Named 'Lizzie'	FX 776. To Bournemouth & District. 10/19 to Wiles, Bournemouth as lorry.
B Named 'Lizzie II'	Later Parnell (dealer) scrap.
C Named 'Lizzie III'	FX 1546. To Bournemouth & District. 1/20 to Wiles, Bournemouth as lorry.
	FX 1080/1870/2139. To War Department as lorries.

An Early Proposal for Trolleybuses in Poole

Before moving to the years following the war, one interesting scheme deserves mention. Apart from the offer of Bournemouth Corporation to provide trolleybuses in Poole described on page 79, a scheme was put forward in 1913. The *Bournemouth Directory* for 1st March, 1913 contained a suggestion for a 'Railless Traction' scheme to meet the needs of Branksome Park, Canford Cliffs, Lilliput and Sandbanks, the extension of the Bournemouth Corporation tramways being considered impracticable. The promoters of the scheme were Messrs Clough Smith, the well known trolleybus manufacturers. The proposed routes were:

1   County Gates to Sandbanks along The Avenue, Western Road, Haven Road, Canford Cliffs Road, Flaghead Road, Haven Road and Banks Road.

1A   from a junction with Haven Road along Ravine Road for 3.78 chains.

2   Poole (Park Gates East) along Sandbanks Road and Lilliput Hill Road to a junction with Haven Road.

2A   from Shore Road to Haven Road.

In conjunction with this scheme (known as the Poole, Sandbanks & Westbourne Railless Traction Co.) a film and talk dealing with trolleybuses was given on 28th February, 1913 at the Electric Theatre, Commercial Road, Bournemouth. Representatives of Bournemouth and Poole Corporations attended, the Mayor of Poole being in the chair. On 3rd January, 1914 the promoters 'formally deposited' their Bill in the House of Commons, but it was later withdrawn.

Chapter Five

Poole Tramway Decline and Replacement

The great changes brought about as a result of the war affected everybody in all walks of life, and their mode of transport was no exception, advancements in motor bus design had changed people's perception towards the tram. The facts that a steel wheel on steel rails offered a low rolling resistance of 5-10 lb. per ton compared with 50 lb. plus of a rubber tyred vehicle, and the rapid effective braking, deceleration and acceleration which was far superior to the motor buses of the period was overlooked in the world of the 1920s. Even a Royal Commission on Transport had little to say in favour of the tram.

There was indecision as to whether to extend the tramways in Bournemouth and Poole or replace them with motor buses or trolleybuses. The neglect of the war years also had to be rectified, in March 1919 it was decided to carry out track repairs on the Poole system and repaint many of the traction poles. At about this time the matter of road works west of County Gates was under discussion; the state of the road was said to be bad and there were large pot-holes in the road surface; all of this (it was said) was due to the deplorable state of the tramway. The weight of increasing road traffic added to the wear and tear, traction engines and later heavy lorries being the main offenders. The section between Park Gates West and Park Gates East having to be relaid again in April 1921.

At the Bournemouth Tramways Committee meeting held on 23rd January, 1925 a letter was read from the Poole Town Clerk stating that his Council was considering the reconstruction of Poole Road between County Gates and Pottery Junction, and possibly Ashley Road from Pottery Junction to Constitution Hill. As a result of this Bournemouth Corporation's Tramways Committee later voted in favour of inviting tenders for the reconstruction of the tramway between County Gates and Constitution Hill and in favour of applying for sanction to borrow the amount of finance required for this work. However, Bournemouth Town Council sounded a cautionary note by referring the matter back to the Tramways Committee for reconsideration and asking for a further report. The Bournemouth Corporation Tramways General Manager produced a report showing that trams were the most efficient form of transport compared with buses and trolleybuses due to their low accident rate and high seating capacity. The decision was therefore taken to proceed with the re-construction of the tramway between County Gates and Constitution Hill, (this being announced in March 1925).

There had been much discussion as to the best material for the reconstruction of the roadway using either concrete or asphalt, with one councillor proposing a wood-blocked road. The council decided to use asphalt. The relaying work did not proceed without problems. Firstly, there was considerably more traffic using the roads than when previous relaying had taken place, and by early November there were complaints regarding the replacement bus service provided by Bournemouth Corporation. Of the three Tilling Stevens 37-seat

A pre-World War I view of a Bournemouth Corporation bogie car ascending Constitution Hill. Although development had already commenced in the area, the view from this point 90 years later shows that many of the fields and open spaces have been developed.   *B.L. Jackson Collection*

Bournemouth Corporation car No. 7 draws the amps as it follows another car up Constitution Hill during 1913. Ironically Poole & District car No. 7 was the only vehicle fitted with adequate brake equipment to operate on this hill at the opening of the system in 1901.   *Andrew Hawkes Collection*

petrol buses, Nos. 13-15, RU 2012-RU 2014, it was observed that the buses had entrances at each end, and instead of these being used as an entrance and exit respectively passengers were allowed to rush in and out by both doors causing congestion, confusion, and a waste of time, and furthermore the entrances were considered too narrow. It also appeared that the drivers were free to act very much as they wished in the matter of where and when the buses should stop *en route*. There were also disputes concerning the fares charged. During the relaying a Poole man came before the magistrates and was fined £3 for stealing a length of tram rail. Messrs A. Stark & Company completed the relaying on 7th June 1926, and normal running resumed the following day.

The General Strike of 1926 was to close the whole system from Tuesday 4th May, when the entire staff of inspectors, drivers and conductors went on strike, as did all of the generating station, permanent way and overhead staff. By midday of Wednesday 5th power had been restored by the use of volunteers, the following morning a basic service commenced in Bournemouth with volunteer tram crews. This service was increased by Saturday, no service being operated on the Sunday. On the morning of Monday 10th a service was commenced between Poole and Bournemouth Square. By the following day all inspectors except one had returned as had six drivers, and gradually the strike crumbled. Men not returning to work by the 17th were informed they would be re-employed if required, and in all 79 employees had their employment cards returned to them.

By 1926 the condition of the track on the Lower Parkstone route was a cause for concern. The original 1906 track, on which only the odd rail had been replaced and a few minor repairs undertaken, now gave a very rough ride and its replacement had become a matter of urgency. Poole Council gave notice of this requirement to Bournemouth Corporation, the Tramways Committee discussed the matter in October and it was agreed that the line should be re-laid, the estimated cost was £30,000. On 11th November it was suggested that Bournemouth and Poole should discuss whether the trains should be replaced by buses on this route, and following this a joint sub-committee (consisting of representatives of Bournemouth and Poole councils) was formed to inquire into the possibilities of such a scheme. In March 1927 the Bournemouth Town Clerk was informed by the Board of Trade that a Provisional Order amending a section in a local Act to permit Bournemouth Corporation to operate outside the Borough would not be granted. It should be pointed out that prior to the 1930 Road Traffic Act, road passenger transport was administered by local authorities, under the Town Police Clauses Act of 1847 (as amended in 1899), the Public Health Act of 1875, and the Hackney Carriage Act of 1832. All having been drawn up in the horse-drawn era, these were outmoded in the present situation which was shortly to highlight their inadequacies.

It was later agreed that Poole should obtain bus operating powers, but in the meantime the Lower Parkstone line was to be put into good repair and continue until substituted by motor buses. The Town Clerk at Poole arranged to prepare a scheme for motor bus operation by Poole between Poole and Bournemouth for consideration by Bournemouth, and on 9th April, 1927 Poole put forward a proposal for powers to operate buses through Lower Parkstone. In September 1927 the final proposal agreed between the Councils of Bournemouth and Poole was that Poole would apply for bus operating powers generally in that Borough as soon as possible. When such powers had been obtained and Poole was in a position to operate buses then Bournemouth would surrender the lease of the Lower Parkstone line and would pay Poole the sum of £20,000 and that Authority would undertake the re-instatement of the road surface following removal of the tram track. At this stage it had not been decided who would remove the rails from the roadway, but it was estimated that the scrap value of the material and old concrete would just about cover the cost of the work. It was agreed that whoever removed the track would be entitled to the old material. Furthermore, it was agreed that if Parliament refused to grant Poole Corporation its bus operating powers, or if Poole withdrew its Bill, then the above-mentioned proposals would be null and void, but Bournemouth would pay Poole half the cost incurred by them in connection with the promotion of the Bill.

On 4th October, 1927 it was suggested that negotiations should commence with regard to allowing buses to run to Bournemouth Square instead of County Gates (as originally planned), and four days later it was suggested that if all fares received between Bournemouth Square and County Gates were paid to Bournemouth then Bournemouth might agree to this proposal.

On 8th December, 1927 Poole started the process of promoting a Bill, which would allow them to run motor buses over the following routes:

County Gates, Canford Cliffs, Sandbanks
Sandbanks, Poole
Poole, Parkstone Station, Penn Hill Avenue, Lindsay Road, County Gates
Poole, Sandbanks Road, Compton Avenue, Penn Hill Avenue, Lindsay Road, County Gates
Poole, Ringwood Road, Newtown
Poole, Oakdale, Newtown
Poole, Hamworthy, Upton
Poole, Oakdale, Upton
Newtown, Sea View Road, Ashley Road, Pottery Junction.
Wallisdown, Alder Road, Pottery Junction

In March 1928 Bournemouth said (on learning that Poole Corporation was proposing to enter an agreement with Hants & Dorset Motor Services Ltd for seven years from 24th June, 1928) it would withdraw its objection to Poole's Bill if certain conditions were met. Among these conditions were that the clauses in the Poole Bill relating to 'Powers to provide and run buses' and 'Working and other agreements' should not be exercised without the sanction of Bournemouth - that a capitation fee of ½d. should be charged per passenger on any part of the tramway between Poole and Park Gates East; buses not to stop within a certain distance of tram stops and a route was also laid down by Bournemouth; from Poole Tram Terminus to Park Gates East over the tram route (via Parkstone Road) or via Longfleet Road then via Lower Parkstone to North Lodge Road, along that road, Lindsay Road, The Avenue, County Gates then via the tram route to Bournemouth Square. This route was unsuitable for double-deck buses because of the low bridge in North Lodge Road

On 15th May, 1928, it was announced that Hants & Dorset Motor Services Ltd would operate the services in Poole including the Lower Parkstone line. The company had to pay £5 per vehicle per quarter licensed by the council, the period of agreement being until 7th June, 1935.

Thus the 'Poole Corporation' Bill was put before Parliament in the summer of 1928. It covered several other domestic issues such as water supply. The omnibus section of the document contained 19 pages of provisions and clauses, the wording of several of them making interesting reading 73 years later:

> 'Omnibus' means any stage carriage moved by animal power or by mechanical power (including in that expression steam, electrical, and every other motive power not being animal power) obtained from some internal source.
>
> Subject to the provisions of this Act the Corporation may provide and maintain (but shall not manufacture) and may run omnibuses within the borough and with the consent of the Minister of Transport and the local authority of the district along any route outside the borough within a distance of ten miles from Poole railway station. Every omnibus moved by electrical power shall be so equipped and worked as to prevent any interference with telegraph communication.

The latter clause in fact meant that Poole had obtained authority to operate trolley buses two years ahead of neighbouring Bournemouth.

At the time there were rumours concerning a 'secret agreement' between Hants & Dorset and Poole Corporation. In its leading article, *Motor Transport* stated that as the information about the agreement had not reached them through official sources, they had taken the precaution of communicating with the Town Clerk in order to ascertain whether it was substantially correct, his reply being that the appropriate committee report was communicated confidentially to the council and it would not be in their interests to publish it at the moment. Noting that the Town Clerk did not imply that it was in any way inaccurate, whilst refusing to confirm its accuracy, the leading article continued: 'While regretting to go counter to the wishes of the Council of Poole, we feel that in the interest of our readers and in view of the fact that the Poole Corporation Bill is now before Parliament, we cannot postpone dealing with the matter'.

They then disclosed that Hants & Dorset proposed to pay Poole Council the quarterly sum of £5 in respect of each bus licensed. Furthermore, the council, so far as they lawfully could, would not grant licences to other persons to run buses in the Borough, except where the renewal of existing licences was concerned. If, however, the licences were to be renewed (other than four specified licences), or if the council were required by any competent authority to make a grant, Hants & Dorset was to be compensated with additional licences. In return for this Hants & Dorset would not oppose the Bill.

The editorial of the same issue, giving an entire page to the subject, commented that it was a matter of particular importance to the passenger carrying industry. The council appeared to proposing to do its level best to refuse licences to anyone else, and should it be compelled to do so, to compensate Hants & Dorset by granting them two free licences. These might conceivably afford the company the opportunity to kill off every single bus under other ownership that had succeeded in obtaining a licence. The editorial asked if an arrangement of this kind was at all consistent with the obligations of a licensing authority. 'The recognised ruling is to the effect that such an authority is bound to act judicially, it must hear and

Bournemouth Corporation car No. 101 stands at the Poole terminus. Beyond an up train passes the level crossing, whilst in the foreground a lady dashes across the road either oblivious of the photographer or the vehicle approaching on the far right.   *R.K. Blencowe Collection*

Bournemouth Corporation car No. 8 passing 'Tennyson Buildings', Ashley Road, Upper Parkstone. The traction pole and span arm clearly show the arrangement of both overhead wires being attached at passing loops, also the street lighting fixed to the traction pole. This pole was also a section breaker, note the distribution/fuse box alongside, the section insulators in the wire being held in the special ears shown suspended from the cross arm.   *R.A. Wright Collection*

determine according to law and bring to that task an open and unbiased mind. In coming to a decision it must put aside preconceived opinions and previous resolutions and act without prejudice and without any partiality. Finally, it must treat all applications fairly and alike'. It concluded that if the Bill became law it would render the council unable to perform its duties as licensing authority properly. The final sentence gave an indication of the future: 'Of course, no such problems as this would arise if the licensing of vehicles were controlled by independent boards'. Indeed, the 1930 Road Traffic Act was soon to remove all such responsibility from local authorities.

There was also much debate in the Poole Council Chamber. One member stated that a lady had given him a copy of the journal and she had a serious grievance against the council because of such an agreement. Councillor Carter asked if, in view of the statements made, compensation would be paid to persons running omnibuses prior to the agreement in respect of losses they might incur through Hants & Dorset obtaining a monopoly. The Mayor replied that such a question could not be answered until such a claim was made. Several Councillors appealed for more sympathy towards small bus operators.

There had already been some uncomfortable moments earlier in the year when the Mayor refused to allow the contents of a letter containing details of Miss Foott's recent agreement with Hants & Dorset to be read. Alderman Cole referred to 'wangling' by members of the committee who were shareholders in Hants & Dorset. One member mentioned that there was a clause in the Tramways Bill under which season tickets could be granted to councillors at a reduced rate, but it was felt that with the bus services nothing should be accepted which could be construed as a bribe.

Giving evidence before the Parliamentary Committee, the Mayor of Poole (Alderman W.P. Hunt) stated that motor buses must eventually supersede the trams throughout the Borough. The corporation thought that their running on the proposed Lower Parkstone route would be a useful guide to possibilities for the remainder. There was much discussion regarding the route to Sandbanks, the council claiming this was rapidly expanding into a resort where they were spending large sums of money, and that there was a need for a regular service to meet great public demand. Replying to a question the Mayor said they were not at present proposing to own and run omnibuses themselves, agreeing that by 1935 the buses may be out of date. This was one of the reasons why they did not want to embark on large expenditure if they could avoid it. Power was being taken to borrow £35,000 for motor omnibuses and garages, but none of this would be required for seven years at least if everything was satisfactory with the company. His Worship agreed with a member of the committee that the running powers sought would give the council a hold over the company in case the latter should fail at any time.

The committee were informed that £10,000 of the sum received from Bournemouth was the estimated cost of restoring that portion of the road and 18 inches each side occupied by the tram lines. This being a County Road, the remainder of the cost (except £1,000) would be met from the Road Fund. The £9,000 remaining would be invested and retained for future transport facilities. Bournemouth Corporation estimated their loss on this tramway route at £3,000 a year and they were glad to get rid of it.

The junction of North Road and Ashley Road, Upper Parkstone, looking towards Bournemouth. A double track section of tramway curves from North Road on the right, into Ashley Road. A motor bus heads towards the junction, a tram appearing in the background. To the left, the junctions of Kipling Road and Cranbrook Road beyond which can be seen a parade of shops.

Andrew Hawkes Collection

The Poole terminus in Towngate Street viewed from the footbridge at the level crossing. Bournemouth Corporation car No. 111, a Brush-built car of 1921, has just arrived. Between Dean's Store and the advert hording can be seen the tramway waiting room.   *R.A. Wright Collection*

There had been many arguments and changes of policy, some never fully explained, during the course of both Council and Parliamentary procedures. However, the Bill progressed through Parliament and became the Poole Corporation Act on 3rd August, 1928. It authorised the corporation to operate buses within the Borough and up to 10 miles outside, with the exception of the County Borough of Bournemouth, no particular routes being specified. It also provided for the abandonment of the tramways and for bus services to be provided by an undertaking other than Poole Corporation.

In October 1928 Poole informed Bournemouth that they were willing to establish a bus service over the Lower Parkstone line as soon as possible but subject to Hants & Dorset being prepared to start operation on an agreed date, and referring to the £20,000 provided for in the original agreement. Bournemouth replied that the necessary arrangements had been put in hand.

Commenting on the proposed new bus service, the *Bournemouth Evening Echo* remarked: 'Until a few years ago the trams only came as far as Park Gates East, and the last tram ran at an absurdly early hour. Continual demand resulted in certain improvements, but at best the service was much inferior to that of the upper route - with the not unnatural consequence that it continued to be an unprofitable concern. To the poor service was added in the last few years decided discomfort in travelling, owing to the condition into which the track had fallen'. Addressing the new service it continued: 'There will be six new vehicles running over the whole route, and the complete journey between the Square, Bournemouth to the Library at Poole will occupy half-an-hour each way. The buses are covered top double deck types, with a seating capacity of 48 passengers each'.

The last tram departed from Bournemouth Square on Saturday 5th January, 1929 at 10.55 pm, a good number of people having waited for the privilege of riding on the last service over the lower road. A reporter from the *Echo* took the ride reporting that:

The last tram between Bournemouth and Poole to run over the Lower Parkstone route, before the substitution of motor buses, left the Square on Saturday night at 10.55 pm. The inside was quickly filled and a fair number of Spartans braved the icy blast on the upper deck. The tram left unheralded and unsung, but not in silence - certainly not when the tram left Pottery Junction. It was only then that the passengers realised exactly how bad a condition the trackway had fallen into as the tram rattled and banged over the worn out lines. The faithful few were making the through trip and became quite friendly and communicative, but certainly not sentimental over the passing of the old order.

The *Poole & East Dorset Herald* did not mourn the closure of the Lower Parkstone route either:

Late on Saturday night the last tramcar crawled with the customary groaning over the worn out track running the Bournemouth and Commercial Roads from Pottery Junction to Park Gates East. No one was sorry that this very unsatisfactory service had come to an end, yet the car carried a fair number of passengers, not of necessity, perhaps. Most of them appear to have taken a ride on it so they might claim the distinction of being the last tram passengers over the route. There are several bad portions on the tram route

A Bournemouth Corporation tram stands in the Albert Road loop in 'The Broadway', Ashley Road, Upper Parkstone, heading towards Bournemouth during the early 1930s. Today the shop fronts have been altered along with the methods of trading. The junction with Madeira Road on the left has now been closed to traffic. *R.A. Wright Collection*

Bournemouth Corporation car No. 117 waits to depart from the Poole terminus on the 11 mile run to Christchurch, travelling out of Dorset, through the County Borough of Bournemouth to the Borough of Christchurch in the County of Hampshire. No. 117, amongst the last trams built for Bournemouth, had the luxury of windscreens from new. *R.A. Wright Collection*

between Poole and Christchurch, but none so bad as that which is now mercifully to be pulled up. It was a source of discomfort and danger and of extreme anxiety to the man at the wheel, who would rather drive anywhere but there.

Thus the first part of the Poole tramway programme had been effected.

On Sunday morning the motor buses of Hants & Dorset commenced to operate over the route between Poole and Bournemouth. To record the event for posterity a reporter from the *Echo* rode on the first bus departing from Bournemouth Square at 10 am, being issued with the first ticket, a 5*d*. single, No. PY1.000. He reported:

The pneumatic tyres of the wheels prevented anything more than a gentle swaying motion, and the leather upholstered spring seats with comfortable back rests made the going travelling de-luxe. I found myself riding in equal comfort to that of a first class coach on a railway train. Our first stop was at County Gates, and our route was then via Lindsay Road to Archway Road, under the railway arch and onto the road followed by the Lower Parkstone tram route, and a few minutes later we were at Poole Park Gates East. Here we turned off towards Longfleet Road, turning at the corner by the Shah of Persia, from whence we ran into Poole to the Library corner in the High Street, the end of the outward journey. When I dismounted from the vehicle it had just turned twenty past ten. Before leaving Bournemouth I noted the number of a Poole bound tram car that left the Square some eight minutes before the bus on which I journeyed. Arriving at Poole I made my way to the tram terminus and waited for the tram. It came along about ten minutes after I had arrived in Poole.

The result of diverting the buses off the main road in Parkstone was demonstrated on the third day of service, when brand new vehicle No. 22, TK 1851, a Leyland TD1 with a Beadle H24/24RO body, was damaged when the driver took a wrong turning out of Archway Road and at a fair speed struck the railway arch over North Lodge Road. Fortunately nobody was injured in the incident, but a *Poole Herald* representative who was a passenger on the bus stated:

I was looking out of the forward window with my fellow passengers when suddenly we realised the bus would not go under the arch. We ran back along the deck for safety and just in time for the windows were smashed and we were lucky to escape from being injured by the flying glass. The passengers left the bus in an orderly manner and in less than a minute it was empty. The vehicle was firmly jammed under the arch, and but for this fact would undoubtedly have turned over with the force of the impact because the off side rear wheel was lifted high off the ground.

Unfortunately over the years a number of double-deck buses off route have had an affinity with this particular bridge.

The above incident apart, the new service was a success, bringing favourable comment from both passengers and traders along the route. This also had an effect on the remaining tram route through Upper Parkstone, passengers travelling direct to either Poole or Bournemouth preferring the motor buses. Also people chose to walk from points as far west as Constitution Hill (on the Upper Road) through to the Lower Road buses!

The tramlines were quickly removed from Pottery Junction to the Sloop Hotel at Park Gates East, Poole Council accepting a tender from the Improved Wood

Pavement Company of £17,895 10s. for wood block-paving the route, and
Tarmac Ltd of £3,768 16s. for asphalt surfacing.

Hants & Dorset timetables of the period had two whole pages devoted to the
replacement bus services:

> By arrangement with the respective Corporations, a Direct Service of Double Deck
> Omnibuses will operate between Bournemouth and Poole. The route will be to and from
> the omnibus stand Avenue Road, operating to Commercial Road via Bournemouth
> Square then via Poole Road to County Gates, Linsdsay Road, Archway Road,
> Bournemouth Road, Parkstone, Park Gates East, Parkstone Road to the Library, High
> Street, Poole. Weekdays, leaving Bournemouth at 5.50, 6.00, 6.20, 6.40, 6.50, 7.00 am and
> then every 10 minutes up to and including 11.30 pm.
>   Sundays, leaving Bournemouth at 9.40 am, then every 10 minutes up to and including
> 11.30 pm.
>   Weekdays, leaving Poole at 5.50, 6.00, 6.10, 6.20, 6.40 am then every 10 minutes up to
> and including 11.20 pm.
>   Sundays, leaving Poole at 9.30, 9.40, 10.00 am, then every 10 minutes up to and
> including 11.10 pm.
>   This service is duplicated during busy periods: 8 am to 9 am and 2 pm to 6 pm.

Condition of Service
  Passengers are most particularly requested to note that the conditions relating to this
service are: That no person can be carried on the above time-tabled Omnibuses who
wishes to commence and finish their journey in the Borough of Bournemouth,
passengers can be picked up *en route* for points outside the Borough, but the first stop
on the outward journey at which passengers will be allowed to alight will be at the
Omnibus Stand, County Gates in the Borough of Poole. Passengers coming into
Bournemouth from outside the Borough can alight at the official stopping places.

Stopping Places
  In the Borough of Bournemouth are: The Omnibus Stand, Avenue Road near The
Square; St Michael's Church; West station entrance (viz: on the Bournemouth side of the
Hospital on the outward journey): and from there direct to County Gates stand. In the
Borough of Poole the stopping places are: County Gates; Corner of Lindsay and
Leicester Roads; Corner of Archway Road and Penn Hill Avenue; Archway Road and
from there to Poole the stops recently used by Trams.

Fares
  For the First Stage out of Bournemouth and the Last Stage into Bournemouth, viz
between Bournemouth and County Gates, the fare will be 2d. Between County Gates
and Poole, intermediate fares on similar stages to the Previous Tram fares will be
charged. The through fare between Bournemouth and Poole and vice versa will be 5d.
Workmen's and Children's Fares similar to those previously in operation.

Poole						
1d.	Park Gates					
2d.	1d.	St Osmund's Church				
3d.	2d.	1d.	Archway Road Junction Bournemouth Road			
3d.	2d.	1d.	1d.	St Aldhelm's Church or Penn Hill Corner		
4d.	3d.	2d.	1d.	1d.	County Gates	
5d.	4d.	3d.	3d.	2d.	2d.	Bournemouth Square

Special Notice
  Additional Omnibuses will leave Poole and Bournemouth at quarter to and quarter past the hours from 9.45 am to 10.15pm and proceed via Penn Hill Avenue. Omnibuses leaving Poole at 10, 30 and 50 minutes past each hour proceed via Longfleet. Also on the return journey, leaving Bournemouth at the hour, 20 minutes and 40 minutes past each hour.

Following the opening of the Hants & Dorset bus station at The Square, on 8th March, 1931, all Hants & Dorset services operated to and from the new facility.

Although Bournemouth, or at least their Tramway Manager Mr Bulfin favoured trams to motor buses or the new 'Trackless Trolley', the fact was that the track and other items were in desperate need of replacement, and to operate an efficient service much of the system would require relaying as double track. Also, nationally Government thinking was starting to go against the tram.

Having visited several towns already operating trolley buses, Bournemouth Tramways Committee decided the time for change had come. The Bournemouth Corporation Act of August 1930 which was primarily obtained to extend the Borough boundaries, also gave authority to operate trolley buses in Bournemouth and Poole, the corporation of the latter not being able to object without good reason.

In January 1933 it was decided to operate an experimental trolley bus service between Bournemouth Square and County Gates, this commencing on 13th May. This being successful, it was decided that the trams would be replaced by the new 'Silent' mode of transport.

Final Tram Closure

The lease of the Upper Parkstone tram route was due to expire on 7th June, 1935. With this event in view Bournemouth offered to operate trolleybuses and also provide 'feeder' services, but Poole preferred motor buses - informing Bournemouth in August 1934 that trolleybuses were unacceptable in Poole. The Ministry of Transport (in an effort to resolve the situation) later invited representatives of Bournemouth Corporation and Hants & Dorset to discuss Poole Corporation's proposed sale of the tramway to Hants & Dorset. Following this meeting the Minister of Transport asked the councils to consider the needs of the area as a whole rather than from the interests of any particular part of it when reconsidering this matter. He also asked the councils to consider the appointment of a mutually acceptable transport expert to examine the matter with a view to finding a satisfactory solution. Bournemouth was in agreement with these proposals and asked the Minister to suggest someone. In the event Bournemouth Council appointed a sub-committee to negotiate with Poole Council. Late in 1934 Bournemouth drew up powers for trolleybus operation, a draft Bournemouth Corporation Act 1935 being prepared for the following route: Poole Road-Ashley Road-North Road-Parkstone Road-Longfleet Road-High Street (terminating on the east side of the level crossing in Towngate Street). In the course of the discussion between the two councils, Poole had asked that Bournemouth should guarantee some minimum amount to be paid annually to Poole in respect of the

The preserved tramway distribution and fuse box, now standing outside Poole Museum at the bottom of the High Street. Note the 'Magnet & Wheel' insignia of the British Electric Traction Group cast into the inspection door.   *B.L. Jackson*

Map of the former Poole & Bournemouth tram system, still on display in a grounded tram body on a farm in the Bridport area in the late 1970s.   *B.L. Jackson*

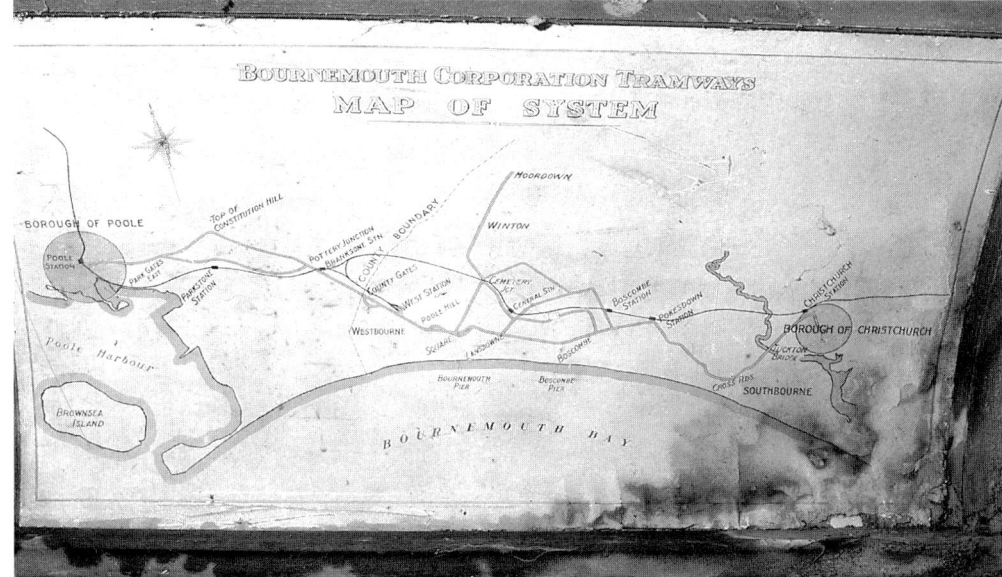

capitation fee offered in connection with the proposal to run trolleybuses in Poole. Bournemouth offered £3,500 per annum. Hants & Dorset, however, offered to pay £75,000 for 40 years in order to obtain the Poole transport rights and Poole accepted this offer. Hants & Dorset applied to the Traffic Commissioners for a Road Service Licence for a bus service over the Upper Parkstone tram route in April 1935. On 9th May, 1935 it was announced that Hants & Dorset had reached agreement with Bournemouth Corporation. Features of this agreement were incorporated into the Poole Road Transport Act 1935 (which received the Royal Assent on 2nd August, 1935) whereby Hants & Dorset purchased the tramway in Poole for £75,000, and was also to pay Poole Corporation ⅒th of the net profit received in respect of the following routes which were operated in place of the trams and which were also specified in the Act:

1   BOURNEMOUTH-POOLE via County Gates, Lindsay Road, Penn Hill Avenue, St Osmund's Church, Park Gates East, Parkstone Road
2   BOURNEMOUTH-POOLE via Poole Road, Pottery Junction, Bournemouth Road, Castle Hill, Commercial Road, Longfleet Road
2A   BOURNEMOUTH-POOLE via County Gates, Lindsay Road, Archway Road, Bournemouth Road, Park Gates East, Longfleet Road
3   BOURNEMOUTH-POOLE via Poole Road, Ashley Road, St Peter's Road, North Road, Park Gates East, Parkstone Road
4   BOURNEMOUTH-POOLE via Poole Road, Ashley Road, St Peter's Road, North Road, Park Gates East, Longfleet Road
5   BOURNEMOUTH-CONSTITUTION HILL via Poole Road, Ashley Road

Bournemouth Corporation was to receive £1,000 per year plus the profit on fares received by Hants & Dorset from passengers travelling wholly within the Boroughs of Bournemouth and Christchurch. Under this agreement Poole Corporation agreed not to operate their own buses provided that the company carried out its obligations. The agreement was for 22 year periods, expiring on 31st December, 1975. The last Bournemouth Corporation tram ran over the Upper Parkstone line on 7th June, 1935.

It was first intended to arrange some ceremony to mark the occasion, but owing to the illness of the Mayor of Poole (Councillor A.J. Dacombe) the proposal was abandoned, and. unfavourable weather reduced the number of sight-seers to a minimum. The *Echo* reported:

> The final five or six tramcars left the Towngate Street terminus bearing the ominous mark 'Depot Only'. Passengers were accepted only as far as the Ashley Road depot, after which they made a through run to Bournemouth. On each there was only one or two passengers. Matters, however brightened up towards 11.30 pm and a little knot of intending passengers assembled at the terminus all intent on being able to say that they had taken the last ticket issued by the tram service in Poole.
>
> With the familiar clanking and rattle which had become all too noticeable during the past few months with the tramlines beginning to show signs of wear, the last tram started. At the Ashley Road depot - now locked up and silent - the last tram made its last passenger stop. The passengers quietly disappeared with a sort of subdued air suggestive of mourners returning from a funeral. The tram service had ended and the last tramcar disappeared towards Bournemouth. Dorset's only tramway system had closed.

The replacement bus service commenced from both Bournemouth and Poole at 5.30 am on Saturday 8th July. On the first departure from Poole, the first ticket was purchased by a Mr A.S. Stokes, whose late father had purchased the first 1*d*. ticket in 1929 when the lower route went over to motor buses. Again there was lavish praise for the new service. The *Echo* reported:

> It seemed like the peace of a Sunday without the screeching and grinding of the trams. The only thing is that probably a number of people overslept. They have been accustomed to rely upon the first tram coming along as a sort of alarm clock to awaken them. Now the only noise is the occasional clip-clop of a horse drawn milk cart, or the rattle of a hand pushed milk pram.

Thus the story of trams in Poole comes to a close, never in the 'big league', even when operated as part of the Bournemouth system. The marriage, like that of the Somerset & Dorset Railway which had running rights over the London & South Western Railway into Bournemouth, was not always the happiest of unions!

The trams did however provide a much needed service for many years until usurped by the more flexible motor bus, and there is little doubt that for Poole to have accepted the Bournemouth trolley bus would have been a blow against civic pride.

On 8th April, 1936 the final tram service in Bournemouth, between the Square and Christchurch, ceased, the trolley bus taking over, the latter being looked upon as the marvel of the age. However, like the tram, with the passage of time it was to fall out of favour, the motor bus ruling supreme!

One of the few surviving photographs of a vehicle in the Bournemouth & District Silver Fleet. No. 6, (FX 4663) a Daimler 'Y' type acquired in June 1919 and fitted with a Kiddle 28-seat char-a-banc body, waits to depart from County Gates with a service to Sandbanks. Later joining the Hants & Dorset fleet, No. 6 was sold in September 1928 becoming a lorry in the Croydon area, until withdrawn in September 1932.				*Hants & Dorset Archive*

Chapter Six

Hants & Dorset 1920-1940

The business was founded by William Wells Graham, who had previously assisted his father with the West Cliff Mews at Bournemouth. Not wishing to continue in the jobmasters profession, and having the foresight to see the future of the motor vehicle, William formed W.W. Graham & Company, opening the West Cliff Garage in 1905. In 1911 premises on Poole Hill (later to become the offices of 'Charlie's Cars') were acquired. As well as the car hire business Graham became an agent for several of the leading manufacturers of the period.

Through this business Graham met Walter Flaxman French, who had been involved in the omnibus industry since the turn of the century and who had contacts in British Automobile Traction, the subsidiary of BET, and was on the management of both Maidstone & District and Aldershot & District Motor Services. Soon the two businessmen were discussing the idea of forming an omnibus company in the Bournemouth area and possible investors were contacted including British Automobile Traction - resulting in 'Bournemouth & District Motor Services' being registered as a private company on 17th March, 1916. French was elected Chairman, and Graham Director and General Manager.

The first operations of the company were private hire and tours, but after six months services had to be curtailed owing to conditions arising out of World War I. Operations recommenced in August 1918 with the Bournemouth to Sandbanks service which had been taken over from George Fox.

There were many difficulties in opening up services following the war, such as shortages of manpower, vehicles, and materials. Added to this there was the Bournemouth Corporation Horse Committee, the appointed body who looked after Hackney carriage affairs, and naturally the interests of the Borough Tramways had first consideration!

By July 1919 services had commenced from County Gates to Canford Cliffs and Sandbanks, at single fares of 6d. and 1s. and from the George Hotel, Poole, to Sandbanks, at 1s. single. 1s. 6d. return. Bournemouth & District was already spreading its wings in the Poole direction. By mid-December a service of four buses a day to Wimborne, via Upper Parkstone, Poole, Newtown, West Howe and Canford Village had commenced operation. In late January 1920 this service was extended to Blandford, and to Shaftesbury two years later.

The summer of 1920 saw three services of Bournemouth & District serving Poole.

1st August, 1918	County Gates-All Saints Church-Canford Cliffs-Sandbanks. Extended periodically to Bournemouth in the early days, but later to become a Bournemouth to Sandbanks service.
23rd May, 1919	Poole-Sandbanks.
December 1919	Bournemouth- Upper Parkstone, Poole, Newtown, West Howe, Canford, Wimborne (extended to Blandford January 1920).

Bournemouth & District Service No. 1 County Gates, Canford Cliffs, Sandbanks.
County Gates *dep.* 9.00, 10.00, 10.30, 11.00, 11.30 am, 12 noon, 12.30, 2.15, 2.30 then every half-hour up to and including 6.30 pm.
Sandbanks *dep.* 9.30, 10.30, 11.00, 11.30 am, 12 noon, 12.30, 2.00 then every half-hour up to and including 7.00 pm.

Bournemouth & District Service No. 2 Poole (George Hotel), Sandbanks.
George Hotel *dep.* 10.15, 11.15, 12.15, 2.15, 3.15, 4.15, 5.15, 6.15 pm.
Sandbanks *dep.* 10.45, 11.45 am, 12.45, 2.45, 3.45, 4.45, 5.45, 6.45 pm.

BOURNEMOUTH & DISTRICT MOTOR SERVICES, LIMITED.

NOTICE.

Service of Motor Omnibuses

BETWEEN

Bournemouth, Poole and Wimborne,

Via NEWTOWN AND CANFORD.

Motor Omnibuses will run Daily (Sundays included) as follows :—

	a.m.	noon.	p.m.	p.m.
Bournemouth Square dep.	9.0	12.0	3.30	6.30
Poole, George Hotel ,,	9.30	12.30	4.0	7.0
Newtown, Albion Hotel	9.35	12.35	4.5	7.5
Canford Village, dep.	9.55	12.55	4.25	7.25
Wimborne, Crown Hotel,the Square, arr.	10.5	1.5	4.35	7.35

	a.m.	p.m.	p.m.	p.m.
Wimborne, Crown Hotel. the Square,dep.	10.15	2.15	5.0	7.40
Canford Village, dep.	10.25	2.25	5.10	7.50
Newtown, Albion Hotel	10.45	2.45	5.30	8.10
Poole, George Hotel, dep.	10.50	2.50	5.35	8.15
Bournemouth Square, arr.	11.20	3.20	6.5	8.45

The ROYAL MEWS, Norwich Avenue,   (By Order) **W. W. GRAHAM,**
Bournemouth.   Telephone **2264.**   General Manager

Bournemouth & District Motor Services timetable December 1919.

Bournemouth, The Square

9d						
9d.	*Albert Road, Upper Parkstone*					
9d.	9d.	*Poole, The George Hotel*				
1s.	9d.	3d.	*Newtown PO*			
1/3	1s.	9d.	6d.	*West Howe*		
1/3	1/3	1s.	9d.	4d.	*Canford Village*	
1/6	1/3	1/3	1s.	9d.	4d.	*Wimborne*

Although not directly concerned with the Poole history, in July 1919 a service had also commenced between Bournemouth and Ringwood via Longham and Ferndown. This, together with the Poole-Wimborne-Blandford service, was the first major challenge to the railways in the area as people forsook the circuitous 'Old Road' in favour of the buses.

In January 1920, a representative of Thomas Tilling Ltd joined the Board, the British Automobile Traction Co. (BAT) at that time holding a controlling

---

BOURNEMOUTH & DISTRICT MOTOR SERVICES, LIMITED.

NOTICE.

Service of Motor Omnibuses
BETWEEN

Bournemouth, Poole, Wimborne and Blandford Daily, as follows :

		Not Sundays.			Not Weds.	Only Weds.
		a.m.	p.m.	p.m.	p.m.	p.m.
Bournemouth Square, dep. -		9.45	12.0	2.50	6.30	8.30
Poole, The George Hotel ,,	-	10.15	12.30	3.20	7.0	9.0
Newtown, Albion Hotel ,,	-	10.20	12.35	3.25	7.5	9.5
Canford Village ,,	-	10.40	12.55	3.45	7.25	9.25
Wimborne, Crown Hotel ,,	-	10.50	1.5	3.55	7.35	9.35
Corfe Mullen, Coventry Arms		11.0	1.15	4.5	7.45	9.45
Sturminster Marshall ,,	-	11.13	1.28	4.18	7.58	9.58
Spettisbury, Railway Inn ,,	-	11.25	1.40	4.30	8.10	10.10
Charlton Marshall ,,	-	11.32	1.47	4.37	8.17	10.17
Blandford Market Place (arr.) Greyhound Hotel		11.45	2.0	4.50	8.30	10.30

		Not Sundays.			
		a.m.	p.m.	p.m.	p.m.
Blandford Market Place (dep.) Greyhound Hotel		9.15	12.30	3.0	5.40
Charlton Marshall	,,	9.25	12.40	3.10	5.50
Spettisbury, Railway Inn	,,	9.33	12.48	3.18	5.58
Sturminster Marshall	,,	9.45	1.0	3.30	6.10
Corfe Mullen, Coventry Arms	,,	9.58	1.13	3.43	6.23
Wimborne, Crown Hotel	,,	10.15	1.35	4.0	6.40
Canford Village,	,,	10.25	1.45	4.10	6.50
Newtown, Albion Hotel	,,	10.45	2.5	4.30	7.10
Poole, The George Hotel,	,,	10.50	2.10	4.35	7.15
Bournemouth Square (arr.)		11.20	2.40	5.5	7.45

The ROYAL MEWS, Norwich Avenue, Bournemouth. Telephone 2264.

(By Order) W. W. GRAHAM, General Manager

Bournemouth & District Motor Services timetable January 1920.

Two early Leylands stand in the doorway of the Wimborne Road garage, Poole, shortly after its opening. On the left PLSC1, B188 (RU 4228) with Leyland B31F body, new in November 1926 and withdrawn in March 1935 when it passed to Gosport & Fareham Omnibus Company as No. 2 until withdrawn in 1944. On the right PLSC3, B270, (RU 8679) fitted with a Leyland B30F body new in January 1929, withdrawn in September 1938 passing to Caledonian Omnibus Company as No. 28 being withdrawn the following year.   *A. Waller Collection*

A Leyland PLSC3 Lion of 1927-9 with a Leyland B35F body. A vehicle of this type inaugurated the Bournemouth-Swanage service via the Sandbanks Floating Bridge in 1927.   *Leyland Motors*

interest. On 27th July, 1920, the company became known as Hants & Dorset Motor Services Ltd, becoming a public company four years later, by which time other changes had taken place at a higher level. In 1922 Tilling acquired a considerable holding in British Automobile Traction, resulting in a joint development policy being pursued. Changes again took place in 1928 when the organization was restructured taking the title 'Tilling & British Automobile Traction Ltd'. The following year the Southern Railway acquired half the share capital of Hants & Dorset. It should be noted that BAT was the motor bus development branch of the BET, therefore the BET was not to be kept out of the Poole transport scene for long!

With the backing of the combine Hants & Dorset rapidly spread its wings, serving Bishop's Waltham, Eastleigh, Lymington, Romsey, Salisbury, Southampton and Winchester from 1920; Fareham, Gosport, Petersfield and Portsmouth from 1922; and Woolston from 1926. It was in the later part of the 1920s that the town service network at Poole was built up. There had been a difficult moment during 1921 when Elliott Bros (Royal Blue) applied to Bournemouth Corporation for licences to operate stage carriage services to Lymington, Ringwood, and Wimborne. Fortunately for Hants & Dorset, domestic matters within the Elliott family caused the scheme to be delayed until late 1923, when the council considered that the original applications had lapsed, and at that late stage were not prepared to grant additional licences. It did however, result in an agreement whereby Hants & Dorset would not operate tours and express services within 10 miles of Bournemouth Square, and Royal Blue would not operate stage carriage services, an arrangement under which the two companies worked well together, and more importantly, Hants & Dorset was free to explore its expansion in the Poole area.

The Poole-Sandbanks service had recommenced following World War I, by the end of 1921 it had lapsed as vehicles were required for other services. In March 1922 Mr Graham attended a Poole Council meeting with reference to bus services between County Gates and Sandbanks and Poole and Sandbanks. In July 1926 Poole Council drew attention to the condition of Banks Road, which they claimed was largely caused by omnibuses with solid tyres, and requested that the company use only vehicles with pneumatic tyres. Although Hants & Dorset was gradually establishing itself in the area, Poole Council were considering the idea of operating their own bus services, a matter being investigated by the General Purposes Committee in November 1926.

The concept of bridging the entrance to Poole Harbour had again been explored, several novel schemes being proposed - including a bridge commencing on the Sandbanks side with a spiral road rising to a height of 120 feet, with the Studland side descending on a gradual slope. Plans for this were abandoned after opposition from Poole Council, by which time the chain ferry had become established. This was provided by the Bournemouth & Swanage Motor Road & Ferry Company, the ferry arriving in 1926. Mechanical problems caused it to be withdrawn within a short time, the service not being resumed until April 1927. In March Hants & Dorset applied to Poole Council for licences for four buses to operate a through service between Bournemouth and Swanage. In March of the following year the local Swanage services of Russell Parsons were acquired, Hants

HANTS & DORSET MOTOR SERVICES, Ltd.

(In association with Southern Railway Co.)

TIME TABLE

Commencing June 8th, 1935

OMNIBUS SERVICE between

POOLE & BOURNEMOUTH

BOURNEMOUTH—
Registered Office: Royal Mews Norwich
Avenue, Bournemouth. Phone 5284

POOLE—
Tecemate Street. Phone 544
Wimborne Road. Phone 417

On and from Saturday, June 8th, 1935, the above Company will operate a Fleet of Double-deck Omnibuses on all Services to and from POOLE and BOURNEMOUTH, including the Route at present operated by the Bournemouth Corporation Trams, also extending the Upper Parkstone Service to the Sea View Hotel.

The Services will be numbered as follows:—

No. 1—From POOLE, via PARKSTONE ROAD, COMMERCIAL ROAD, CASTLE HILL, ST. OSMUNDS CHURCH, PENN HILL AVENUE, LINDSAY ROAD, COUNTY GATES, BOURNEMOUTH.

Time Table.
Weekdays. Depart Poole—
8.15 a.m., 8.30, 8.45 and then on each Hour, 15, 30 and 45mins. past each Hr. up to and incl. 10.45 p.m.
10 a.m. and then as on Weekdays (10.45 p.m. last bus)

Sundays.
8.15 a.m., 8.30, 8.45 and then on each Hour, 15, 30 and 45 mins. past each Hour up to and incl. 10.45 p.m.
10 a.m. and then as on Weekdays.

Weekdays. Depart B'mouth—

Sundays.

No. 2—From POOLE, via LONGFLEET ROAD, ASHLEY ROAD, CASTLE HILL, BOURNEMOUTH ROAD, ARDMWAY ROAD, LINDSAY ROAD, COUNTY GATES, BOURNEMOUTH.

Time Table.
Weekdays. Depart Poole—
5.50 a.m., 6 a.m., 6.10 a.m., 6.20 a.m., 6.40 a.m. and then every 10 mins. up to and including 11.30 p.m.
8 a.m., 8.30 a.m., 9 a.m., 9.30 a.m., 9.40 a.m. and then every 10 mins. up to and including 11.30 p.m.

Sundays.

Weekdays. Depart B'mouth—
5.50 a.m., 6 a.m., 6.20 a.m., 6.40 a.m. and then every 10 mins. up to and including 11.30 p.m., then every 10 mins. up to and including 11.30 p.m.

Sundays.

No. 3—From POOLE, via PARKSTONE ROAD, NORTH ROAD, ST. PETER'S ROAD, VIEW ROAD ASHLEY ROAD, POOLE ROAD, BOURNEMOUTH.

Time Table.
Weekdays. Depart Poole—
5.30 a.m., 5.55 a.m. and then every 10 mins. up to and including 11.35 p.m.
8.35 a.m., 9.5 a.m., then as on Weekdays (last Bus 11.35 p.m.)

Sundays.

Weekdays. Depart B'mouth—
5.30 a.m., 5.55 a.m. and then every 10 mins. up to and including 11.35 p.m.
8.5 a.m., 9 a.m., then as on Weekdays (Last Bus 11.35 p.m.)

Sundays.

No. 6—To and From CONSTITUTION HILL (Sea View Hotel), via ASHLEY ROAD, POOLE ROAD, BOURNEMOUTH.

Time Table.
Weekdays. Dep. Sea View Hotel—5.45 a.m. and then every 10 mins up to and including 11 p.m.

Sundays. 2 p.m. then as on Weekdays until 11 p.m.

Weekdays. Depart B'mouth—5.30 a.m., 6.10 a.m. and then every 10 mins. until 10.40 p.m.

Sundays. 1.40 p.m. then as on Weekdays until 10.40 p.m.

SPECIAL NOTICE.—It is the Company's intention when their permanent Licences are granted to run a Service between Upper Parkstone, along the following Route:—POOLE, Longfleet Road, North Road, Park Road, View Road, Ashley Road, Longfleet Road, Poole Junction, Poole Road, Bournemouth. This will mean that every other Omnibus on No. 3 Route will proceed between Bournemouth and Poole in the usual manner, the other proceeding via Upper Parkstone. ALSO No. 2 Service, at present proceeding via Bournemouth Road, Archway Road and Lindsay Road will then be run via Bournemouth Road, Pottery Junction, Poole Road to Bournemouth.

HANTS AND DORSET MOTOR SERVICES, LIMITED.

NOTICE.

By arrangement with the respective Corporations a Direct Service of Double Deck Omnibuses will be operated between

BOURNEMOUTH and POOLE

Commencing on the Morning of SUNDAY, the 6th day of January, 1929.

The Route will be to and from the Omnibus Stand, Avenue Road, Bournemouth, round the Square, and then via Poole Road to County Gates, Lindsay Road, Archway Road, Bournemouth Road, Parkstone, Park Gates East, Parkstone Road to the Library, High Street, Poole.

Time Table.

Week Days leaving Bournemouth at 5-50, 6-0, 6-20, 6-40, 7-0 and then every 10 minutes up to and including 11-30 p.m.
Sundays " " 10-0 a.m. and then every 10 minutes up to and including 11-30 p.m.

Week Days leaving Poole at 5-50, 6-0, 6-20, 6-40 and then every 10 minutes up to and including 11-20 p.m.
Sundays " " 10-0 a.m. and then every 10 minutes up to and including 11-20 p.m.

Conditions of Service.

Passengers are most particularly requested to note that the conditions relating to this service are :—That no person can be carried on the above time-table Omnibus who wish to commence and finish their journey in the Borough of Bournemouth, passengers can be picked up en route from points outside the Borough, but the first stop on the outward journey from Bournemouth at which passengers will be allowed to alight will be at the Omnibus Stand, County Gates, in the Borough of Poole ; passengers coming into Bournemouth from outside the Borough can alight at any of the official stopping places.

Stopping Places.

IN THE BOROUGH OF BOURNEMOUTH are :—The Omnibus Stand, Avenue Road, near the Square ; St. Michael's Church ; West Station Entrance (viz., on the Bournemouth side of the Hospital on the outward journey, and opposite the Hospital on the inward journey) ; and from there direct to the County Gates Stand. IN THE BOROUGH OF POOLE the stopping places are County Gates ; Corner of Lindsay and Leicester Roads, Corner of Archway & Penn Hill Avenue ; Archway Road ; and from there to Poole the stops recently used by the Trams.

Fares.

For the First Stage out of Bournemouth and the Last Stage into Bournemouth, viz., between Bournemouth & The County Gates the fare will be 2d. Between the County Gates and Poole intermediate Fares on similar Stages to the previous Tram Fares will be charged.

The Through Fare between Bournemouth and Poole and vice-versa will be 5d.
Workmen's and Children's Fares similar to those previously in operation.

Registered Office, The Royal Mews,
Norwich Avenue,
Tel. 2264. Bournemouth.

Poole Depot,
Wimborne Road,
Tel. 417 Poole.

By Order,
W. W. GRAHAM,
Director & General Manager.

Above: Hants & Dorset timetable for services between Poole and Bournemouth, 6th January, 1929.

Right: Hants & Dorset imetable for services between Poole and Bournemouth, 8th June, 1935.

& Dorset thus establishing a foothold in the Isle of Purbeck. The road mileage between Bournemouth and Swanage via the ferry was 13½ compared with 22 by the main road or by train via Wareham, and the floating bridge was to play an important part in future transport developments. It is also one of the few places in the British Isles where a service bus puts to sea on part of its regular route!

At a General Purposes Committee meeting on 10th July, 1928 it was reported that Hants & Dorset was willing, in view of the existing demand on the Poole-Sandbanks route, to run a service at once without waiting until the date when the agreement with the company came into operation, the sub-committee agreeing to this offer. Indeed, 1928 was a year of rapid expansion. Apart from the matter of the Lower Parkstone tramway replacement (covered on page 69), during the year the company opened its first garage in Poole, which was situated in Wimborne Road next to the George Hotel. It was a small structure capable of holding only four vehicles, but it established Hants & Dorset in the town.

On 4th September the council formed an Omnibus Committee, which replaced the General Purposes Committee on all affairs concerning omnibuses, there being little doubt the problems of the tram replacement and the developing bus services had caused matters to be put on a more formal footing. Even at that early date the parking of buses was becoming a problem, and at the December meeting a councillor complained that Hants & Dorset was not keeping within the limit of its stand in Kingland Road.

The principal routes commenced in Poole by the company between 1922 and 1929 were:

11.4.23	Bournemouth-Wareham via Upper Parkstone, Poole, Fleets Bridge, Upton, Lytchett Minster, Holton Heath, Sandford. Re-routed via Poole Quay and Hamworthy 10.4.27 (following the opening of Hamworthy Bridge).
17.3.24	County Gates-All Saints Church-Canford Cliffs-Parkstone Golf Links. Lilliput-Park Gates East-Poole. Later extended to Bournemouth, and later still curtailed to form a Poole-Canford Cliffs service.
5.7.24	Winton-Wallisdown service acquired from S.W. & C.L. Bushby. Later transferred to Bournemouth Corporation who numbered it Service 9.
10.4.27	Poole-Oakdale-Fleet's Corner-Upton.
10.4.27	Newtown-Oakdale-Poole-Hamworthy. Later extended to form Newtown to Upton service.
4.27	Bournemouth-Swanage, via floating bridge.
1.2.28	County Gates-Penn Hill Avenue-Lower Parkstone-Poole
1.2.28	County Gates-Penn Hill Avenue-Woodside Road-Parkstone Golf Links-Lilliput-Park Gates East-Poole.
1.2.28	Wallisdown-Branksome (Pottery Junction) via Alder Road. Extended from Branksome to Branksome Chine during the Summer months.
3.1.29	Bournemouth, (Avenue Road) Poole Road, County Gates, Lindsay Road, Archway Road, Bournemouth Road, Lower Parkstone, Park Gates East, Parkstone Road, Poole Library. (Lower Parkstone Tramway replacement service.)
30.3.29	County Gates-Branksome Dene, Branksome Chine-Canford Cliffs-Lilliput-Parkstone Golf Links-Junction. Woodside Rd/Penn Hill Avenue.
4.29	Bear Cross-Newtown-Oakdale-Tatnam or 'Shah of Persia'-Poole-Hamworthy-Upton.
1.7.29	Newtown 'Albion'-Sea Road-Madeira Road-St Osmund's Church-Ashley Cross-Lilliput-Sandbanks.

County Gates bus station, built in the mock-Tudor style so popular at that period. This superb view taken shortly after opening in the Autumn of 1932 shows Leyland TD2 G118 (TK 7286) one of a batch of 11 Eastern Counties L26/26R vehicles delivered in the Spring of that year. Behind stands a 1928 Leyland TD1 with a Short Bros O27/24RO body. Today the whole scene has changed with redevelopment, the bus station closing during 1953. Ironically G118 survived longer, rebodied by ECW in October 1945 and renumbered 947 in 1949. Following withdrawal in March 1952, it passed to a showman in Westmorland.

Brian Botley Collection

The closure of the Upper Parkstone tram route and the previous removal of most other operators in the Poole area gave Hants & Dorset a clear run for the town services. Although the Easter holiday accounts for Poole in 1936 recorded 20,017 miles run and £1,192 12s. 11d. taken in revenue, the previous year with trams still running on the Upper Parkstone route the figures had been 18,732 miles, for £1,093 3s. 3d. in revenue, which meant that an additional 2,157 miles of running had earned just £99 9s. 8d.

The small garage in Wimborne Road was replaced in January 1932 by a new one with offices in Towngate Street capable of garaging 40 vehicles, although the Wimborne Road premises remained as a parcel office, and just somewhere to park buses off the road during layovers, such was the congestion near the George Hotel. At the same time a small bus station was under construction at County Gates, this opening in the late summer of 1932. The County Gates property was built on land leased from Walter Dinnivan, a former Bournemouth char-a-banc owner who was murdered in May 1939. All three properties were constructed by Wilson & Company, a local building contractor. The former tram depot at Parkstone was also taken over, and at a Board meeting in July 1935 it was reported the company was currently paying £7 a week for outside garage space, and it was therefore urgent that Parkstone be made suitable for use as a bus garage. The final cost of alterations was £853.

The problems caused by buses loading and unloading around the George Hotel area and the Public Library in Lagland Street were causing concerns from the late 1920s, and the need for a central bus station became a pressing issue for both the company and Poole Corporation. The situation was not helped by indecision concerning plans for a bridge to cross the railway, thus alleviating the problems of Poole's two level crossings. As far back as 1924 a scheme had been considered for a bridge over the line at the White House Laundry site (later Kingland Crescent) but in 1936 the scheme was still being considered, the council making no decision on a bus station until the bridge matter was finalised! In February 1938 the company approached South Coast Theatres Ltd with a view to purchasing a piece of land they owned in the same area, and by the end of the year agreement had been reached between both parties and the corporation, after which the preliminary works commenced.

During the 1930s there was still a measure of acrimony between the authorities of Bournemouth and Poole particularly over the provision of buses along Wallisdown Road which had sections in both Boroughs. Problems arose when Bournemouth Corporation sought powers to operate trolleybuses along Wallisdown Road - a matter to which Hants & Dorset and Poole Council objected. After much discussion the matter was resolved by the Traffic Commissioners, whereby Hants & Dorset and Bournemouth Corporation had to co-ordinate their timetables for services along this road. Trolleybuses were never introduced along the proposed section of route from Wallisdown Cross Roads to Bear Cross.

COUNTY GATES—WINSTONE AVENUE

```
County Gates
1    Branksome Station
1½   1    Bourne Valley Gas Works
2    1½   1    Guest Avenue
2½   2    1½   1    Winstone Avenue
```

Workmen's Return Fare 4d. Return available up to 8-45 a.m.

UPPER PARKSTONE (Sea View Hotel)—WEST HOWE and BEAR CROSS

```
Sea View Hotel (5)
1    Old Wareham Road (3)
2    1    Alderney Hospital (2)
2    1½   West Howe (Shoulder of M.) (1)
4    3    2    1    Bear Cross (23)
```

COUNTY GATES—BRANKSOME CHINE

```
County Gates (2)
1    Tower Road (3)
2    1    Branksome Chine (4)
3    1    Canford Cliffs (5)
```

RETURN FARES—
Gates— Branksome Chine 3d.

BOURNEMOUTH—

COUNTY GATES and SANDBANKS

```
    Bournemouth Omnibus Station
30  1    County Gates
29  2    1    Chester Road,
28  3    2    1    All Saint's Church or Martello Road
27  3    2    1    Canford Cliffs
26  4    3    2    1    Bottom West Hill
25  5    4    3    2    1    Sandbanks Pavilion
24  6    5    4    3    2    1    Sandbanks, Haven Hotel
23  7
```

RETURN FARES—Bournemouth Stn. to Sandbanks ... 1/-
County Gates to Sandbanks ... 10d.

Residents' Tickets (in Books of one dozen) can be obtained from Charmbury's Ltd., 3 Bay View, Sandbanks, Suppliers of Confectionery, Drugs, Patent Medicines, Photographic Materials, and Arts and Crafts, Agents for Poole Pottery:—
Canford Cliffs—Bournemouth 4/6
Sandbanks—Bournemouth 9/-
Or from—F. Holloway, Estate Agent, Canford Cliffs.—
Or from the Company's Inspector at County Gates Omnibus Station.

POOLE and SANDBANKS

```
Poole (10)
1    Park Gates East (2)
2    1    Ashley Cross or Salterns Road (3)
3    2    1    Lilliput Square (4)
4    3    2    1    Top Evening Hill (5)
5    4    3    2    1    Shore Road (6)
6    5..  4    3    2    1    Pavilion (7)
7    5    4    3    2    1    Sandbanks Ferry (8)
```

RETURN FARES
Park Gates East—Sandbanks 10d.
Poole—Sandbanks 1/-
Poole—Pavilion ... ... 10d.

WALLISDOWN—PENN HILL.

```
Wallisdown
1    Winston Avenue
2    1    Alder Road
2    1½   1    Penn Hill Corner
4    3    2    1    Woodside Road
4    3    2    1    Compton Avenue Junction of Lilliput Road.
```

WALLISDOWN—CANFORD CLIFFS.

```
Wallisdown (1)
1    Winston Avenue. (2)
2    1    Alder Road (3)
2    1    1    Penn Hill Corner (4)
3    2    1    Haig Avenue (9)
4    3    2    1    Canford Cliffs (10)
```

Children's Fare: Penn Hill Corner—Branksome Chine 1d.

POOLE, PARKSTONE AND BOURNEMOUTH SERVICES.

Bournemouth Omnibus Station.   Special Fare:
Grand Cinema   Ashley X.—Poole 1½d.

```
1    County Gates
1    1    Branksome Station
2    2    1    Pottery Junction
3    2    1½   1    St. Osmond's Ch. or Mansfield Rd.
4    3    2    1    Park Gates East
5    4    3    2    1    Poole (The George or Library
```

Bournemouth Omnibus Station   Special Fares:
Grand Cinema   B'm'th Sq.—Spur Hill   2½d.
                                     County Gates—   1½d.
                                     Penn Hill Cr.—   1d.

```
1    County Gates
1    1    Penn Hill Corner
3    2    1    St. Osmond's Ch. or Mansfield Road
4    3    2    1    Park Gates East
5    4    3    2    1    Poole (The George, or Library)
```

Bournemouth Square   Special Fares:
Grand Cinema   B'mouth Sq.—Bourne Valley Road   1½d.
                                     Poole—Branscourt Rd.   1½d.
                                     B'mouth Sq.—Chah of Persia   4½d.

```
1    County Gates
2    1    Pottery Junction
3    2    1    Branksome Station
2½   1½   1    1    Albert Road
3    3    2    1    Police Station
3    3    2½   2    1    Top Constitution Hill or Sea View. B
4    4    3    2½   2    1    Park Gates East
4    4    3    2    2    1    Poole (The George or Library)
```

Extracts from Hants & Dorset fares tables, 1936.

Pre-War Ticket System

In the later days of Bournemouth & District and the early days of Hants & Dorset, fareboard single tickets were issued, these having the names of the fare stage points printed down the sides of the ticket, the value of the ticket being printed in the centre towards the top; as routes were added and fare changes took place the system became impractical. By October 1924 the first tickets with numbered fare stages printed down the sides appeared (sometimes referred to as 'Deaf and Dumb Tickets'), the fareboards being phased out. However before this, return tickets had been introduced during 1922, classed as 'Geographical Returns' and like the fareboards they also carried printed fare stage names. Again problems arose with inflexibility, and to counteract fraud, within a short while exchange tickets were issued on the return journey, the conductor withdrawing the original return ticket, this being accounted for against the exchanges issued.

From 1921 residents of Sandbanks and Canford Cliffs could purchase a book of 12 prepaid tickets to travel to County Gates, offering a substantial reduction on separate tickets. Following the 1935 agreement these tickets were extended into Bournemouth Square. By the end of April 1929 residents' tickets at reduced fares were available on the Poole-Sandbanks route, and by the October Hants & Dorset stated that workmen's tickets were available throughout the Borough except from County Gates to Sandbanks, where special 'Staff Tickets' for workmen were available upon application to the company by the employers of such men. It must be added the tickets themselves were a little more socially discreet; they did not actually spell things out in quite such class-ridden language.

Five-day scholars' tickets were also issued in the Poole area, these were just below 2½ inches square, as were the normal weekly tickets of the period. During World War II the scholars' ticket was restyled as a normal single bell punch ticket, no doubt as a paper saving measure.

The withdrawal of the trams from the Lower Parkstone road in 1929 created a special set of tickets to give accountancy details of the various sections of the route. These tickets were again of the fareboard type with the fare stage names printed down the sides, four types of ticket were issued, adult, child, workmen's singles, and early morning returns. To complicate matters there were different tickets for sections of the route still covered by the tram service, and for roads without trams! Those still covering the tram route had a coloured vertical stripe down each side, it being estimated 36 different tickets were in use at one stage. A situation which fortunately for the conductor only lasted a short while, from 1st October, 1933, ordinary tickets with side printed fare stage numbers were introduced; however, just to be different all tickets had a large 'X' overprinted across the face issued on the Poole-Bournemouth route.

Advertising on the backs of tickets had from the earliest days been a source of revenue to bus companies, and the traders of Poole and Bournemouth were frequent advertisers. Perrins, tailors and outfitters, Poole, offered 3*d*. off every 5*s*. for cash purchases upon presentation of an 8*d*. ticket.

Hants & Dorset came to an agreement with Bournemouth Corporation during 1930 to collect fares from passengers travelling entirely within the Bournemouth Corporation area on two routes. On journeys operating into the Bournemouth

Corporation Transport Area conductors issued special Bell Punch tickets over-stamped 'BCT'. These tickets were issued to Hants & Dorset by Bournemouth Corporation from their bulk ticket stores (at Southcote Road depot when your C.G. Roberts, was employed there). This arrangement was necessary under an agreement with Bournemouth Corporation of 1930 and under the terms of the Poole Road Transport Act 1935, following the closure of the last Poole tram route. Initially 'BCT' tickets were 'geographical', but from about 1940 a standard set of 'fare stage' tickets to cover all Hants & Dorset services operating in the BCT Area was introduced. It should be noted that the 1*d*. (green) was the only BCT ticket in use for many years up to about 1950 for the fare from County Gates to Bournemouth Square, although as the years went by other values were used following various fares increases. The 'BCT' tickets with 'Child Ret.' on them date from 1956, the Traffic Commissioners granting a Bournemouth Corporation fares revision at a Public Sitting held at the Law Courts at Bournemouth (which C.G. Roberts attended whilst working for BCT) where the introduction of Child Returns was sanctioned and so the 'BCT' tickets had to be altered accordingly.

On journeys from Poole to Bournemouth the BCT Area started at the bus stop immediately to the west of County Gates (i.e. the last stop in the Borough of Poole) and referred to as 'Dorset Loop' in the company's fare tables. Two interesting features of this arrangement were that BCT inspectors could board Hants & Dorset buses in the BCT Area and that Hants & Dorset buses travelling to or from the west of Bournemouth were not permitted to stop in the Square (other than the Bus Station), hence the stops in Avenue Road (inward from Poole), and on Poole Hill (Royal Victoria Hotel) (located near the traffic lights on Poole Hill) - this being the first Hants & Dorset stop after the Bus Station for journeys to Poole.

Between 1938 and 1946 trials were carried out with various ticket machines, insert Setrights were used and at least one Willebrew machine was in use at Poole; a machine rarely seen in the South of England it guillotined a pre-printed ticket below the fare issued, the guillotined portion dropping into sealed container, later to be checked against the cash taken.

The Pre-War Fleet

With a company the size of Hants & Dorset and the frequent exchange of vehicles between depots, it would be impossible either to list or give details of all vehicles that have been based at Poole and Parkstone depots. Added to this, Bournemouth-based vehicles operated a percentage of services into Poole and those passing through the Borough.

The first vehicles operated by Bournemouth & District on stage carriage services were those acquired from Eugene Poulain, FX 776 and FX 1546, and the two Milnes-Daimlers, SD 503/4 from the Canford Cliffs Motor Omnibus Company - all fully described on page 59. These veterans were quickly joined in 1919 by a Leyland, two AEC, and a Daimler, (FX 4519/86, 4626/63), all fitted with 28-seat char-a-banc bodies by Messrs Kiddle of Christchurch.

In July 1919 the die was cast for Leyland to become the principal chassis supplier to the company, with nine Leylands numbered 10-26. The first two were also bodied by Kiddle - No.10 as a 28-seat char-a-banc, and No. 12 as a 28-seat bus. The remainder received Dodson CD19 type 28-seat saloon bus bodies. By fitting fold-down seats in the gangway the vehicles could actually carry 34 passengers, a point missed by Bournemouth Council. Also in service at Poole in the early 1920s was No. 28, CD 3885, a Daimler 'B' type.

In July 1920 the company became Hants & Dorset, and 12 more Leylands with Dodson B34R arrived, numbered 30-52, followed in 1922 by five Leyland 'G' types, four with Beadle B34R bodies Nos. 60-66, and No. 68 with a Beadle CH28 body. These vehicles formed the backbone of the services in Bournemouth, Poole, and the remainder of the fast-growing company. An idea retained from Bournemouth & District days was the use of only even fleet numbers, which gave the impression of a much larger fleet.

Prior to the 1930 Road Traffic Act all Hackney vehicles (which buses were classed as until the Act) had to be licensed with the local authority of the town in which they operated, hence many Hants & Dorset vehicles were licensed in both Bournemouth and Poole. It is from the remaining Poole Council records that an outline of some of the vehicles operating in the Borough at that period can be identified.

Three vehicles granted licences early in 1924 could well be Nos. 82, 84 and 86, EL 8771/2/3, from a batch of 12 Daimler 'Y' types. Originally these ex-WD chassis had been shipped back from France by Royal Blue and fitted with Dodson 28-seat Charabus bodies, with the intention of operating stage carriage services as described on page 87. In February 1924 the vehicles passed to Hants & Dorset, the three Poole licensed vehicles being put on the Sandbanks service.

In September 1925 four lightweight Morris chassis with Kiddle B13F bodies joined the fleet, three being licensed to operate in Poole. The first Leyland PLSC 'Lions' were acquired in 1926, the first three being delivered in May with the intention of operating the Bournemouth-Swanage service, but owing to the ferry being withdrawn Nos. 160, 162, 164, RU 3152/3/4, were placed on other duties. Two Leyland PLSC3s Nos. 38 and 42, RU 5394/5, arrived in May 1927, these being purchased especially for the ferry route. Fitted with Tilling 33-seat coach bodies, the Cape-Cart type hood could be rolled back along the waist rails to convert the vehicle into an open coach in fine weather. Each vehicle had cost £1,263, actually £1 less than a normal enclosed all-Leyland saloon. The novelty of the open air soon faded, both vehicles being rebodied by Beadle in 1932 with conventional 32-seat bus bodies. After withdrawal in 1938 No. 42 went to the Caledonian Omnibus Company as No. 229, where she served until 1944, and the body of No. 38 was fitted to Leyland LTI No. BB220 in 1937, surviving until 1950.

Poole Council were not accommodating in April 1927 when they refused licences to No. 68, EL 6673-a 1922 Leyland G5, and No. 92, EL 8901, one of the ex-Royal Blue Daimler 'Y' types. The following month, No. 76, EL 7509 a 1923 Leyland G5, was also refused a licence, the grounds being that all three vehicles required a repaint. No. 76 had obviously deteriorated since last licensed the previous August! No. 76 was one of a batch of six vehicles with Beadle bodies supplied to the company in 1923.

Six new Leyland PLSC3 with Leyland B35F bodies were licensed in July 1928, Nos. 244, 246, 248, 250, 254, 256, RU 7556/7/8/9/60/1. These vehicles were at the time the finest Leyland produced, and they served well, No. 244 became

E12 (TK 2591) was Hants & Dorset's first lowbridge double-deck with sunken side gangway in the lower saloon and was new in May 1929. This view, taken at Sandbanks in the early 1930s shows the outside staircase of this Leyland L27/24RO bodied Leyland TD1. *Below*, the near side of this type of vehicle is clearly shown in this Leyland Works photograph of 1929.

Andrew Porter/Leyland Motors

Caledonian Omnibus Co. No. 226 in 1938, giving 11 years further service, whilst Nos. 250 and 254 went to Newbury & District in 1938 as Nos. 29 and 41, remaining in service until 1946. No. 256 went into private ownership in 1936 and was still with a showman in the Eastern Counties in July 1953.

Whilst the newest vehicles in the fleet were making their debut on the roads of Poole, several older members of the fleet were taking their farewells. FX 4663, a 1919 Daimler 'Y' type of the former Bournemouth & District fleet, was licensed for the last time by Poole Corporation in June 1928, to be withdrawn three months later. No. 22, EL 4498, a 1920 Leyland, also licensed in June was withdrawn at the end of the year, both vehicles giving other owners three years' use as lorries.

For tram replacement on the Lower Parkstone route, six Leyland TD1 double-decks Nos. 22, 228, 258, 66, 88, 260, TK 1851, - 6 were acquired. Fitted with Beadle 'Highbridge' 24/24R0 bodies, they were the first covered-top double-decks purchased by the company. Owing to difficulties caused by lamps fitted to the tram poles in Parkstone Road, four open-top double-deck Leyland TD1, Nos. 20, 90, 96, 240, RU 7687/7686/7671/7471, were also used to commence the service. Whether the lamps were moved, or cured on the arrival of six TD1s with Leyland Lowbridge L27/24R0 bodies in April and May, Nos. 12, 52, 68, 100, 276, 278, TK2591-6, is not recorded. However, at the time of their licensing with Poole Council, it was stated that they were in substitution of the original six Highbridge Titans.

In March 1930 the first nine Titans with Leyland L24/24R bodies arrived, these being the first to be purchased with enclosed stairs (Nos. 206, 210, 304, 306, 310, 320, TK 388 1-6, and 324, 122, 134, LJ 1302/3/4). As new vehicles arrived others were allocated to less prestigious duties. During 1932 and 1933 the improved Leyland TD2 joined the fleet, followed by the TD3 in 1934. One of these (A132) was fitted with a torque converter, it was the prelude to the pending closure of the remainder of the Poole tramway system. In March 1935, four TD3s fitted with torque converters arrived, but the production of the TD3 was short. The main replacement programme saw 18 Leyland TD4c chassis fitted with hydraulic converters purchased in 1935, those supplied to Hants & Dorset being amongst the first production batch and were unusual in having a 7.6 litre petrol engine, the chassis costing £785 7s. 7d. each.

The Leyland torque converter was the first automatic transmission system fitted to buses in the Country, and it eliminated the conventional gearbox, gear lever, and clutch pedal. There was a single control lever identical to a gear lever having four positions, neutral, converter, direct, and reverse. To drive the bus the lever would be placed in the converter position, and engine revolutions quickly built up. On attaining a road speed of around 20 mph the driver moved the lever to the direct position. Although the system gave a very smooth ride, little noise, and placed less strain on the driver, it was not a world leader in fuel economy.

Distinguishing features of the TD4c were the 'Gearless Bus' badge in chrome block letters affixed to the radiator grill, the header tank for hydraulic fluid mounted alongside the autovac on the bulkhead behind the front nearside mudguard, and for those who saw the underside of the vehicle, the much smaller gearbox unit and the heat exchanger to cool the hydraulic oil, mounted on the outer side of the nearside chassis frame. The other modification of note with the TD4 chassis was the provision of Lockheed vacuum hydraulic brakes, replacing the previous triple servo system.

An early 1930s view of the junction of Wimborne Road and Poole High Street outside the George Hotel shown extreme left where one of the 1929 Leyland TD1 with Leyland 27/24RO bodies is loading before departing for Sandbanks. To the right Leyland TD1 324 (LJ 1302) new in March 1930 with a Leyland L24/24R body was amongst the first batch of double-deckers with enclosed staircases purchased by Hants & Dorset. Extensively rebuilt by ECW in late 1946, renumbered 926, withdrawn in December 1950 passing to Hedon Motor Coaches of Hull, it gave a further two years' service. Apart from the George Hotel the view has completely changed, the buildings in Upper High Street replaced by the alignment of the new Kingland Road and a much larger roundabout occupies the foreground. *Yellow Buses*

A works photograph of a 1930/1 Leyland TD1 with the enclosed staircase version of the Leyland 48-seat lowbridge body. *Leyland Motors*

The Brush L27/25R bodies each cost £650 and were of six bay construction, they had a single seat at the front of the lower saloon on the near side, and had an emergency door at the front off side of the lower saloon. These were removed during the major body overhauls carried out by Eastern Coach Works between 1942 and 1945. Two-aperture destination boxes were originally fitted at the front, but later number boxes were fitted to many of the batch.

The petrol engines came under scrutiny for running costs as early as January 1936. Engineers from Leyland had visited the area and went over the routes used by the vehicles, and a set of 4 inch cylinders and pistons and a 5.5 to 1 differential were tried on a vehicle employed on the Poole-Bournemouth route. It was decided that four of the vehicles should be fitted with oil engines as soon as possible. Gradually the torque converter transmissions were replaced by conventional clutches and four-speed gearboxes, the original 'P' prefix of the original fleet numbers being changed to 'A' upon replacement. As later vehicles entered the fleet, the Leylands were used less on the principal Poole-Bournemouth routes. They served well, the entire batch being withdrawn between May 1950 and February 1952, No. 998 being the last in service. With the exception of 990 and 998, most survived a few more years with other owners, 991/2 still being with showmen in the summer of 1962, and 981 still travelling the fairs in March 1966.

Torque Converter Leylands

No	No	Reg No.	Chassis No.	Built	Clutch	Oil Engine	W/drawn	Notes
A132	974	LJ 9405	3909	3/34	8/46		11/50	A
A184	981	ALJ 778	5743	3/35	8/39	1/38G	8/50	A
A186	982	ALJ 779	5744	3/35	11/46	11/46G	3/52	A
A188	983	ALJ 780	5745	3/35	8/46	4/47G	12/51	A
A190	984	ALJ 781	5746	3/35	8/46		8/50	A
P216	985	ARU 160	6601	6/35	11/38	1/37L	12/50	
P218	986	ARU 161	6602	6/35	46?	12/36L	12/50	
P222	987	ARU 162	6603	6/35	7/39	4/38G	11/50	
P336	988	ARU 163	6604	6/35	8/46		8/50	
P340	989	ARU 164	6605	6/35	8/46		4/50	
P344	990	ARU 165	6606	5/35	11/46	11/46G	9/51	
P346	991	ARU 166	6607	5/35	/46?	2/37L	12/51	
P368	992	ARU 167	6608	6/35	9/46	5/47G	10/51	
P108	980	ARU 168	6609	6/35	8/46		4/50	
P410	993	ARU 169	6610	6/35	/46?	10/47G	12/51	
P514	994	BEL 389	7945	8/35	2/39?	2/39G	10/51	
P518	995	BEL 391	7947	8/35	8/46		11/50	
P520	996	BEL 392	7948	8/35	8/46		6/50	
P522	997	BEL 393	7949	8/35	9/41?	5/39G	7/51	
P524	998	BEL 394	7950	8/35	10/41?	6/39G	2/52	
P526	999	BEL 395	7951	8/35	8/46		10/50	
P528	1000	BEL 396	7952	8/35	7/39	7/39G	11/50	B
P534	1001	BEL 390	7946	8/35	3/39	10/36L	4/50	

Notes
A   These vehicles were Leyland TD3c chassis, the remainder being Leyland TD4c chassis.
B   Operated on producer gas September 1939-May 1941; unit fitted under staircase.
G   Gardner 7 litre, five cylinder, 5LW.
L   Leyland 8.6 litre, six cylinder.

The first Leyland TD2 purchased by the company in February 1932, No.G56 (TK 7281). Fitted with an Eastern Counties L26/26R body, and six-cylinder 7.6 litre petrol engine, replaced by a Gardner 5LW oil engine in September 1937. The body was extensively overhauled by Hants & Dorset in July 1949, although the vehicle was withdrawn the following year passing to Wroot (Showman) Notts and eventually withdrawn in March 1960. *Below*, Leyland TD4c Gearless No. P534, BEL 390, the last of the torque converter models delivered during 1935. Details of the Brush body include the lower deck emergency door behind the driver's door, and the route number box added as an afterthought. As No. 1001 the vehicle was withdrawn in May 1950 and sold the following January to D.T. Davies of Tonmawr, Neath. Finally purchased by a showman during 1953. *(Both) A. Waller Collection*

Photographed when new in April 1938 Bristol K5G TD 628 with Brush L28/26R bodywork. This batch of double-decks being the first Bristol chassis and last Brush-bodied vehicles purchased by the company. Clearly shown is the front-end detail, the destination blind box displaying 'Bournemouth' and 'No. 4' in the route number-box which looks like a 'bolt on accessory'. The fleet name is displayed in the pre-war curved style. The body was rebuilt in October 1945 by Beadle, and rebuilt again by Hants & Dorset in April 1950, as No. 1017 withdrawn in May 1957, but served several contractors as works transport until the end of 1963. *East Pennine Transport Group*

TD 725 (ERU 601), a 1939 Bristol K5G with ECW L27/26R body delivered new in March 1939 departs down the ramp from Bournemouth bus station with service No. 4 bound for Poole. These vehicles operated the Poole area services for many years. *The Omnibus Society*

During 1932 a batch of Leyland LT5 single-decks were acquired, followed by further LT5A models in March 1935, the latter having Brush B34F bodies, several of which replaced the older Leylands on the Sandbanks Ferry crossing. As these did not have the ground clearance of the older high chassis vehicles, this resulted in the rear ends of the bodywork being cut away to clear the ramp of the ferry. This was to remain a feature of vehicles used on that route for many years, at least four LT5A being so altered, (BA2/78/102/170). Although Bournemouth-based vehicles, the fact that they and most of the route they operated was within the Borough of Poole brings them and other ferry buses into our story.

With the increasing influence of the Tilling Group, the Bristol chassis was introduced into the fleet during April 1938, by which time the 'K' and 'L' chassis were in production. These were without doubt the two finest chassis produced by Bristol, ranking alongside the Leyland and AEC chassis of the period. Many thought it superior. It was known as 'The Engineer's Bus' because of its ease of maintenance.

The first batch to arrive were Bristol K5G double-decks fitted with Brush L28/26R bodies, and they were also the last Brush-bodied vehicles ordered by the company, signifying the change to Tilling influence. Two further batches were delivered in 1939 and 1940, these having bodies supplied by Eastern Coachworks, thus adding further to the Tilling connection. Vehicles from all three batches were allocated to Poole and Bournemouth to operate the Poole-Bournemouth routes. Fitted with the Gardner five-cylinder oil engine and a conventional gearbox, they were a vast improvement mechanically and economically to their predecessors. During the same period three batches of Bristol 'L' type single-deck chassis with Beadle bodies were also purchased by the company.

Leyland LT5A No. BA 78, (ALJ 783), and an unidentified sister arrive at Shell Bay on the Sandbanks ferry. These vehicles, new in March 1935, were the first on account of their low chassis to require alterations to their rear end panels to allow clearance of the ferry ramps, a feature of 'ferry vehicles' for many years after.   *A. Waller Collection*

Chapter Seven

Poole Independent Operators Post-1920

By the end of World War I the motor vehicle had proved itself to be a reasonably reliable machine and, whereas pre-1914 the char-a-banc was something of a novelty, it now opened up a new industry. Many were to try their luck with either a char-a-banc or motor omnibus. Some were successful, some failed, whilst others struggled on until either lack of finance and resources prevented them obtaining replacement vehicles or the forthcoming 1930 Road Traffic Act brought their activities to an end.

Those who were licensed for tours only do not concern this book except that they formed part of the passing scene, and Poole Council also licensed many of the Bournemouth operators. The Poole operators were: H. Burdett, F.W. Collings, A.H. Condon (Minuet Coaches, Hamworthy), J.R. Drewett, Arthur Jacobs, F.J. Lovelace, J. Morris, P.A. Parkes, F.W.Parnell (Parkstone), Helen Reeves (Sandbanks), W.H.R. Scott (Parkstone), Snell & Prosser, W. Southgate, J.H. Wilson (Parkstone).

Although it is not intended to give a full account of all operators running stage carriage services with vehicles of 14 seats and upwards, the following details give a clear picture of the events of the period.

One of the first to succumb was Messrs Addis and Venner who commenced trading as taxi owners and haulage contactors in August 1920 from the yard of the London Hotel, High Street, Poole. The following year a third partner, Mr Eversfield, joined, and a Dennis char-a-banc was acquired and the trading title was altered to 'The London Garage Company'.

In November 1921 Eversfield died, having terminated the partnership only the previous day. The business was already having financial problems, and ceased trading in May 1922 when Addis and Venner were declared bankrupt. However, Venner reappears later in our story.

J.P. Wells of Corfe Mullen had a single-deck bus licensed for passengers and goods between Corfe Mullen and Poole, from 1921 until 1923. Other proprietors from surrounding villages operating into Poole included Vacher of Bere Regis, and Davis of Bloxworth, both described on page 111.

Of more significance was N.S. Rose of Poole who traded under the fleetname of 'Rosebud' and operated a service between County Gates and Sandbanks. In 1921 he had one char-a-banc licensed for tours and stage carriage, but the following year three motor buses were listed for tours and stage work. Between 1926-28 five char-a-bancs were licensed for the work.

The County Gates-Sandbanks service passed to Herbert Rendell of Parkstone in 1927 who, conceding defeat to Hants & Dorset, withdrew on 11th May, 1929 to concentrate on his 'Cosy Coaches' business based at Ashley Road, Upper Parkstone.

Another early operator between Poole and Sandbanks was Arthur Howard of Poole, who also had licensed services to both Broadstone and Lytchett Minster. Three motor buses were licensed for stage carriage work in 1922, but from

POOLE AND DISTRICT MOTOR SERVICE.

Commencing Monday, 1st July, 1929.

DAILY BUS SERVICE.

Wimborne, Corfe Mullen Broadstone and Poole.

	N.S. a.m.	a.m.	Noon.	S.O. p.m.	p.m.	p.m.	p.m.	p.m.	p.m.	Wed,Sat Sun. p.m.
Poole Quay ...	8-30	10- 0	12- 0	12-30	2- 0	4- 0	6- 0	7-30	Regent	10-30
Poole Station ...	8-33	10- 3	12- 3	12-33	2- 3	4- 3	6- 3	7-33	8.35	10-33
Oakdale ...	8-40	10-10	12-10	12-40	2-10	4-10	6-10	7-40	8-40	10-35
Waterloo ...	8-45	10-15	12-15	12-42	2-15	4-15	6-15	7-45	8-45	10-40
Broadstone ...	8-50	10-20	12-20	12-45	2-20	4-20	6-20	7-50	8-50	10-45
Corfe Mullen Sch'l	8-58	10-28	12-28	...	2-28	4-28	6-28	7-58	8-58	10-48
Lake Gates ...	9- 0	10-30	12-30	...	2-30	4-30	6-30	8- 0	9- 0	10-50
Wimborne ...	9- 5	10-35	12-35	...	2-35	4-35	6-35	8- 5	9- 5	10-55

	N.S. a.m.	a.m.	p.m.	S.O. p.m.	p.m.	p.m.	p.m.	p.m.	p.m.	Wed,Sat Sun. p.m.
Wimborne ...	9-20	10-50	12-50	...	2-50	4-50	6-50	8- 5	9-20	11- 0
Lake Gates ...	9-23	10-53	12-53	...	2-53	4-53	6-53	8-10	9-25	11- 5
Corfe Mullen Sch'l	9-28	10-58	12-58	...	2-58	4-58	6-58	8-15	9-28	11- 8
Broadstone ...	9-35	11- 5	1- 5	12-45	3- 5	5- 5	7- 5	8-20	9-35	11-15
Waterloo ...	9-40	11-10	1-10	12-48	3-10	5-10	7-10	8-25	9-40	11-18
Oakdale ...	9-45	11-15	1-15	12-50	3-15	5-15	7-15	8-30	9-45	11-20
Poole Station ...	9-55	11-25	1-25	12-55	3-25	5-25	7-25	8-35	9-55	11-25
Poole Quay ...	10- 0	11-30	1-30	...	3-30	5-30	7-30	...	10- 0	...

N.S.—Not Sundays.   **S.O.—Sundays only.**

Dept.—3, Commercial Road, Parkstone.

Telephone—Parkstone 555.

H. VENNER, Manager

A. E. RUSSETT, Secretary.

W. S. Hallett, Printer, 22, Market Street, Poole.   Tel. 48.

remaining records it appears that 1924 was the last year of stage carriage operation, although the vehicles were licensed for tours up to 1926.

A non-starter, was A.J. Wilkins of Imperial Motor Services. Having sold his Aberdare-based company to Red & White, he moved to Bournemouth and obtained licences to operate a service to Wimborne in 1928. This was extended to Blandford the following year, when application was also made for six licences for a service between Bournemouth, Poole, Wareham, Dorchester and Weymouth, and a Bournemouth-Swanage service. The application was refused on the grounds the area was already well served. A fierce battle over the Wimborne road resulted in the interloper selling out to Hants & Dorset in May 1930.

During 1929/30 Messrs Tilling Stevens & Company of Maidstone had one motor bus licensed in Poole, but no records remain of the actual service it operated. In view of its owners, there is little doubt that the vehicle was a demonstrator working in the area.

Poole & District Motor Services

H.W. Godfrey had commenced in October 1925 with one bus. Three were licensed the following year, and five in 1927, trading from No. 3 Commercial Road, Parkstone, as 'Poole & District Motor Services'. He was also listed in the trade directories as a motor engineer. In November 1928 Poole & District had four buses licensed for various routes in the Poole area. They were the originators of the service between Poole and Upton, Oakdale, and Waterloo, this service being later extended to Newtown, and on Sundays to Broadstone.

By 1928 Hubert Venner and his wife Mrs V.W.A. Venner became involved with the company, although owing to Venner's bankruptcy he could not become proprietor in his own right. Godfrey disappeared from the scene shortly after, and by March 1929 the business styled as Poole & District Motor Services Ltd had passed into the ownership of a Bristol-based company, Russett Brothers, who operated coaches under the fleet name of 'Premier'. They were also involved in bus operations at Aylesbury as 'Aylesbury & District' and had run a service at Coombe Martin in North Devon. The Poole business was run with H. Venner as manager and A.E. Russett as secretary, the latter residing in a house next to the garage.

At this point the progress of the company's activities takes an interesting turn, with Poole Council finding difficulty in granting any licences to them. The subsequent arguments again bring to the fore many of the underlying matters of the 1928 Poole Transport Act.

In March 1929 Poole & District submitted timetables for existing routes and proposed additional services between Poole and Sandbanks, and between Kinson, Wallisdown, Poole, Lytchett, and Bailey Gate. The additional services were refused on the grounds that the routes were already well served. One objecting Councillor declared it was the public and not the committee who were the persons to say whether routes were sufficiently served, whilst another was worried that, by licensing a large number of buses, there would be heavy compensation to pay in the event of the council wishing to run its own services. Another stated, 'The best thing we can do is to ask Hants & Dorset to buy all the small companies up'. Alderman Hunt remarked that 'Poole & District was now owned by a Bristol firm who were trying to obtain vested interests in Poole and the committee had to consider it from that point'.

The following month application was made to open two new routes: (a) Park Gates East to Poole Library via Fernside Road, Stanley Green Road and Sterte Road; and (b) Oakdale to Sandbanks via Tatnam. The committee were of the opinion that both services were unnecessary and that Stanley Green Road was not in a safe condition for omnibus traffic, and therefore refused the application for both routes. However, timetables for the following existing routes were approved:

Poole Quay to Waterloo via Oakdale
Poole Quay to Newtown via Longfleet Road
Poole station to Upton via Hamworthy
Poole Quay to Broadstone via Wimborne Road

Poole & District soon appealed to the Ministry of Transport against the refusal of the council, for the two new routes, resulting in an inquiry at Poole Municipal Offices on 25th July, 1929.

The reason given for the refusal was that the council considered the vehicle unsatisfactory and the committee disapproved of the bus being run on the Poole to Sandbanks Route. The vehicle (NU 8443) was a 1926 model, which had been licensed in the Borough for the past 2½ years and held the usual engineers certificate as to its fitness. Councillor W.K. Field, a member of the Omnibus Committee and a motor engineer of 35 years experience, said he considered the vehicle in question unsafe and unsuitable though he admitted he made only a superficial examination. Mr A.J. Brixey, of Westminster Garage, Parkstone, examined the bus and found no mechanical defects. In cross-examination he declared that the braking and steering systems were perfectly satisfactory.

The Inspector considered that many irrelevant issues were being raised, and ruled that only the question of mechanical efficiency of the vehicle could be considered, as no amount of talk about queues of waiting passengers at Sandbanks would make an unsound vehicle sound.

However, much interesting information was brought to light during the enquiry. The so-called 'Secret Agreement' between Hants & Dorset and Poole Corporation was discussed and the actions of council members made public. Mr D'Angibau, Counsel for the appellant, said that Councillor R. H. Stokes who was chairman of the Hackney Committee up until October 1928, after which he ceased to be a councillor, had during his chairmanship a financial interest in Hants & Dorset, that company's list showing he held 300 shares. A clause from the Road Traffic Bill disqualified persons financially interested in transport companies from adjudicating in the granting of licences. Mr D'Angibau, continued by stating that during Stokes' chairmanship, his son, Mr R.S. Stokes, had been appointed assistant Hackney Carriage Inspector. He suggested that such inspectors were vested with a good deal of power and there were occasions when licences were granted subject to these inspectors' approval of time tables, and the inspector who was the son of a shareholder of one company, was very likely to be prejudiced against another company.

A.E. Russett, Secretary of Poole & District stated that numerous complaints had been received from residents that the present Sandbanks service was inadequate. On one occasion Poole & District ran two unauthorised buses on this route, and even then people had to wait. In one case an unauthorised bus had on board hospital collecting boxes and no fares were charged, but in the other case a charge was made.

Mr D'Angibau submitted that 'the committee was so prejudiced that they would not license any vehicle other than that belonging to Hants & Dorset, and that they sheltered behind one of three grounds: that a proposed new service was unnecessary; that an existing service on which it was required to run was adequately served; or the vehicle put forward had mechanical defects'. He continued, 'By reason of the agreement with Hants & Dorset the committee could not function as a judicial body'.

Giving evidence for the appellant, Councillor Sansom said, 'several councillors have told me that to grant new licences to firms other than Hants & Dorset would be to the financial detriment of the borough. After that, I feel in my mind that one could not expect the very best of vehicles to be licensed'.

Cross-examined, he would not say that the committee was incapable of dealing with licensing, but he would admit to unreasonable bias.

The Inspector: 'Do you think this is the attitude of the council as a whole?' Councillor Sansom replied: 'Yes'.

Inspector: 'Of what does the bias consist?' - Sansom: 'One company is refused permission to open up a new route, and then soon afterwards Hants & Dorset start the route'.

Counsel for Poole Corporation, referring to the Poole Corporation Bill and the replacement of the Lower Parkstone trams with a bus service stated:

Here was Hants & Dorset a large company with wide connections, well able to run the service and there was no evidence that any other company was in a position to run it. If the corporation ran the service itself it would mean a large capital outlay, and it seemed good business to enter into negotiations with Hants & Dorset which would itself take the financial risk.

Questions were also asked about the involvement of the General Manager and Traffic Manager of Hants & Dorset at various meetings of the Hackney Carriage Committee.

Following the inquiry, relationships failed to improve between the two parties. At the August 1929 Omnibus Committee meeting the Town Clerk reported that the Minister of Transport, having considered the evidence at the enquiry, was not prepared to make an order upon the council. At the same meeting a licence for vehicle TK 3312 was deferred until September when it was refused on the grounds that the routes authorised to be operated by the company were already sufficiently provided with omnibuses for the approved timetables. An application for the approval of a timetable relating to a new service between Poole and Wimborne was refused on the grounds that the portion of the route within the Borough was already sufficiently served.

A rare photograph of a Poole & District Motor Services vehicle. A destination board in the side window reads, 'Poole Station, Tatnam, Oakdale'. The vehicle is a Morris 'D3' type bus, also known as the 'T' Type Tonner, powered by a four-cylinder side valve engine, fitted with a three-speed gear box, rod operated rear wheel brakes and a scuttle mounted 7½ gallon petrol tank, specifications that quickly lost favour for PSV use, and as with many lightweight chassis of the period an overweight body usually assisted in their swift demise.   *Andrew Hawkes Collection*

Former Poole & District Motor Services Leyland PLSC3, TK 2334, new in March 1929, passing to Hants & Dorset Motor services in September 1930. Numbered 74 in the Hants & Dorset fleet, it later passed to showmen as living accommodation carrying its original Leyland 32-seat dual door body until withdrawn in 1957.   *P. Davies Collection*

The Town Clerk reported on the summonses against Poole & District for plying for hire with an unlicensed vehicle. The offences had been admitted, and the Bench in view of the special circumstances had dismissed the case on payment of the cost of one summons, and that the summonses for a breach of one of the conditions of their licence had been dismissed.

Although it would appear the courts took a more sympathetic view towards the company than the council, in December the licence for TK 3312 was again refused. The company appealed to the Ministry of Transport against the council's refusal to license this vehicle for its Poole-Corfe Mullen-Wimborne service and to approve their Tatnam-Sandbanks service. The inquiry was held on 24th March, 1930.

This time the council relented and agreed to a compromise and licensed TK 3312, and approved the Poole-Corfe Mullen-Wimborne timetable, on condition that Poole & District withdraw its application to ply between Tatnam and Sandbanks.

However the fragile peace was short lived, for in late May the Hackney Inspector reported that on several recent Saturdays the buses between Newtown and Upton were not running to their timetables, being supplemented by additional vehicles which were driven at times in a dangerous manner. The Town Clerk was instructed to caution the company, and bring the question of dangerous driving to the attention of the police.

In June application was made to licence TK 2333 for a proposed new service between Poole and Sturminster Newton, but this was refused on the grounds that transport facilities on the route were adequate for the needs of the travelling public. Finally in August, the committee disapproved of two amended timetables on the grounds that they would tend to increase traffic congestion in the Borough, that the proposed additional services were totally unnecessary, and also that the routes proposed were already amply served by existing transport facilities.

How much longer the battle could have continued is open to question, as the forthcoming introduction of the 1930 Road Traffic Act could have seen changes. However, Poole & District sold out to Hants & Dorset in September 1930, the battle for local services was over, and Hants & Dorset ruled supreme.

Little appears to have survived on record of the Poole & District fleet. Under the ownership of Godfrey the small Morris saloon buses of the period sufficed, being as good as any others of the type available at the time. The purchase of a Guy (TK 1309) in February 1928 was a natural progression from the previous vehicles, and with the Russett involvement further Guys were acquired, although two Leyland saloons were obtained for the heavier traffic. Several vehicles were transferred from Bristol, but again full details have not been recorded. The livery of the fleet was maroon and white.

In addition to the bus services, tours were operated from Park Gates Garage (the Commercial Road Premises) and Poole Library. Of the people involved, Venner, discharged from his bankruptcy in December 1930, continued with the Commercial Road premises as a car dealer, whilst the Russett family withdrew from the omnibus business except for their Bristol operations. The family later returned to Poole in the road haulage business trading as Pioneer Transport with premises in Rosemany Road, Parkstone, as a branch of the Bristol-based company. Ironically big brother was to strike again. With the nationalisation of parts of the road haulage industry in 1948 the Poole depot became British Road Services unit No. F23.

Although Poole & District was only small, it was an important part of the transport history of Poole. It well portrays the difficulties faced at that period, and certainly proved the need for the 1930 Act where the rules were nationwide and consistent.

H.W. Godfrey
Poole & District Motor Services

Reg No.	Chassis	Chassis No.	Body	Type	Built	Acquired	Sold	Notes
WU 5166				B18				
PR 5661	Morris				10/25			
PR 5827	Morris			B14	11/25	11/25		
PR 7970	Morris				12/26			
PR 7975	Morris				12/26			
NU 8443	Morris	Wilkinson		B14	3/26	b4/28		
TK 1309	Guy			B	2/28			
TK 2333	Dodge			B26	3/29	3/29	9/30	A
TK 2334	Leyland PLSC3		Leyland	B32D	3/29	3/29	9/30	A
TK 2740	Guy OND	OND9218	Guy	B20F	5/29	5/29	9/30	A
TK 3201	Guy OND	OND9376	Guy	B20F	7/29	7/29	9/30	A
TK 3312	Guy OND	OND8984	Guy	B20F	8/29	8/29	9/30	A
TK 4687	Leyland LT1	50671	Brush	B32F	5/30	5/30	9/30	A
GD 3033						b3/30		B
HW 5200	Dodge			20	5/29		/30	

Notes
A   To Hants & Dorset upon purchase of company.
B   Originally registered in Glasgow.
b   by [applies in subsequent tables also].

Previous Owners
NU 8443   New to Tailby & George, Willington, Derby (Blue Bus). 9/27 to Miles, Potterdown.
HW 5200   Russett (Premier) Bristol.

Disposals
PR 5661   LO E.P. Hall, Wimborne Road, Winton, Bournemouth.
PR 5827   LO H.W. Godfrey.
PR 7975   LO at Walsingham, Norfolk, taxed as goods Morris lorry.
TK 1309   LO Mrs Evans Shirley, Southampton. LL 1936 as Guy truck.
TK 2333   To Hants & Dorset. LO G. Blackwell, Caversham, Reading.
TK 2334   To Hants & Dorset as No. 74.   LO H. Smith, (showman) Reading. WD 1957.
TK 2740   To Hants & Dorset. To Mrs Kent (Kingsclare Coaches) sold with business 4/37 to Newbury & District, No.8. Sold 1938. Hosking, Helston, Cornwall, as lorry LL 12/42.
TK 3201   To Hants & Dorset, LO Showman at Epsom WD 9/47.
TK 3312   To Hants & Dorset as No. 344. LL by Kent, Baughurst, to E.G. Hunt Baughurst 1936, not operated.
TK 4687   To Hants & Dorset as No. 220, rebodied 1937 with Beadle B32 body from vehicle No B38. 1950 to Barnby (dealer) Southampton, scrap.

The Bere Regis Area

At the same time as Hants & Dorset was securing its position in Poole, it was looking westwards towards Bere Regis. Apart from the road to Wareham via Holton Heath, Hants & Dorset had not conquered the area towards Dorchester, which remained firmly in the hands of the country carriers and independents. Although Hants & Dorset had applied for and been granted a licence by Weymouth Town Council in September 1920 to run into the town via Dorchester, the service was not taken up owing to more pressing matters elsewhere.

The first service between Weymouth-Dorchester-Bere Regis-Poole and Bournemouth was commenced by the Weymouth Motor Company Ltd in June 1921. When that company went into liquidation in 1924 George Vacher took over the route operating between Dorchester and Poole, with a Friday service extended to Bournemouth, trading as 'Bere Regis Motor Service'. Services were also run mostly to coincide with market days, by 1927 he operated to Blandford, Bournemouth, Dorchester, Poole, Wimborne, and Wareham.

Vacher sold the business to Hants & Dorset on 20th August, 1930, thus giving the company a foothold in the area. Agreement was quickly reached with Southern National, and in September a joint service between Bournemouth and Weymouth (11) commenced. Vacher was placed in charge of the company's operations at Bere Regis, the garage in North Street being retained until the war, although the vehicles acquired were only operated for a short while, never receiving fleet numbers or a repaint, being replaced by Chevrolet LQ saloons, which were in turn quickly replaced by Dennis Ace saloons in 1934. These vehicles were often known as 'Dennis Pigs' owing to their bonnet which protruded like a pig's snout!

Looking back with hindsight a glorious opportunity was missed by Hants & Dorset in 1933 when the business of Messrs I. Davis & Sons, 'Bloxworth & Morden Motor Service' of Bloxworth, was investigated with a view to purchase, the company details for 1932 being as follows:

Service Operated	Length of Route (miles)	Miles	Gross receipts £	s.	d.	Receipts per car mile
Dorchester-Poole	27.7	67,104	1228	9	11	4.39d.
Morden-Blandford	23.2	2,076	82	19	7	9.59d.
Morden-Wimborne	20.1	1,812	62	7	1	8.25d.
Bloxworth-Wareham	9.2	1,055	50	7	8	11.46d.
Totals		72,047	1424	4	3	4.74d.

However the Hants & Dorset Board agreed not to proceed, a decision that cost the company dear, as events that later unfolded were at the time unforeseen. In October 1929 R.W. Toop who previously had been a driver for Vacher, commenced his own operations from Bere Regis with a 14-seat model 'T' Ford. The following year W.J. Ironside, a carrier-cum-bus operator who ran services from Winfrith to Dorchester, Weymouth, and Wareham, sold out to Toop and the combined service then operated under the fleet name of 'Pioneer'. In 1936 P.W. Davis joined Toop, and Ironside who had been out of the industry since 1930 acquired a financial interest. The fleet name 'Bere Regis & District Motor Sevices' was adopted.

In almost new condition No. K408 (LJ 9415), a 1934 Dennis Ace with a Harrington B20F body, stands in the main Street of Bere Regis before departing for Poole. The Dennis 'Pig' enjoyed a brief popularity as a small country bus before being ousted by the Bedford. Converted for OMB operation in early 1952, by July of the following year it was in use as a non PSV with Stevenson of Birmingham, and a showman at Brighton by late 1954, being withdrawn the following March.

B.L. Jackson Collection

The Bere Regis outstation Bedford OB parked up in the village, No. 562 (JEL 276), new in May 1949 as No. 981 was fitted with a Beadle B27F bus body. The original Bedford six-cylinder petrol engine, was replaced by a Perkins P6 diesel in November 1952. Withdrawn in September 1957, passing to Express Motors of Rhostryfan in February 1958, being withdrawn at the end of the year.

Brian Botley

The acquisition of Law's of Briantspuddle in June 1940 and the withdrawal of Caundles 'Puddle Queen' service from Puddletown, secured more traffic on the Poole-Dorchester road. During the peak years following the war double-decks were often employed on this route. The combined set of routes was Bere Regis services:

Service 1   Bere Regis-Poole via Bloxworth, East Bloxworth, Whitefield, East Morden, Park Corner, Organford Cross, Lytchett Matravers, Upton, Fleets Bridge.
Service 1A   Bere Regis-Dorchester via Briantspuddle, Affpuddle.
Service 2   Bere Regis-Poole via Winterbourne Kingston, Winterbourne Zelstone, Marsh Bridge, Mapperton, Almer, Park Corner, thence as Service No.1 into Poole.

However the later decline in traffic followed by the reduction of local services resulted in those routes being handed over to Hants & Dorset on 12th July, 1959.

Services 1 and 2 were absorbed into Hants & Dorset Services 91 and 90 respectively and 1A became 11A. Today these services form part of Wilts & Dorset services 186, 187, 188 and 189.

G. Vacher, Bere Regis

Reg No.	Chassis	Chassis No.	Type	Built	Acquired	Notes
FX 6037	Commer 35hp				8/20	C
PR 5768	Chevrolet		B11F		11/25	
MW 1313	Chevrolet		B10	2/28	b10/29	A B
PR 7099	Chevrolet		B14	6/26	6/26	
PR 6867	Chevrolet		B14F	5/26	5/26	A
TK 523	GMC			3/28	3/28	A
TK 4130	Chevrolet	LQ54031	B14F	2/30	2/30	A

Notes
A   To Hants & Dorset 8/30.
B   Licenced by Poole B.C. subject to removal of drop seat in gangway 10/29.
C   Described in register as lorry PC 3t 15 cwt.

Previous Owners
MW 1313   New to J. Cockle, Salisbury.

Disposals
FX 6037   To H. Turk Sturminster Newton.
PR 5768   To Hawker Piddletrentide.   LL 1935.
PR 6867   LO Gillard, Christchurch.
PR 7099   LO J. Sherwood, Parkstone.
TK 522   LO R.W. Toop Bere Regis.
TK 4130   LO Ministry of Supply, WD 1940.

Photographed during 1928, local schoolchildren stand with Mr George Vacher's 1926 Chevrolet (PR 6867), fitted with a Pitt 14-seat body. Vacher, seated at the wheel, became the Bere Regis manager for Hants & Dorset when his 'Bere Regis Motor Service' was acquired in August 1930.
Colin Morris Collection

Davis's Motor Service

Commencing—
MONDAY, JULY 9th, 1934.

Poole - Bere Regis - Dorchester Service.

	am	WS am	am	WS pm	pm	WS pm	SO pm	WS pm	SO pm	MTTH & WFS pm
Poole depart		9 45	11 45	1 30	3 20	4 45	7 15	9 0	9 30	10 R 25
Fleets Corner		9 50	11 50	1 35	3 25	4 50	7 20	9 5	9 35	10 40
Upton Cross		9 55	11 55	1 40	3 30	4 55	7 25	9 10	9 40	10 45
Lytchett Matravers		10 5	12 5	1 50	3 40	5 5	7 35	9 20	9 50	10 55
Organford Cross		10 10	12 10	1 55	3 45	5 10	7 40	9 25	9 55	11 0
Morden	9 0	10 15	12 15	2 0	3 50	5 15	7 45	9 30	10 0	11 5
Bloxworth	9 10	10 25	12 25	2 10	4 0	5 25	7 55	9 35	10 5	11 10
Bere Regis arrive	9 15	10 30	12 35	2 15	4 10		8 0	9 45	10 15	11 15
Bere Regis depart	9 20		12 45		4 10		8 20			
Tolpuddle	9 30		12 55		4 20		8 30			
Puddletown	9 40		1 5		4 30		8 40			
Dorchester arrive	9 55		1 20		4 35		8 50			

	am	WS am	am	WS pm	SO pm	WS pm	MTTH pm	WFS pm
Dorchester depart		10 0		1 45		5 30		9 0
Puddletown		10 15		2 0		5 45		9 10
Tolpuddle		10 25		2 10		5 55		9 20
Bere Regis arrive		10 35		2 20		6 5		9 30
Bere Regis depart		10 35	12 40	2 20		6 5	8 30	9 30
Bloxworth	8 45	10 40	12 45	2 30	3 45	6 15	8 35	9 40
Morden	8 55	10 50	12 50	2 35	3 50	6 20	8 40	9 45
Organford Cross	9 0	10 55	12 55	2 40	3 55	6 25	8 45	9 50
Lytchett Matravers	9 5	11 0	1 0	2 45	4 0	6 35	8 50	9 55
Upton Cross	9 15	11 10	1 10	2 55	4 10	6 45	9 5	10 0
Fleets Corner	9 25	11 20	1 20	3 5	4 15	6 50	9 10	10 5
Poole arrive	9 30	11 25	1 25	3 10	4 25	6 55	9 15	10 15

WS Wednesdays and Saturdays only.   SO Saturdays only.

R Waits for Regent Theatre at Poole.   MTTh Mondays, Tuesdays and Thursdays only.

WFS Wednesdays, Fridays and Saturdays only.   No Services operate on Sundays.

Every endeavour will be made to keep to times stated above, but no responsibility will be taken for any loss or injury arising from any cause.

Phone: ~~BERE REGIS 25~~ *MORDEN 41.*   I. DAVIS & SONS.

A. J. Mason, Printer, Poole

Davis, Bloxworth

Reg No.	Chassis	Chassis No	Type	Built	Acquired	Sold	Notes
PR 5556	Ford			1925	9/25		
PR 7788	Chevrolet	LM18127	14?	1/26	11/27		
SG 7525			B	1924	b3/29		
PR 8517	Chevrolet		B	3/27	b3/29		B
TK 4366	Chevrolet	LQ60606	14	3/30	3/30	6/34	A
YC 3293	Chevrolet	LO42022	14	1928		3/33	
GC 5860							
RU 5789	Star		20	1927	?33		
TM 3082	Reo	FAX 5804	20	1928	1933		
UP 4717	Chevrolet	72576	20	1931	4/34	3/36	

Notes
A   LO P. Davis Bloxworth.
B   Registered with DCC as Chevrolet van.

Previous Owner
PR 7788   New to Stroud, Wimborne.
YC 3293   Couchman, Codford, Wilts.
RU 5789   New to Rawlins & Norman, Bournemouth, to Ellwood, Bradford Abbas.
TM 3082   New to National Omnibus & Transport Co. 12/29 as No. 2924 then to Eastern National also as No. 2924, to Ideal, Luton.
UP 5717   New to Pole, Bedlington, to United.

Disposals
TK 4366   To Bere Regis & District 6/34.
PR 7788   LL as goods Heyward Bros Builders Wardcliffe Road Weymouth.
UP 5717   To Bere Regis & District Fleet.
PR 8517   LO M. Pitts & Co. (dealer) Amesbury, Wilts.
TK 5366   Became part of the Bere Regis & District fleet.

Toop

Reg No.	Chassis	Chassis No.	Body	Type	Built	Acquired	Sold	Notes
	Ford T			14		10/29	b/34	
TK 3897	Chevrolet			B14	1930	1/30	3/36	
MR 7761	Chevrolet	X10538		14	1926	1930		
RU 9455	Star Fly.	VB4 998		26	1929			
TK 4140	Chevrolet	LQ 61454		B14F	2/30	b/34	3/36	
MP 54								
VW 6745	GMC T40E	404728		B26F	9/28	10/35	3/36	
MY 3052	Star VB4	1007	Strach/Brown	C26D	1931		b/36	A
TK 2299	Star VB4	1041		27	1929	12/34	3/36	
CUL 588	Dodge PLB	1070		C20F	1936	1936	3/36	
VJ 6462	Dennis Lancet	170699	Willowbrook	32	1934	7/36	3/36	

Note
A   At some stage operated by Toop 1934-1936.

Previous Owner
MR 7761   White, Netheravon, Wilts.
RU 9445   Down & Smith, Bournemouth, to Vatcher Bere Regis.
TK 4140   Dean, Chickerell, Weymouth.
VW 6745   F. Matravers Coggershall, 7/31 to Hicks, Braintree.
MY 3052   Kinch & Gee, London. To Ewer, London.
TK 2299   R.W. Austin, (Greyhound), Weymouth.
VJ 6462   Morgan (Wye Valley) Hereford.

Disposal
TK 3897   To Bere Regis & District Fleet, LO Cutler Dewlish, Dorchester.
RU 9445   To Fox, Bere Regis, as non PSV, 1938
TK 4140   To Bere Regis & District fleet. To Purnell, Rogerstone, LL 30/9/40. LO Lancashire Motor Traders.
VW 6745   To Bere Regis & District fleet.
TK 2299   To Bere Regis & District fleet. 9/40 to Ministry of Supply.
CUL 588   To Bere Regis & District fleet. Scr. 4/42.
VJ 6462   To Bere Regis & District fleet.

PR 1274, a 1925 Fiat char-a-banc operated by Miss Foott, photographed at the head of a line up of other assorted vehicles for a tour of land boundaries organised by the Society of Poole Men. The name 'Mentone' is carried on the dashboard, whilst 'Miss Foott Sandbanks' is displayed on the bonnet panel.   *Poole Local History Museum*

Transport for the ceremony of Beating The Bounds of the Borough of Poole in 1926. Front left is a 1919 AEC 'YC' type char-a-banc EL 3606, No. 9 in the Royal Blue fleet., whilst front right is PR 1274, a 1925 Fiat char-a-banc operated by Miss Foott. The procession was photographed outside Poole Town Hall before departure.   *Ian Andrews Collection*

Prior to this Bere Regis & District had expanded with the acquisition of small operators around the county, particularly during the war years when many literally surrendered! Locally the coach operations of Robertson of Longham were acquired in June 1951, and Elliot's Garage of Sturminster Marshall in June 1965. Expansion then slowed up, Elliot & Potter of Wimborne not being acquired until 1982. In its heyday Bere Regis & District was one of the largest independent coach operators in the Country. With over a hundred vehicles in a colour scheme of two shades of brown, their vehicles were a familiar sight throughout the County of Dorset.

Changes within the industry conspired against this firm, and on 17th March, 1994 the company - then based at Dorchester - was sold to the Cawlett Group who controlled Southern National. The former owners retained a small section of the original business, amounting to nine vehicles based at Blandford and Wimborne , trading as 'Bere Regis Coaches', but its life was short.

Miss Louie Foott, The Rossmore Bus Company Ltd

The story of Louie Dingwell Foott is one of perseverance against the odds in the days when a woman running a bus company was almost unheard of, and she was the sole independent to operate a stage carriage service within the Borough of Poole after 1930. Louie Foott was born at Exeter in June 1893, and by the commencement of World War I was living in Weston-super-Mare. During the conflict she joined the Women's Legion and was attached to the Canadian Forestry Corps based in Berkshire, where she was a motorcycle despatch rider and ambulance driver. Demobbed in October 1919, this popular lady was presented with a Ford 'T' car by her friends.

By that time the family had moved to Parkstone, and Louie travelling around in her car soon became captivated with Sandbanks. The area was then slowly developing, but apart from about 30 or 40 large houses it mainly consisted of a collection of huts and old railway carriages that were so popular at budding seaside developments at that period. Louie rented one of these huts, and made it her home. Realising the transport needs for the area, with her mechanical skills and her car she established a taxi business, for which a Poole hackney licence was granted in 1923. Other taxis were acquired and by June 1925 a hackney licence was granted for a Fiat char-a-banc, PR 1274, by which time the lady was in the business of running a bus service to this rapidly expanding community, from Poole and County Gates.

As Sandbanks developed the days of the shanty huts were drawing to a close, Louie moved into a bungalow and opened a garage and petrol station in Panorama Road, 'Miss Foott's Motor Service' had become established. This caused concern to Hants & Dorset who wished to gain full control of the Poole-Sandbanks Road, and indeed every other route in the area. The competition between the two operators was intense, and there are stories of the struggle between the opposing camps, many no doubt embellished in the passage of time. Cat and mouse tactics were employed as both operators scrambled for

Foott's Time Table

Albert Road—Brixey Road.

Leave Albert Road		Leave Brixey Road	
7 50 a.m.	10 10 a.m.	8 0 a.m.	10 20 a.m.
8 8	10 30	8 15	10 40
8 23	10 50	8 30	11 0
8 38	11 10	8 45	11 20
8 53	11 30	9 0	11 40
9 10	11 50	9 20	12 0
9 30	and every 20 mins.	9 40	and every 20 mins.
9 50	till 10 50 p.m.	10 0	till 11 0 p.m.

Sundays
1-50 p.m. till 10-30 p.m.
as above.

Bank Holidays from 8-50 a.m.

Sundays
2-0 p.m. till 10-40 p.m.
as above.

Bank Holidays from 9-0 a.m.

FARE CHART.

Albert Road							
1	Heatherlands School						
1	1	Alcester Road					
1	1	1	Sunnyside Road				
$1\frac{1}{2}$	1	1	1	Hill Top			
2	$1\frac{1}{2}$	1	1	1	Stanfield Road		
$2\frac{1}{2}$	2	$1\frac{1}{2}$	$1\frac{1}{2}$	1	1	Good Road	
$2\frac{1}{2}$	2	$1\frac{1}{2}$	$1\frac{1}{2}$	1	1	1	Brixey Road

Children (travelling to and from School) $\frac{1}{2}$d. fare.

A. J. Mason, Printer, Poole.

passengers along the route. Fisticuffs between the crews were not unknown, and a Hants & Dorset employee was thrown into the sea when he upset Louie's supporters. When one of her lightweight Fords was trapped nose to tail by the opposition the passengers and bystanders dragged it out sideways! Hants & Dorset mounted a campaign encouraging passengers to 'patronise the green buses', whereupon Louie and her employees repainted their fleet green overnight! Hants & Dorset then complained   that her action constituted unfair competition!

In November 1928 Poole Council Omnibus Committee granted Louie licences for three omnibuses on the Poole-Sandbanks route, the condition being that only two were to be used at any one time, the other being a spare. However when it came to licensing the actual vehicles (there were seven in the fleet at that time) 'the committee were of the opinion that the omnibuses did not attain the standard they considered necessary for public service vehicles, and whilst they granted licences on this occasion in respect of three omnibuses, they resolved that the applicant be informed that the licences will not be renewed in April next'.

The matter was debated in the local press, followed by letters and petitions from residents along the route. At the Omnibus Committee meeting for February 1929, a letter was read from the Borough of Poole Ratepayers Association.

Re Miss Foott's Omnibus Service between Poole and Sandbanks.
A resolution of protest against the decision of Poole Borough Omnibus Committee whereby they decided not to grant licences to any of Miss Foott's omnibuses running between Poole and Sandbanks after March 31st next. Recognising the valuable and effective transport services, which have been carried out by this lady during the past eight years, we realise that this decision of the Licensing Committee will deprive the public of a very necessary service and in addition will deprive her and her employees of their sole livelihood. We as ratepayers of the Borough of Poole ask the Committee to reconsider their decision in this matter.

There had also been disagreement with the committee concerning the timetable submitted by Miss Foott, a letter from her stating that Hants & Dorset was willing to amend its timetable on the same route so that she might continue to run at the original times proposed by her. The committee decided to defer the matter until a timetable had been received from Hants & Dorset so services on the Sandbanks route could be considered as a whole.

It was clear that Hants & Dorset with its greater resources could undercut her and eventually win the battle, so bowing to the inevitable a compromise was reached and from 6th March, 1929 Hants & Dorset took over the route.

Having already established a service between Upper Parkstone and Rossmore, the Omnibus Committee minutes of the 22nd March, 1929 fully explain Miss Foott's future plans. In a letter she reported that she had disposed of her omnibus undertaking on the Poole and Sandbanks route, and now proposed to provide a new service between Parkstone Joinery Works in Bournemouth Road, along Vale Road, Alexandra Road, Madeira Road, crossing Ashley Road and along Albert Road to the Rossmore Gospel Hall. The Bournemouth Road-Madeira Road section of the route was not granted neither was an application to extend the

Miss Louie Foott gives Bedford 'WTB' JT 3594 attention with the paint brush. A lady full of vigour and determination who was successful in the omnibus business for almost 50 years, and for 43 years the sole independent operating wholly within the Borough of Poole.

Ian Andrews Collection

service from Parkstone Joinery Works to Branksome Chine, although the existing Albert Road-Rossmore section was agreed. Her buses were produced for inspection on the 25th, and approved by the committee as being satisfactory and suitable for the district, and licences were granted for two buses to run until the end of the current licensing half year.

At a sub-committee meeting held on 28th March one licence was granted for vehicle XP 9506, whilst applications for PW 1071, PW 1078, and PR 1274 were refused, although in December permission was given for the temporary use of vehicle KK 2601 during the repainting of TK 2631.

Having received cash as compensation for loss of the Sandbanks route, Louie also struck a bargain with Hants & Dorset to obtain exclusive rights to operate a service from Upper Parkstone northwards to Rossmore, an area which at that time contained little housing but a large gipsy encampment. Louie saw the potential for development, and indeed over the next 20 years several thousand houses were built. In 1933 the route was extended from the Rossmore Hotel to Brixey Road.

This hilly but busy route of 1¾ miles started at the end of Albert Road, near the shops in Upper Parkstone, and ran down Albert Road through 'Heavenly Bottom' and then up another very steep hill to 'Monkeys Hump' before turning left to run along Rossmore Road to terminate at the corner of Brixey Road.

Louie acknowledged the part her husband Archibald Dingwell had played in its success. His medical studies at Edinburgh had been disrupted by service during World War I, and he decided to seek pastures new. Taking employment with the fledgling Sandbanks business, he proved to be a first class mechanic and driver, and also won the heart of his employer. After marriage he took on the administrative side of the business leaving Louie to the practical side she loved best, maintaining and driving the vehicles. She was one of the first women to obtain a PSV driving licence. It also allowed her to resume her interest in horses, becoming a well-known racehorse owner and trainer, also a sports woman who played for Parkstone Ladies Hockey Club until World War II.

The war years put a strain on the small fleet, which also suffered from a shortage of staff, materials, and vehicles. This all added to the difficulties of working a service carrying more passengers than ever. An utility Bedford OWB was allocated to the company in 1943.

Following the war the operation was put on a more formal basis. Until then she had traded under her maiden name, but now the Rossmore Bus Company Ltd was registered on 10th December, 1946. In the February of that year a suggestion was made to Poole Council Transport Committee that if the portion of road between Brixey Road and Upperby Road was made up, the Rossmore service could become a circular one by using Ashley Road. Enquiries were also made about improving the existing service, to include Sunday buses, and increase the service during the times school children travelled. In reply Miss Foott said she hoped shortly to extend the service until 10.30 pm, and was prepared to purchase another vehicle as soon as possible and improve the service for the large numbers of school children in the area, with the introduction of half fare tickets for children during school hours excluding Saturday. A timetable with additional services had also been submitted for which approval was awaited.

Unloading at the end of Albert Road on 30th October, 1954 this former Birmingham Corporation Daimler CO5G, No. 1097 (CVP 197), was new in 1937, during 1949 the original Met-Cam body was replaced by an English Electric body of Manchester specification, one of 20 acquired by Birmingham in 1942 when the chassis intended for them were lost owing to enemy action. Withdrawn in 1951 and sold to Rossmore it survived until broken up locally in 1959.

(Both) The late R.B. Gossling

In March 1947 proposals were submitted for a new service forming a circular from Albert Road into Sunnyside Road and up Churchill Road into Ashley Road returning to Albert Road. Although approved by Poole Council little further progress was made, although a short circular route commenced the following year, but was withdrawn from 1st January, 1949. In the July of that year it was proposed to extend the original route a short distance along Rossmore Road to serve the post-war council housing at Trinidad Estate, and this was quickly agreed, the route mileage being increased to one and three-quarters.

Churchill Road eventually got its bus, but only between 1952 and 1954, and then only five or six times a day. It started from Jubilee Road by the Regal Cinema and the Ashley Road shops, and went down Churchill Road and Victoria Crescent to the bottom of Southill Road - a point in Heavenly Bottom about ¼ mile west of the main route running along Albert Road.

At that time the main Rossmore service warranted double-deck operation on a 15-minute headway. In 1954 plans were made for a route to serve the new council housing development at Bourne Estate, about a half-mile north of the existing route along Rossmore Road. Whilst the Churchill Road route was often served by pinching a bus off the main Rossmore route for 20 minutes, the proposed service to Bourne Estate would have its own bus allocated to run at a basic half-hour frequency. Hants & Dorset also saw good reason to link the Upper Parkstone shops to the new Bourne Estate, and proposed a new route 23A. This would start in Bournemouth Square, run almost the full length of Ashley Road through Parkstone, and then proceed along Cranbrook Road and Brixey Road towards Bourne Estate. Both operators would therefore link the Parkstone shops to the new housing, but by substantially different routes. Coincidentally the plan for a new route to Bourne Estate came at the same time as the withdrawal of the Churchill Road runs. With hindsight, one wonders why the Bourne Estate route might not have served Churchill Road instead of, (as proposed in the application), duplicating two-thirds of the length of the main route along Albert and Rossmore Roads.

The competing applications went to the traffic court to be heard by the Traffic Commissioners in the autumn of 1954. And in the end neither service started- apparently because of the poor condition of one of the roads which both services needed to use to reach Bourne Estate. Ironically this was Good Road - only about ¼ mile long, but having two right angle corners in its short length. Although Bourne Estate had Hants & Dorset services to both Bournemouth and Poole town centres by this time, it was to be over 30 years later, after deregulation, that a regular bus service eventually ran from there directly to the Upper Parkstone shops. One cannot help but wonder if the simplest expedient might not have been for the Borough council to have improved the short stretch of road in question, or was that reason put forward simply as a face- saver so that both the competing companies would withdraw their respective applications!

The fleet relied greatly on vehicles that had seen service with other operators, and the principal livery had been brown and cream, (apart from the green episode). In later years the livery often depended on the colour the vehicle arrived in; the Thames Valley acquisitions for example remained red.

Still showing signs of its Birmingham Corporation ancestry as No. 1108, CVP 208 a 1937 Daimler CO5G with Met-Cam H30/24 body loads at the top of Albert Road, Parkstone before departing for Rossmore Estate on 17th August, 1953. *A.B. Cross*

Awaiting departure from Albert Road is DTF 267 a Roe-bodied Leyland TS8 of 1939. New to Lancashire United as No. 166, later passing to Hills of Tredegar, before entering the Rossmore fleet, eventually being withdrawn in October 1961. *B.L. Jackson Collection*

GJB 261 a Bristol LWL6B was new to Thames Valley in 1952 as No. 623, being sold to Rossmore in August 1964. Converted to front entrance OMB operation the vehicle also maximised its earning potential by carrying a mass of adverts. *East Pennine Transport Group*

The indefatigable Bedford, the first in the fleet new in 1935 - was one of the prototype WTB models. Later four wartime utility models (OWB) appeared, one being purchased new in 1943, with the others second-hand, the last as late as 1954.

Apart from the early vehicles, the most interesting had to be the three former Birmingham Corporation Daimler double-decks with their Birmingham specification Met-Cam bodies with straight staircases. Likewise the two Sentinel STC saloons acquired in 1961 from Ribble Motor Services which although interesting were not an operating success, DRN 351 only gave six months service, and DRN 347 never turned a wheel in revenue earning service.

Vehicles often remained in the yard off Rossmore Road for a considerable time after being taken out of service. The operational fleet during 1962 consisted of two pre-war vehicles, WS 4516 (a 1935 AEC Regal), and CTF 429 (a 1939 Leyland TS8), whilst two former Thames Valley, Bristol LWL6B saloons, FMO 963/7 were the newer vehicles mainly responsible for operating the service. By May 1965 the operational fleet was entirely former Thames Valley, Bristol LWL6B, FMO 963/7, GJB 252/61, with double-deck K6A, DBL 154 mainly used for school contract work.

Like most small operators Rossmore used the Bell Punch ticket system, it being on record that during World War II Bell Punch stock tickets were carried but seldom used. There was also a 7*d*. scholar's weekly return headed 'Miss L. Foott'. The stock tickets were used more frequently after the war. However exactly what arrangements for fare collection were used at times is a little vague, but it would appear that one man operation was in use during 1948. A complaint from Poole Council to the Traffic Commissioners brought forth the following reply: 'There is no evidence that the absence of conductors is prejudicial to the proper operation of omnibus services in the area'. Later, 'Ultimate machines' were used with stock 'Transport Services' rolls, but by 1964 'pay as you enter' was in operation without tickets being issued. After sale to Rendell this method continued until Speed Setright machines arrived, which printed the 'Rendell' title on stock rolls, but instead of the ticket class, the destinations of excursions, e.g. 'Dean Ct' and 'Soton', were printed!

Miss Foott, Rossmore Bus Company (known fleet)

Reg No.	Chassis	Chassis No.	Body	Type	Body No.	Built	Acquired	Sold	Notes
EL 6336	Unic			CH14		10/21	9/26		
EL 8217				CH14			b10/26		
BK 6749				CH14			b10/27		
PR 1274	Fiat			CH			b6/25		
PW 1071									
PW 1078									
YB 9506	Dennis			CH14		5/27	b1/29		
KK 2601							b12/29		
TK 2631	Chevrolet			B14		4/29	4/29		
TK 2333	Dodge			B26		3/29	3/29	9/30	1
TK 5455	Chevrolet			B		11/30	11/30		
JT 3594	Bedford WTB	402135		B		10/35	10/35		10
DL7552	Bedford WLG	113391	Grose	B20F		7/31	10/39	3/48	
HHW 780	Bedford OWB	14126	Duple	UB30F	32145	1943	2/51		
CVP 187	Daimler CO5G	10053	Met Cam	H30/24R		1937			
CVP 197	Daimler CO5G	10063	E. Electric	H28/26R		1937	1951	1959	
CVP 200	Daimler CO5G	10068	Met Cam	H30/24R		1937			
CVP 208	Daimler GO5G	10069	Met Cam	H30/24R		1937	5/53	3/56	
HL 9070	Leyland TS8	301090	Roe	B35F		1939			
HD 7176	Leyland TS8	304322	ECW	B34F	6706	1940			
BFX 936	Bedford OWB	27007	Duple	B26F		1945	1945		1 2
GRU 43	Bedford OB	41982		C26F		1946	1946		
BDW 14	Leyland Tig.TS8	14620	Weymann	B35F		1937	9/56	10/58	
BFX 79	Bedford OWB	14560	Duple	B26F		1943	1943		1 2
DTF 267	Leyland TS8	302167	Roe	B32F		1939		10/61	
FEH 815	Leyland TS8		Burlingham	B35F		1938	9/58	2/61	3 11
BFX 32	Bedford OWB	13911	Duple	UB28F		1943	1954	9/57	4
HL 7519	Leyland TS7	10677	Roe	B34F		1936	1/60	9/61	
CTF 429	Leyland TS8	14966	Roe	B34F	GO1750	1939	3/59	2/63	
CTF 433	Leyland TS8	14953	Roe	B32F		1939	10/58	5/62	
ERX 724	Bedford OB	54091		C25F		1949		10/55	
BYD 72	Bedford WTB	110743	Duple	26		1936	11/50	6/53	
WS 4516	AEC Regal	0662	1689 Alexander	B35F		1935	10/61	5/65	
CAG 806	AEC Regal 2	6821A132	Burlingham	B35F		1949	1/62	4/65	
FMO 963	Bristol LWL6B	85015	ECW	B39R	4736	3/51	5/62		5
FMO 967	Bristol LWL6B	85019	ECW	B39R	4740	3/51	3/63	b9/71	5
DRN 347	Sentinel STC	6/44/45	Sentinel	B44F		1951	11/63		12
DRN 351	Sentinel STC	6/44/49	Sentinel	B44F		1951	11/63	6/64	6
GJB 261	Bristol LWL6B	87003	ECW	B39R	5370	1952	8/64	9/71	5 7
GJB 252	Bristol LWL6B	85043	ECW	B39R	5361	1952	11/64	b9/71	
DBL 154	Bristol K6A	62014	ECW	L27/28R	1180	1946	4/65	1/72	
GFM 882	Bristol L6A	67115	ECW	B35F	1646	1947	6/66	b12/71	
FMO 22	Bristol LL5G	79090	ECW	FB39F	11400	1950	6/68	b9/72	8
KRU 995	Bristol LWL6B	85102	ECW	FB39F	5531	7/51	3/69	9/72	
JRU 66	Bristol LL6A	73060	ECW	FB39F	12074	12/49	8/70	10/77	
KEL 122	Leyland PD2/3	500048	Weymann	FH33/25D	M4266	1953			9
NLJ 269	Ley. PSU1/13	532051	Burlingham	B42F	5644	1953			9
NLJ 270	Ley PSU1/13	532052	Burlingham	B42F	5645	?53			9
RRU 903	Ley. PSU1/13	553657	Park Royal	B40F	37664	1955	5/72	9/74	13
UFX 520L	Bedford YRT	452904	Plaxton	C53F	733634	1973	1973	1/78	14
UFX 521L	Bedford YRT	452920	Plaxton	C53F	733635	1973	1973	5/78	14
XJT 205M	Bedford YRT	CW453198	Plaxton	C53F	733638	8/74	8/74	11/75	14
XJT 206M	Bedford YRT	CW 453173	Plaxton	C53F	733637	3/74	3/74	11/75	14
XJT 207M	Bedford YRT	CW453646	Plaxton	C53F	733636	3/74	3/74	3/76	14
CHD 606	AEC Regent 5	LD3RA447	Met Cam	H39/31F		/58		11/77	14

Notes
1.   Was UB32F.
2.   When sold converted to furniture van.
3.   Rebodied 1949.
4.   Fitted with seats from Manchester Corporation bus by Bere Regis & District.
5.   To B39F by Rossmore.
6.   Not operated by Rossmore.
7.   Broken up at Parkstone.
8.   New body fitted 1958.
9.   On loan from Bournemouth Corporation.
10. One of the prototype Bedford WTB.
11. Scrapped by 7/62.
12. Withdrawn 6/64, still in yard 1966.
13. To B40F 10/72.
14. Operated by Rendell, included for completeness.

Previous Owners

EL 6336   New to Charlies Cars, Bournemouth No. 4.

YB 9506   New to D.T. Patten, Weston-super-Mare 5/27.

DL 7552   New to Browns Bus Service, Carrisbrooke IOW. 3/35 to Southern Vectis as No. 701, renumbered 31 1937. To Hodge & Childs, (Bembridge & District Motor Services) 1937. 10/39 to Rossmore.

HHW 780   Ex Bristol Tramways & Carriage Co. No. 274 WD 1950. 1/51 to Stokes, Weston-super-Mare, 2/51 to Rossmore.

CVP 187   Ex Birmingham Corporation No. 1087. WD 1951.

CVP 197   Ex Birmingham Corporation No. 1097. WD 1951.

CVP 200   Ex Birmingham Corporation No. 1100. WD 1951.

CVP 208   Ex Birmingham Corporation No. 1108. WD 1951.

HL 9070   West Riding Auto. No. 541, via Hill of Tredegar.

HD 7176   Yorkshire Woollen District No. 479.

BDW 14   Newport Corporation No. 61, via South Wales Motors.

DTF 267   Lancashire United No166, via Hill, Tredegar

FEH 815   Ex PMT No. SN110.

BFX 32   New to Sheasby, Corfe Castle. To Bere Regis & District.

HL 7519   West Riding, to Hill Tredegar.

CTF 429   Lancs. United. No 120, via Hill Tredegar.

CTF 433   New to Lancs United Transport No. 152, to Hill Tredegar.

ERX 734   Ex Chandler.

BYD 72   Ex Dawson, Weston-super-Mare.

WS 4516   Ex SMT No. B168.

CAG 806   Ex Western Scottish Motor Traction Co. No. 578.

FMO 963   Ex Thames Valley No. 581.

Previous Owners (continued)

FMO 967   Ex Thames Valley No. 585.

DRN 347   Ex Ribble No. 291.

DRN 351   Ex Ribble No. 294.

GJB 261   Ex Thames Valley No. 623.

GJB 252   Ex Thames Valley No. 614.

DBL 154   Ex Thames Valley No. 446.

GFM 882   New Crossville No. SLA 73. 1963 to Thames Valley No. 302

FMO 22   Ex Thames Valley No. 818. Rebodied 1958 by ECW as FB39F.

KRU 995   Ex Hants & Dorset No. 694.

JRU 66   Ex Hants & Dorset No. 663.

RRU 903   Ex Bournemouth Corporation No. 89.

NLJ 269   Ex Bournemouth Corporation No.91.

UFX 520L   Ex Cosy Coaches, Parkstone.

UFX 521L   Ex Cosy Coaches, Parkstone.

CHD 606   Ex Hall, North Benfleet.

11 AFC   New to Stoddard & Cheadle as RLJ 426C?

Disposals

TK 2631   LO Trent (dealer) Parkstone.

TK 5455   LO Trent (dealer) Parkstone.

JT 3594   LL 6/43 G. Light, Wingfield Avenue, Poole.

DL 7552   To Crapper, Oxford.

CVP 197   Broken up locally 1959.

CVP 208   To Bird (dealer) scrapped 6/56 also reported with contractor by 5/58.

GRU 63   To Cornes & Sons (Contractors) Handley 1958.

BFX 32   To Rogers Transport, Parkstone for spare parts.

ERX 734   To Meatyard, Porchester. 10/57 to Mobile shop Cardiff.

DBL 154   To Ward, High Wycombe, for preservation.

GFM 882   To Hyper, Poole for preservation. By 1997 with Mac Ewan Amisfield.

RRU 903   To Allan, Bournemouth for preservation. By 1997 with Cooper, Sutton Coldfield.

In the late 1960s Louie Foott was still firmly in charge, and would often arrive without warning in her horsebox to check on buses and drivers. Having run the 'Rossmore Flyer' for many years, aged 80, in the early months of 1973 she sold the still thriving business to Cosy Coaches of Parkstone, owned by Simon Rendell, the son of founder Herbert. That the route was still good business is evidenced by the sale price of £20,000. Although Cosy's 20 plus fleet of coaches was primarily involved in private hire and foreign language student work, the bus route was not neglected and there were again plans made to extend the route to the Alderney East and Alderney West housing estates, but nothing came of these proposals which would have needed a three bus-operation on a 15-minute headway (and a two-hourly frequency on Sundays). Instead the original route was reduced in 1976 from its long-standing 15-minute frequency - needing two buses in service all day - to a one-bus shuttle on a 20-minute frequency. In a shrewd piece of marketing Cosy Coaches displayed the name 'Monkey's Hump and Heavenly Bottom Express' on the headsign of UFX520L, one of the two grant assisted 53-seater Bedfords working the service. The other was UFX 521L. School journeys were operated by double-deckers CHD 606 and KEL 122. Cosy Coaches continued all the Rossmore routes for 10 years, and the service then passed to the Stanbridge and Crichel Company in December 1983 (following financial difficulties at Cosy and the subsequent demise of the business).

After six years of operating the route as a one bus shuttle which stopped for half-hour mid-morning and for an hour at lunchtime to allow the driver meal breaks, it was usually operated by KUF 239F, ex-Southdown No. 239, a 1968 Marshall-bodied Bristol RE, B45F, the service passed to its fourth incumbent when the Stanbridge and Crichel business was acquired by Oakfield Travel of Blandford in 1989. Oakfield did extend the Rossmore route to serve the new Tower Park shopping and leisure centre development, half a mile past the original Trinidad Estate terminus. By deploying one extra vehicle for a short while they introduced new morning shoppers' routes linking Upper Parkstone to Talbot Heath, Bloxworth Road and Alderney East housing developments, but these did not last long. Oakfleld sold its business to Guildford and West Surrey, which after a short time sold the ex-Oakfield and ex-Stanbridge businesses (including the Rossmore route) to Wilts & Dorset on 1st November, 1993. Running one midibus as their routes 168 and 169, the extensions which had been contemplated at various times over the years to Alderney East and Bourne Estate were now covered on alternate journeys from Upper Parkstone, albeit with slightly slower running times owing to an extensive traffic calming project with various sleeping policemen and speed humps which now cover the entire length of Albert Road and half of Rossmore Road. Indeed the title 'Monkey's Hump and Heavenly Bottom' could not be truer!

Louie Foott passed away in 1982, aged 89, and spared the knowledge that her old adversary had acquired the business, after 64 years of independent operation.

Chapter Eight

Hants & Dorset 1940-1983

The War Years

The international events of 1938 and 1939 precluded any further expansion of services except those of an essential nature. Like many other companies, Hants & Dorset was preparing for the possibility of war during the early part of 1939. By June ARP, ambulance and fire fighting parties had been organised, and Poole Council commenced the construction of an air raid shelter under the grass plot next to the County Gates bus station, whilst the company converted a 1933 Leyland Tiger Cub No. L110, LJ 7516, with a Brush B20F body into an ambulance which they presented to the corporation.

The outbreak of war on 3rd September brought an immediate reduction in services. The 'Wallisdown Circular' (Upper Parkstone-Wallisdown-Upper Parkstone) was withdrawn immediately. A shortage of staff ensued as many joined the services resulted in conductresses becoming a common sight on the buses. The increase in passenger numbers were not helped by fuel rationing, and the blackout with its 20 mph speed restriction. By early October the cream roofs of Bournemouth and Poole buses had been painted grey, and the windows had a dark blue coating to allow some interior illumination.

At the December council meeting the Town Clerk was instructed to convey to the company the council's appreciation of the skill and courtesy of the bus drivers and conductors in carrying out their duties under the present difficult conditions. In January 1940 the council asked if, owing to the blackout conditions, trafficators could be fitted to the buses, the company replying that it was impossible at the present time, but it would consider the provision of white armlets for their drivers.

Following the fall of France there were further reductions in the frequency of services, in particular those between Poole and Bournemouth, and as the prospects of air raids increased the following instructions were issued to staff: 'When the air raid is sounded omnibuses are to proceed to the nearest shelter, and that on the "all clear" being sounded, conductors are to wait for their passengers to rejoin the vehicles, and then complete the journey. In the event of an air attack in the late evening, the normal last services of the day will be operated, if necessary, after the "all clear" signal had been received'. However it took until January 1941 to decide to disperse vehicles at night in case of air raids! By this time the bus service had been reduced by 25 per cent, and by November there were still further reductions, the last buses departing from both Poole and Bournemouth at 9.30 pm.

Sandbanks became a restricted area in June 1940, the ferry being taken over by the military, and later the Studland Bay area become a training ground in preparation for the invasion of France. By November the War Department had the use of both Parkstone garage and the Wimborne Road garage in Poole, the latter at a rent of £250 per annum. At Parkstone about ¾ of the garage was taken

Leyland LT1, No. BB70 (LJ 516) of 1929 vintage, photographed outside the Hants & Dorset garage at Southampton on 22nd August, 1943. 'Poole' is showing on the blind although no service between the two towns existed; although not technically a Poole picture it does convey the atmosphere of the war years, note the shielded headlights and white-edged mudguards. The original Leyland B35F body survived until May 1947 when a new Beadle B32R body was fitted. When withdrawn in November 1950, this body was exchanged with vehicle No. 745, allowing the older body to go to the scrap-yard with No. 70 in January 1952.   *J.C. Gillham*

Leyland Tiger Cub No. L110 (LJ 7516) of 1933-vintage still working in Poole during June 1948 when photographed turning into Wimborne Road from High Street. Used by Poole Corporation as an ambulance during the war, returned to Hants & Dorset in April 1947, finally being withdrawn in September 1950, it had a short reprieve with Lockerley Motor Services, and was finally scrapped in August 1953.   *A.B. Cross*

over, a partition being erected the full length of the garage which allowed Hants & Dorset to store coaches in its remaining part. Later the premises were taken over by Wessex Electrical Industries of Poole for the duration.

The Poole bus station scheme was making slow progress. In February 1940 the cinema company was proceeding with its scheme having commenced building the first shop of its Kingland Crescent development. It was intended that, when complete, the tenants of an old shop would move in, their previous property being demolished as the bus station scheme proceeded. By August the plans were abandoned owing to war conditions, the only developments being the use of the old shop as staff toilets and an air raid shelter was erected at the rear, only part of the site being used as a temporary bus station from November 1942.

As the war developed Poole became part of the war machine with many extra workmen and servicemen drafted into the area. In June 1941 'RNAS Sandbanks' a basic seaplane training school opened, flying boats having already moved to Poole harbour from Southampton. 'HMS Turtle', an amphibious warfare centre opened at Hamworthy, involving 4,000 personnel at its peak, Bolsons shipyard, the British Power Boat Company, Dorset Yacht Company and Newman's along with many other companies, were all involved with war work, requiring the transport of workers, as did the RN cordite factory at Holton Heath. The latter had its own railway station but still required the transportation of some workers from outlying areas by bus.

During 1942 many normal services ceased to operate on Sunday mornings, in March the corporation discussed the difficulties arising from the number of school children using buses during the rush hours when workers were travelling, the situation being exacerbated by evacuee children from Southampton and other towns also using the schools. The matter was resolved by opening the schools at 9.30 am and closing them at 4.15 pm. In an effort to curb the undignified rush at bus stops, queue rails were erected at various places within the Borough.

Within the bus industry there was also a war brewing, the 14-year-old Tilling and British Automobile Traction Group were disagreeing over various matters, resulting in the partnership being wound up in September 1942. This left the two parties free to pursue their individual policies, Hants & Dorset joining the Tilling Group.

As the war progressed the service deteriorated further, and there were complaints from the public and the council towards the hapless bus company which was in no position to improve matters. A novel idea suggested by Hants & Dorset was the temporary use of beach huts as bus shelters!

Although Bournemouth Corporation Transport had not operated into Poole since the tramway closure, the war was to prove the exception when BCT operated the following works' services:

Christchurch-Moordown-Poole-Hamworthy (Bolson's shipyard & Wallis Tin)
Ashley Road (Boscombe)-Moordown-Bear Cross-Upton
Ashley Road (Boscombe)-Moordown-Creekmoor

The latter continued until 20th March, 1953.

The first crossing of the reopened Sandbanks ferry took place on Friday 12th July, 1946 with Leyland Lion No. BA 2 (ALJ 782), photographed landing on the Sandbanks side with the 9.40 am from Swanage. The cut away rear end of the vehicle and the angle of the ferry ramp are clearly demonstrated.   *Hants & Dorset Archive*

An interesting bus and shops in upper Poole High Street form this classic street scene of the late 1940s. TS 806 (760) FLJ 433, a 1940 Bristol L5G with a Beadle B34F body awaits to depart for Bere Regis on 15th June, 1948. Rebodied the following year with an ECW B35F body and fitted with a PV2 radiator, No. 760 was withdrawn in December 1958, surviving as a contractor's bus until the end of 1963.   *A.B. Cross*

The long-running affair to provide Poole with a bus station continued. In March 1943 the council considered the establishment of a bus station adjacent to the new un-named street (later Kingland Crescent) extending between High Street and Kingland Road, and a month later it was decided to move certain services into Kingland Road to relieve congestion in the High Street area. In June 1944 the council acquired a compulsory purchase of land for improvements in Kingland Crescent, and by January 1945 Kingland Crescent was in use by certain services, the junction with the Crescent and Kingland Road having been improved. The council considered the provision of an omnibus station in Kingland Road for country and long distance services desirable.

Peace, Prosperity and Decline

With the end of the war, the public expected immediate improvements, but with the austerity conditions prevailing they were to be a long time coming. On 14th September, 1945 both the General Manager and Traffic Manager of Hants & Dorset discussed with the Council Transport Committee 'the unsatisfactory position in relation to the bus services in Poole'. The company stated,

> . . . that the position has been greatly aggravated by the temporary release to war service of a large number of the company's regular servants and vehicles, the general labour shortage and other wartime demands upon the company. There is in fact a greater number of omnibuses running in the borough now than before the war but a number of these have to be used to convey essential workers and thus cannot be used on the public routes. The position is however, gradually improving; regular servants are slowly returning to the company's service, the factories are gradually reducing staff, and the buses thus released are being put onto the public routes. Night shifts have ceased at the RNC factory at Holton Heath and the ROF Creekmoor, whilst the Lagonda Factory at Upton has closed down.

The removal of the anti-invasion devices and the rebuilding of the Sandbanks-Studland Road following its near destruction by tanks during wartime exercises took time to complete. The ferry service was reinstated on 31st January, 1946, but the through bus service did not commence until 12th July when Leyland No. BA2, ALJ 782, made the first crossing with the 9.40 am from Swanage to Bournemouth.

In 1940 the company numbered its services, and re-numbered them again into a new post-war series in 1946. Set out below are details of the 'numberings' of the services appropriate to our story.

1940 No.	1946 No.	Route
1*	1	Bournemouth-Penn Hill-Lower Parkstone-Parkstone Road-Poole
2*	2	Bournemouth-Pottery Junction-Lower Parkstone-Longfleet Road-Poole
2A*	2A	Bournemouth-County Gates-Lindsay Road-Penn Hill-Archway Road-Lower Parkstone-Longfleet Road-Poole. This is the route followed by the buses which replaced the Lower Parkstone trams.
3*	3	Bournemouth-Upper Parkstone-Parkstone Road-Poole
4*	4	Bournemouth-Upper Parkstone-Longfleet Road-Poole

A pre-1950 view showing three generations of vehicle at Kingland Crescent. On the left a 1946 Bristol K5G No.TD 781, FRU 826 with an ECW L27/28R body, in the centre an unidentified Leyland TD1. On the right a 1934 Leyland TD3 No. A130 (LJ 9404) still with its original Brush L26/26R body, A130 was withdrawn in April 1950 passing to Kaye of Leeds. TD 781 as No. 1115 was converted into a driver training vehicle in November 1964, and sold for scrap in May 1972.

R.K. Blencowe Collection

Towngate Street garage photographed in June 1953. Built in 1932 to replace the small Wimborne Road garage, Towngate Street itself was cramped and short of space by the late 1940s.

The late R.B. Gossling

1940 No.	1946 No.	Route
5*	5	Bournemouth-Constitution Hill (Sea View Hotel)
6	6	Bournemouth-County Gates-All Saints Church-Canford Cliffs-Sandbanks
6A	6A	Bournemouth-County Gates-Branksome Chine-Canford Cliffs-Sandbanks
	8	Bournemouth-Branksome-Herbert Ave-Upper Parkstone. Commenced 9th June, 1946. This service was originally 66 and renumbered in October 1946.
	9	Bournemouth-Penn Hill-Canford Cliffs. Commenced 9th June, 1946. This service was originally 65 and renumbered in October 1946.
	10	Bournemouth-Upper Parkstone-Constitution Hill-Waterloo Farm-Broadstone. Commenced 5th November, 1945. This service was originally 5A and renumbered in October 1946.
14	14	Bournemouth-County Gates-Penn Hill Corner-Compton Avenue- Lilliput
14A	14A	Bournemouth-County Gates-Upper Parkstone-Lilliput
12	-	County Gates-Branksome Chine-Lilliput. Commenced 1940, withdrawn 1944.
12	-	County Gates-Winston Avenue. Replaced by 12 below.
	28	County Gates-Branksome-Bourne Valley-Alder Rd-Wallisdown. Commenced 9th June, 1946. This service was originally 12 and renumbered in October 1946.
12A	28A	County Gates-Bourne Valley Road-Guest Avenue-Wallisdown
13	-	Wallisdown-Pottery Junc.-Penn Hill-Canford Cliffs-Branksome Chine. Replaced by 13 below.
13	30	Bear Cross-Wallisdown-Canford Cliffs-Branksome Chine
	29	(Circular Route) Upper Parkstone-Wallisdown-Ringwood Rd-Cranbrook Rd-Upper Parkstone. Commenced 9th June, 1946. This service was orignally 13B and renumbered in October 1946.
	29A	(Circular Route) Upper Parkstone-Cranbook Rd-Ringwood Rd-Wallisdown-Upper Parkstone. Commenced 9th June, 1946. This service was originally 13C and renumbered in October 1946.
	31	County Gates-Branksome Chine-Canford Cliffs-Lilliput-Poole. Commenced 9th June, 1946. This service was originally 14B and renumbered in October 1946.
27	32	Poole-Lilliput-Sandbanks
15	-	Bear Cross-Oakdale-Poole-Hamworthy-Upton. Withdrawn 1946.
15A	-	Poole-Hamworthy. (Previously Stanley Green-Poole-Hamworthy. Stanley Green to Poole section incorporated into Poole-Wimborne service from 1st July, 1940.)
15B	33	Bear Cross-Alderney-Constitution Hill-Stanley Green-Poole
-	34	Alderney-Constitution Hill-Oakdale-Poole-Hamworthy-Upton

Note: Those services marked * were numbered in 1935. The reader should note that the above list does not give a complete route history of the period.

During 1946 one of the principal matters discussed by Poole Council Transport Committee was the bus services, or the lack of them, but little could be done as austerity conditions continued to affect all walks of life. The Parks Committee wished to reinstate the beach huts that had been in use as bus shelters, three along the Wimborne Road and one in Kingland Crescent bus station, the latter still being on site in January 1947. Hants & Dorset asked for it to remain until a building licence could be obtained to construct a proper bus shelter, and the committee allowed it to remain until 25th March (or if required for a longer period), at a rent of £17 per annum. In July the Council reported that bus shelters were being erected at various places around Poole.

The beginning, and the end, of an era, the flags are flying on the Sandbanks Ferry on 13th June, 1953, it's Coronation year. For Bristol L5G No. 731 (BOW 164) it is the beginning of the end, still carrying its original Beadle B31F body it was withdrawn at the end of the month. Sold to a showman it gave another 13 years' service. *The late R.B. Gossling*

Bristol LWL6B No. 698 (KRU 999) drives off the Sandbanks ferry onto the Sandbanks shore. New in August 1951 as a FC35F ECW bodied coach, the vehicle was down graded in March 1964 to a one man operated bus, fitted with 39 second-hand bus seats and painted in green bus livery. *PM Photography*

Although limited facilities were in use at Kingland Crescent, there was pressure to move the bus stops from High Street and the George Hotel. The recommencement of Royal Blue and other express services saw these operating from a stopping place in Kingland Road, to which point the services of Bere Regis & District were moved from the George Hotel, the situation at the latter point having become chaotic. In October 1948 it was reported that during the winter months 30 routes picked up and set down at that point, a total of 953 vehicles per day. Adding an average of 30 relief journeys the total came to over 983 - and exceeded 1,000 a day during the summer months. The Borough Engineer was instructed to prepare a scheme for additional accommodation at Kingland Crescent in time for the November meeting, agreement being reached in February 1949 for bus station extensions.

At Parkstone the company had managed to regain use of its garage from the wartime tenants who had wished to purchase the property, Hants & Dorset not agreeing to sell the site. Neither was it willing to convert the garage into a bus station as requested by traders and residents of Upper Parkstone. Space was at a premium, and although the company during the war had purchased 16 properties in Chapel Lane, North Street, and Towngate Street with the intention of enlarging its Towngate Street garage, there was little chance of evicting the tenants and demolishing the property in the foreseeable future.

The nationalisation of the railways was to have an effect on Hants & Dorset. As the result of the 1947 Transport Act the Southern Railway shareholding was acquired by the British Transport Commission, and the Tilling group decided to sell their bus interests to the British Transport Commission, who acquired them on 5th November, 1948, but as from the close of business on 31st December, 1947 Hants & Dorset became a nationalised concern.

Hants & Dorset had written to Bournemouth Council in March 1947 to ask if they had any objection to its application to the Traffic Commissioners for a service between Herbert Avenue and the Square via Surrey Road. Early in 1948, following agreement with Poole Corporation - who permitted BCT Service 19, Square-Surrey Road - Borough Boundary to be extended to Surrey Road (Bourne Valley Road) - Bournemouth agreed to the 'H&D' application provided that timetables were co-ordinated. An interesting point was that at the time of accepting Poole's agreement to the extension of Service 19, Bournemouth Corporation stated that they wished to extend their service to Wroxham Road at some stage in the future. The 'H&D' Service 8 (Bournemouth - Upper Parkstone via Bourne Avenue, Surrey Road, Branksome, Herbert Avenue and Cranbrook Road) was first noted in that company's timetable for 4th April, 1948 - the same date as the extension of service 19 commenced operation.

The late 1940s and early 1950s were the years when bus services reached their peak, many considering 1952 to be the peak year. The traffic returns for Poole depot for that golden year show revenue taken as £296,761 and 2,981,841 car miles operated, an increase of £30,335 on 1951. However, all this traffic caused increased congestion of buses using the adjoining streets, which was not eliminated until 27th June, 1954 when an improved network of Poole town services was introduced. All services ran to and from the bus station at Kingland Crescent (not to be confused with the present bus station). From that date the queuing points near the George

Kingland Crescent, Poole on 1st June, 1953, 758 (FLJ 430) arriving from Wimborne. New in February 1940 as TS 803 a Bristol L5G with a Beadle B34F body. Rebodied by ECW in April 1949 with a B35R body, being withdrawn in October 1957 passing to Edmunds of Rassa as No. 8 surviving until July1962. The shelter in the background was constructed during the late 1940s as soon as a building licence could be obtained, replacing a beach hut previously used.

The late R.B. Gossling

Bristol L5G No. 752, formerly TS 705, (ERU 516), conceals its age under the 1949 ECW B35R body, and a PV2 radiator. Built in March 1939 it originally had a 1939 Beadle B34F body. Awaiting to depart from Kingland Crescent with a service for Swanage via Wareham and Studland. Note the conductor standing in characteristic pose, complete with speed Setright ticket machine.

Photobus

Hotel in the High Street were removed and an improved network of Poole town services was introduced the details of which are summarised below:

1   Bournemouth-Penn Hill-Lower Parkstone-Parkstone Road-Poole (no change)
2   Bournemouth-Pottery Junction-Lower Parkstone-Longfleet Road-Poole (no change)
3   Bournemouth-Upper Parkstone-Parkstone Road-Poole (no change)
4   Bournemouth-Upper Parkstone-Longfleet Road-Poole (no change)
5   Bournemouth-Constitution Hill-Oakdale-Poole re-routed through Foxholes Estate, via Foxholes Road, Dale Valley Road and Oakdale Road, replacing Service 33 from Foxholes Estate to Poole (Library)
5A   Bournemouth-Upper Parkstone-Trinidad Estate extended to Alderney Ave via Ringwood Road and re-numbered 23
6   Bournemouth-Branksome Chine-Canford Cliffs-Sandbanks (no change)
7   Bournemouth-All Saints Church-Canford Cliffs-Sandbanks-Swanage
8   Bournemouth-Surrey Road-Herbert Ave-Constitution Hill-Upper Parkstone (no change)
9   Bournemouth-Penn Hill-Canford Cliffs (extended Summer months to Branksome Chine) (no change)
14   Bournemouth-Upper Parkstone-Lilliput (no change)
23A   Bournemouth-Upper Parkstone-Cranbrook Road-Trinidad Estate (new service)
28   Poole-Oakdale-Wallisdown-Westbourne (Seamoor Road) (new service)
28A   Wallisdown-Alder Road-Trinidad School introduced. School journeys previously on 34 timetable.
29   Poole-Longfleet Road-Lower Parkstone-Upper Parkstone-Alder Road-Wallisdown (no change)
30   Poole-Stanley Green-Waterloo Estate-Broadstone (new service)
31   Poole-Lilliput-Canford Cliffs-Branksome Chine-Wallisdown curtailed to operate Poole-Westbourne (Seamoor Road)
32   Poole-Lilliput-Sandbanks (no change)
33   Poole-Hamworthy-Upton (new service)
33A   Poole-Hamworthy (Hamilton Road) (new service)
34   Bournemouth-Bourne Estate-Poole introduced operating via Branksome, Alder Road, Bourne Estate, Oakdale
95   Poole-Broadstone-Wimborne re-routed via Dunyeats Road, Broadstone instead of Station Rd, Moor Rd and Golf Links Rd

Services withdrawn:

33   Foxholes Estate-Stanley Green Road-Hamworthy
34/34A   Wallisdown-Alder Road Parade-Poole-Upton

The completion of the two-storey office block at the junction of High Street and Kingland Crescent (near the present level crossing) in 1955 marked the fulfilment of a promise made to Poole Council by Hants & Dorset as long ago as 1935, the war and the subsequent restrictions on building work being the main reasons for the delay. The two-storey block housed the local offices of Hants & Dorset, which included general office, cashiers' office, conductors' paying-in room, ticket office, inspectors' office, parcels' office, enquiry office and provision for the local management and secretarial staff. The bus station was operated in an anti-clockwise direction with buses entering from the High Street, and at the eastern end of the station (alongside the Ladies Walking Field) two-way operation took place, but all buses left via Kingland Road.

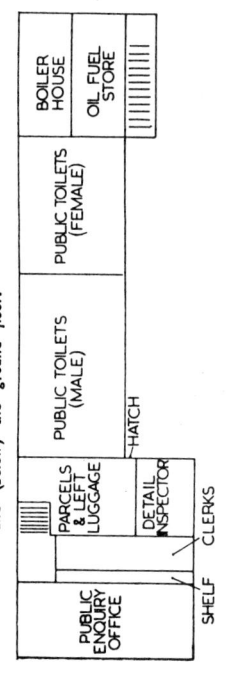

The new bus station as depicted in *Bus & Coach* December 1955.

The layout of the station and its buildings showing (above) the first floor and (below) the ground floor.

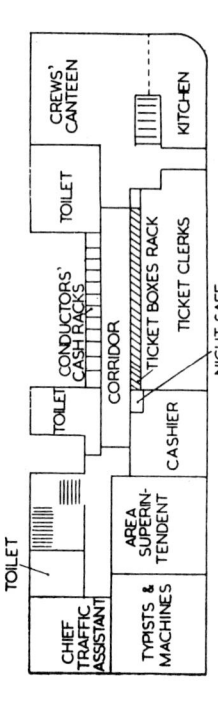

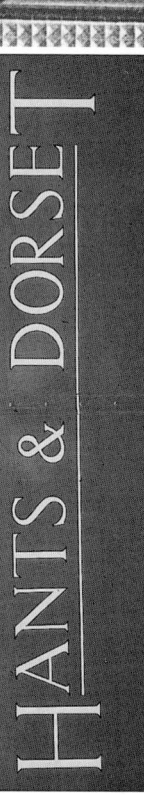

HANTS & DORSET

The Hants & Dorset fleet name as applied to vehicles in the 1950s and 1960s.

B.L. Jackson

Already bus patronage was in decline, the Suez crisis of 1956 with subsequent fuel rationing causing many cuts in services and several sharp fare increases. Some services were not reinstated, as social changes were taking place. Television was becoming popular, replacing the trip to the cinema and many other social events, resulting in less evening travel. Private motoring was also on the increase resulting in an even greater loss of passengers. Traffic figures for 1957 show revenue at £316,710 for 2,971,488 car miles operated, a decline of 12,572 on the previous year. Although the revenue figure is higher than five years previously, the cost of operating a bus had risen from 1s. 8¼d. to 2s. 1d. per mile as the cost of providing services continued to spiral.

Further economies and cuts were made to services resulting in Parkstone garage being closed in September 1958, the majority of the vehicles and staff being transferred to Poole. Parkstone then became the Western Area bus overhaul works, a decision that had been made as far back as September 1953 when authorization for two extra pits and other equipment was made to save buses having to go to Southampton. Bournemouth bus station was also reconstructed during 1957-58, the ramp and turning within the building being à la mode in 1931 but quickly becoming impractical. As early as 1937 an opening was provided in the rear wall allowing use of extra land behind that had been acquired. The rebuilding allowed this area to be used as a horseshoe-shaped bus station with a large parking area in the centre. No longer would the ramp mark the beginning or end of a Poole journey!

Ironically in 1955 - the year Poole bus station was completed - it was resolved to clear Poole of all its slums within five years, the majority of this property being in the oldest part of the town below the two level crossings. Objections caused the time scale to be increased and other developments were also brought to the fore. During 1958 the first proposals for a new shopping centre north of the railway was put forward, and by 1963 schemes for new roads had been added to the plans.

Following much debate, on 1st February, 1967 work commenced on the construction of the Arndale Centre, as the new shopping complex was originally named. Buses moved from Kingland Crescent to a temporary site at what is now the front of the bus station from 9th April, 1967. Thirty-eight acres of land were cleared north of the railway, this including the Kingland Crescent bus station, Kingland Road and the loss of Ladies Walking Field. Construction of the long-awaited bridge over the railway at Towngate Street commenced in 1969, whilst the main Arndale Centre opened in 1970, including the 14 bay bus station on the north side. Shortly after a parking yard and maintenance area situated behind the multi-story car park at the rear of the Arndale came into use, allowing Towngate Street garage to close. The latter was used for a short while as a store by Messrs Aish Electrical before demolition with other properties in connection with the new bridge which opened in September 1971. Additions to the shopping centre were later constructed, the end of the former tram route disappearing under Falkland Square. Over a 20 year period the face of Poole had changed out of all recognition, and the town had the finest bus station along the south coast.

Recently there have been some adverse comments by members of the public about the present bus station, but in 1983 Wilts & Dorset won an award for this as being one of the five best kept bus stations in the Country.

Bristol K5G No. 1033 (JT 9361) stands in Kingland Crescent bus station before departing for Hamworthy. As No. TD 660 this chassis was in July 1938 the last double-deck supplied to the company with Brush bodywork, whilst the chassis was from the first batch of Bristols purchased. In March 1954 the original L28/26R body was replaced by an ECW H32/28R 8 ft wide body; fitted to the 7 ft 6 in. chassis the wheels have a 'countersunk effect'.   *P. Yeomans*

Bristol K6A No. 1170 (HLJ 27) stands at the High Street end of Kingland Crescent bus station. To the right, the bus station offices completed in 1955, in the background is High Street. Today the left background is occupied by W.H. Smith, Argos stands on the site of the bus station offices. Falkland Square is around the corner to the right. No. 1170 survived 24 years. New in December 1948 as No. TD878 it was delivered to London Transport Godstone Garage on loan until March 1950. Withdrawn by Hants & Dorset in June 1966 it passed to Atomic Power Constructors of Dungeness until February 1970, then to Chiswick & Wright of Culceth until withdrawn in August 1972.   *A.B. Cross*

681 (KEL 409) a 1950 Bristol L6G coach with a 31-seat Portsmouth Aviation body awaits its next duty at Kingland Crescent bus station. In December 1961 the chassis was lengthened to 30 ft, an ECW FB39F body being fitted in May 1962 with cut away rear panels for use on the Sandbanks ferry service. In February 1972, 681 passed to Spencer of High Wycombe. *Photobus*

Waiting to depart from Kingland Crescent is No. 793 (NRU 6) a Bristol LS5G delivered new in November 1953. The ECW B43D body had an entrance at the front and the rear, the latter being removed when the vehicle was converted for OMB use in February 1959. Withdrawn during 1970, No. 793 passed to a dealer in October 1971. *P. Yeomans*

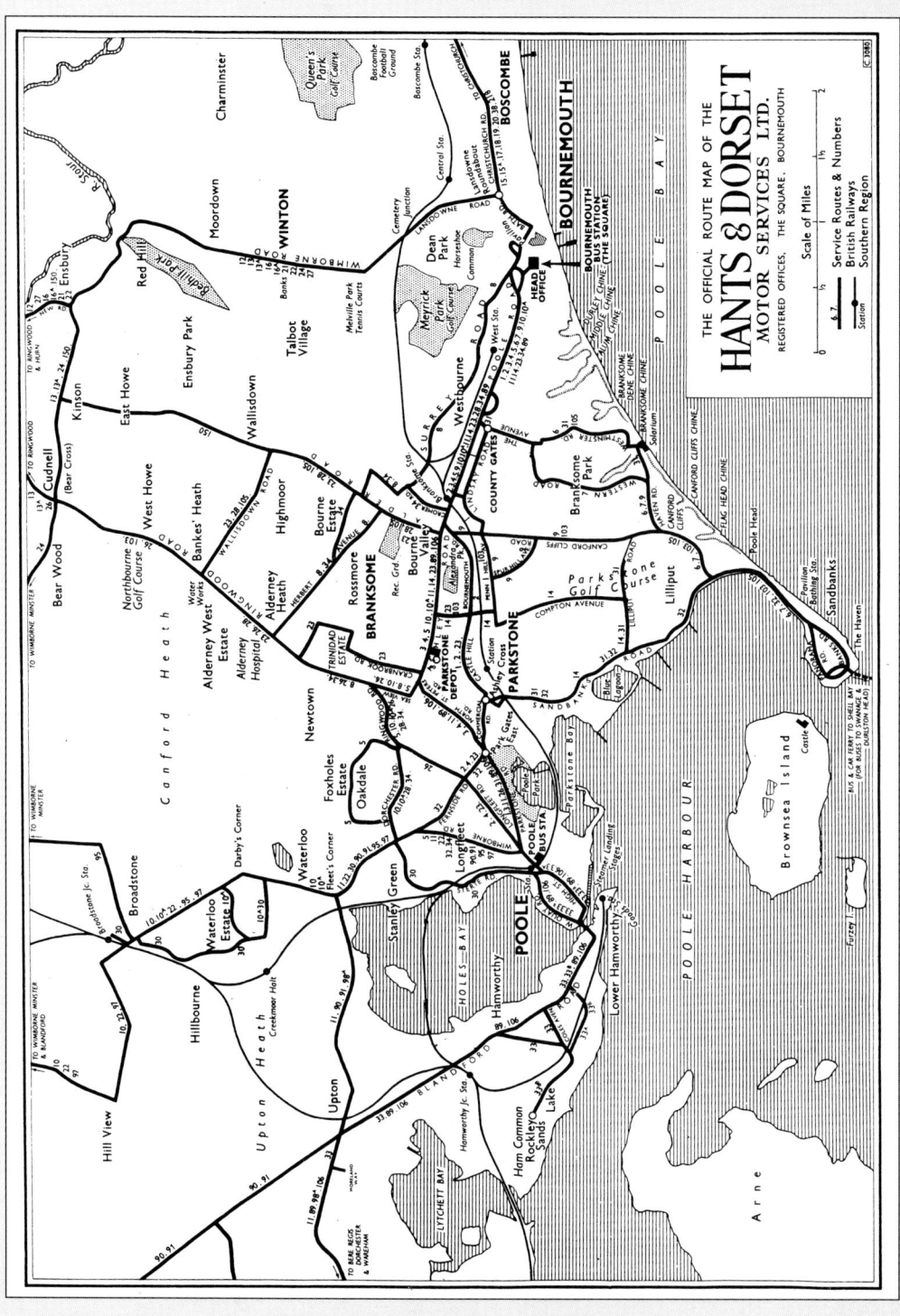

Change and Change Again

Whilst the reconstruction of Poole was taking place changes were occurring within the bus industry, which had fortunately not suffered the management upheavals of other nationalised industries. Little change came with the passage of the 1962 Transport Act which abolished the British Transport Commission, Hants & Dorset and other Tilling companies remaining nationalised and placed under the control of the Transport Holding Company which was set up under the Act. From 1963 a start was made by the Tilling group on the rationalisation of its management structures within its bus companies. First of all the Hants & Dorset General Manager became Managing Director of both Hants & Dorset (whose head office was at The Square, Bournemouth) and Wilts & Dorset Motor Services Ltd (whose head office was at 8 Endless Street, Salisbury) and not to be confused with the present Wilts & Dorset. The merging of management posts continued as vacancies arose in both companies until 1972, when Wilts & Dorset Motor Services Ltd was merged into Hants & Dorset Motor Services Ltd and all buses and coaches then carried Hants & Dorset fleet names.

However, in the meantime the political scene had changed in its policy towards the bus industry and nationalised transport in general, several Government reports during 1967 highlighting the problems faced by the industry. The Transport Holding Company offered to buy out the British Electric Traction Company's bus interests. Following legislation, from 1st March 1968 the BET's bus operations became a wholly owned subsidiary of the Transport Holding Company. The 1968 Transport Act allowed the creation of the National Bus Company which took over the bus interests of the Transport Holding Company from 1st January, 1969. It was the beginning of a new era in bus operation where many sweeping changes were to take place.

Apart from the visual impact caused by the change to Poppy red livery (fully explained on page 171), and the enlarged fleet name in white block capitals with the new 'double N' insignia next to it - which was just as derisory as the infamous 'go to me-come from me' device used by British Railways several years earlier - the internal problems of the company started to mount. Late delivery of new vehicles and spare parts was aggravated by staff shortages. The situation worsened when disaster struck the bus station at Bournemouth Square in the form of a fire on 25th July, 1976 causing severe structural damage. Following the fire services terminated at the Triangle, and later at other points around central Bournemouth. The bus departure area at Bournemouth bus station had also been the open parking area for Bournemouth depot, but following the fire buses were temporarily housed at Bournemouth Transport's Mallard Road depot. Subsequently Hants & Dorset moved some buses to Rutland Road (the old 'Royal Blue' depot) and in 1978 Royal Mews, Norwich Avenue, Bournemouth was repurchased and opened as a depot. From 1st January, 1977 a small number of services returned to the bus station, using the solid area next to Exeter Road.

The next major development took place on 26th February, 1978 when both Hants & Dorset and Bournemouth Transport (alias Bournemouth Corporation Transport) services were revised. The new service pattern was introduced to

Yellow Buses (Bournemouth Transport) Leyland Fleetline No. 138 (VJT 138S) waits at Sandbanks before departing for Christchurch Quay on 20th August, 1997. This convertible Alexander CO43/31F vehicle carries overall advertising for Condor Ferries of Poole, until the mid-1960s Bournemouth Corporation would not allow advertising on the outside of their vehicles.   *J.D. Ward*

Where once Bournemouth Corporation trams travelled along Ashley Road, today the wheel has turned full circle as Yellow Bus (Bournemouth Transport) Dennis Dart No. 458 (M458 LLJ) operates on the 68 service between Christchurch and Alderney. Behind the Safeway supermarket, which occupies the site of the former Parkstone tram depot, later the Hants & Dorset bus garage, their successors Wilts & Dorset have a small travel office situated in the end of the building. *B.L. Jackson*

reflect the growth of Poole and changing passenger demand. According to Hants & Dorset, the South East Dorset Structure Plan gave the company an indication of future needs and this was taken into account in designing the new network. The result of these changes was that Bournemouth Transport once again served the Borough of Poole (proper, as opposed to terminal workings and the section of Wallisdown Road which was in that Borough) and Hants & Dorset served Moordown and West Howe Estate from Poole.

The new services replaced the network which dated from June 1954 which had been added to from time to time, but which did not reflect the traffic needs of the late 1970s and early 1980s. Bournemouth Corporation route 30, Boscombe-Poole, and route 68 serving Upper Parkstone commenced, and a new seasonal Bournemouth Corporation Service 11 was introduced between Christchurch and Sandbanks commencing on 28th May. To mark the historic event, on Monday 27th February, 1978 the Mayor of Bournemouth boarded a 'Yellow Bus' Service 30 bus travelling to Poole and the Mayor of Poole boarded a Hants & Dorset Service 163 bus towards West Howe via Canford Avenue, where the buses, met so that the Mayors could greet one another in celebration of the new cross-boundary services. Historically, apart from the war years and a few slight wanderings around the Borough boundaries, it was the first time since the tramway closure in 1935 that Bournemouth Corporation buses had operated regular services within the Borough of Poole. The most significant change from a historical point of view was the loss of the Hants & Dorset open top service between Bournemouth and Sandbanks, the Bournemouth Corporation Christchurch Quay to Bournemouth Pier and Square service being extended to Branksome Chine and Canford Cliffs to Sandbanks.

Hants & Dorset services

No.	Route
101	Poole-Bournemouth (Lansdowne) via Longfleet Rd, Park Gates, Lower Parkstone, Penn Hill Ave, Branksome, Westbourne, Square
102	Poole-Bournemouth (Lansdowne) via Parkstone Rd, Park Gates, Lower Parkstone, Bournemouth Rd, Branksome, Lindsay Rd, Westbourne, Square
103	Poole-Bournemouth (Lansdowne) via Longfleet Rd, Park Gates, Lower Parkstone, Upper Parkstone, Branksome, Westbourne, Square
104	Poole-Bournemouth (Square) via Longfleet Rd, Park Gates, North Rd, Upper Parkstone, Branksome, Westbourne
105	Poole-Bournemouth (Lansdowne) via Tatnam, Oakdale Sch., Foxholes Est., Ringwood Rd, Sea View, Upper Parkstone, Branksome, Westbourne, Square
106	Creekmoor-Bournemouth (Lansdowne) via Fleets Bridge, Oakdale Sch., Foxholes Est., Ringwood Rd., Sea View, Upper Parkstone, Branksome, Westbourne, Square
107/108	Canford Heath-Bournemouth (Lansdowne) via Oakdale Rd, Dorchester Rd, Ringwood Rd, Sea View, Upper Parkstone, Branksome, Westbourne, Square
109	Corfe Mullen-Bournemouth (Lansdowne) via Broadstone, Waterloo Est., Fleets Bdg., Oakdale Sch., New Inn, Park Gates, North Rd, Upper Parkstone, Branksome, Westbourne, Square
110	Corfe Mullen-Bournemouth (Lansdowne) via Highfield Estate, Broadstone, Darby's Corner, Fleets Bdg., Oakdale Sch., New Inn, Park Gates, North Rd, Upper Parkstone, Branksome, Westbourne, Square

Hants & Dorset services (continued)

No.	Route
129	Poole-Wimborne via Tatnam, Oakdale Sch., Fleets Bdg., Darby's Corner, Broadstone, Merley, Rempstone Rd.
130	Poole-Wimborne via Tatnam, Oakdale Sch., Fleets Bdg., Waterloo Estate, Broadstone, Merley, Queen Anne Drive, Merley Lane
131	Poole-Roman Road via Sterte, Stanley Green, Oakdale Sch., Fleets Bdg., Waterloo Estate, Broadstone
132	Poole-Bournemouth (Triangle) via Poole Hosp., 'Shah of Persia', Oakdale Sch., Fleets Bridge, Sopers Lane, York Rd., Broadstone, Corfe Mullen, Wimborne, Leigh Park, Ferndown, Winton
133	Poole-Bournemouth (Triangle) via Tatnam, Oakdale Sch., Fleets Bdg., Darby's Corner, Broadstone, Highfield Est., Corfe Mullen, Wimborne, Colehill, Ferndown
149	Canford Cliffs-Bournemouth (Bus Stn) via Compton Acres, Penn Hill Ave, Branksome, Westbourne
150	Sandbanks-Bournemouth (Bus Stn) via Compton Acres, Sandecotes Rd, Upper Parkstone, Branksome, Westbourne
151	Poole-Bournemouth (Bus Stn) via Park Gates, Ashley Cross, Lilliput, Compton Acres, Canford Cliffs, Branksome Chine, Westbourne
152	Poole-Sandbanks via New Inn, Park Gates, Ashley Cross, Lilliput
153	Poole-Upton (Moorland Way) via Hamworthy, Coles Ave, Turlin Moor
154	Poole-Rockley Sands via Hamworthy, Ashmore Ave
156	Poole-Creekmoor via Park Gates, New Inn, Oakdale Sch., Fleets Bridge
157	Poole-Canford Heath via Park Gates, 'Shah of Persia', Sweet Home, Dorchester Rd, Johnston Rd
158	Poole-Canford Heath via Tatnam, Oakdale Sch., Oakdale Rd
159	Poole-Bournemouth (Bus Stn) via Tatnam, Oakdale Sch., Dorchester Rd, Ringwood Rd, Alderney, Wallisdown, Alder Rd, Bourne Estate, Herbert Ave, Bourne Valley, Westbourne
160	Poole-Bournemouth (Bus Stn) via Tatnam, Oakdale Sch., Foxholes Est., Newtown, Herbert Ave., Bourne Est., Bourne Valley, Surrey Rd
161	Poole-Kinson (extensions to Ferndown) via Park Gates, 'Shah of Persia', Constitution Hill Rd, Sea View, Newtown, Alderney, Bear Cross
163	Poole-West Howe Estate via Longfleet Rd, Park Gates, North Rd, Upper Parkstone, Alder Rd, Wallisdown Estate, Canford Ave, Turbary Pk Ave
164	Poole-West Howe Estate via Longfleet Rd, Park Gates, North Rd, Upper Parkstone, Alder Rd, Wallisdown Estate, Canford Ave., Montgomery Ave
165	Poole-Moordown via Longfleet Rd, Park Gates, North Rd, Upper Parkstone, Alder Rd, Wallisdown Crossroads, Winton
166	Poole-Talbot View Estate via Parkstone Rd, Park Oates, North Rd, Upper Parkstone, Alder Rd
167	Poole-Alderney East Estate via Parkstone Rd, Park Gates, Lower Parkstone, Upper Parkstone, Sea View Rd, Newtown
168	Wallisdown-Bournemouth (Bus Stn) via Alderney, Trinidad Estate, Sea View, Upper Parkstone, Branksome, Westbourne
169	Alderney-Bournemouth (Bus Stn) via Wallisdown, Alder Rd, Bourne Estate, Herbert Ave, Bourne Valley, Westbourne

Bournemouth Transport Services

No.	Route
30	Poole-Boscombe via Tatnam, Oakdale Sch., Dorchester Rd, Ringwood Rd, Trinidad Estate, Alderney, Wallisdown, Winton, Charminster
68	Wallisdown-Bournemouth Square via Alderney, Herbert Ave., Stanfield Rd, Rossmore Rd, Sea View, Upper Parkstone, Branksome, Westbourne
69	Alderney-Bournemouth Square via Wallisdown, Winton, Lansdowne

This list does not include Hants & Dorset country services, although the reader may note that some services (not mentioned earlier) have been included in this list as they can be said to be 'town services' as Wimborne now forms part of the Bournemouth, Christchurch, Poole conurbation.

The Hants & Dorset town services immediately prior to these changes were:

No.	Route
1	Bournemouth-Poole via Penn Hill, Lower Parkstone, Parkstone Road
2	Bournemouth-Poole via Branksome, Lower Parkstone, Longfleet Road
3	Bournemouth-Poole via Branksome, Upper Parkstone, Parkstone Road
4	Bournemouth-Poole via Branksome, Upper Parkstone, Longfleet Road
5	Bournemouth-Poole via Constitution Hill, Foxholes Estate, Oakdale
5A	South Canford Heath-Poole via Oakdale, Fernside Road, Park Gates East, Parkstone Road
5B	Bournemouth-South Canford Heath via Constitution Hill, Foxholes Estate
8	Bournemouth-Parkstone via Bourne Valley, Herbert Avenue and Constitution Hill
10	Bournemouth-Corfe Mullen via Upper Parkstone, Broadstone and Highfield Estate
10A	Bournemouth-Corfe Mullen via Upper Parkstone, Waterloo Estate, Broadstone
23	Bournemouth-Wallisdown-Poole via Upper Parkstone, Trinidad Estate, Alderney, Alder Road
26	Poole-West Moors/Poulner via Park Gates, Bear Cross, Ferndown, Ringwood
28	Poole-Westbourne via Newtown, Wallisdown, Branksome
33	Poole-Upton via Hamworthy, Coles Avenue, Lake Road, Turlin Moor
33A	Poole-Rockley Sands via Hamworthy, Ashmore Avenue, Lulworth Avenue, Napier Road
34	Bournemouth-Poole via Branksome, Bourne Estate
91A	Poole-Creekmoor via Park Gates East, Oakdale, Fleets Corner
91B	Poole-Creekmoor via Wimborne Road, Oakdale, Fleets Corner
94	Poole-Talbot View Estate
130	Poole-Broadstone via Stanley Green, Sopers Lane, York Road
131	Poole-Broadstone via Stanley Green, Waterloo Estate
132	Poole-Wimborne-Bournemouth via Corfe Mullen, Leigh Park, Ferndown
133	Poole-Wimborne-Bournemouth via Merley, Colehill, Ferndown
138	Bournemouth-Wimborne via Parley Cross, Dudsbury, Longham, Hampreston
148	Bournemouth-Sandbanks Ferry via Branksome Chine, Canford Cliffs
149	Bournemouth-Sandbanks Ferry via Branksome, Penn Hill, Compton Acres, Canford Cliffs
150	Bournemouth-Poole via Branksome, Upper Parkstone, Lilliput
151	Bournemouth - Poole via Branksome Chine, Canford Cliffs, Compton Acres, Lilliput
152	Poole - Sandbanks Ferry via Lilliput

During the next year it became clear that Bournemouth bus station would never completely reopen, and it was decided to vacate both that site and

Norwich Avenue garage and close Bournemouth depot with all buses operating from Poole depot on both town and country services from 30th November, 1980. At the same time further route developments took place on 30th November, when the services of both Bournemouth Transport and Hants & Dorset were altered to bring them into line with passenger demand which had been revealed following the conducting of the National Bus Company's travel survey (Marketing Analysis Project - MAP) in the area. The Hants & Dorset services adopted the brand name 'South Wessex' and the existing Hants & Dorset network needed few changes. Changes to the Hants & Dorset services were:

102	Diverted to operate via Longfleet Road instead of Parkstone Road (this change took place on 21st May, 1978)
103	Diverted to operate via Parkstone Road instead of Longfleet Road (this change took place on 21st May, 1978)
104	To operate: Bournemouth-Poole via Upper Parkstone, Lower Parkstone, Longfleet Road
105	Withdrawn
106	(New service) Bournemouth-Wallisdown via Westbourne, Upper Parkstone, Alderney
107	To operate: Bournemouth-Canford Heath/Creekmoor via Upper Parkstone
109	To operate: Bournemouth-Corfe Mullen via Upper Parkstone, Constitution Hill, Foxholes Estate, Oakdale, Waterloo Estate, Broadstone
110	To operate: Bournemouth-Corfe Mullen via Upper Parkstone, Constitution Hill, Foxholes Estate, Oakdale, Broadstone, Highfield Estate
129/130	Withdrawn
131	To operate: Poole-Corfe Mullen/Wimborne via Stanley Green, Waterloo Estate, Broadstone
150	Extended from Sandbanks to Swanage
156	Diverted to operate via Tatnam from Poole to Oakdale
159	To operate: Poole-Bournemouth via Foxholes Estate, Alderney, Westbourne
160	To operate: Poole-Bournemouth via Foxholes Estate, Alderney, Bourne Valley, Westbourne
163	To operate: Poole-Wallisdown via Upper Parkstone
166/167/168/169	Withdrawn

The remaining services were unchanged or had minor alterations.

The massive rise in car ownership since the mid-1950s had changed people's travel habits, a Government report stating that only 39 per cent of households did not have the regular use of a car, and in the past 30 years bus and coach passenger miles had halved and the bus share of total travel had dropped from 42 per cent to 8 per cent. It was clear that the Government wanted to devolve itself of the bus industry. In line with the then current National Bus Company policy, in March 1983 the Hants & Dorset company was broken up into four smaller companies: the Hampshire Bus Co. Ltd (with headquarters at Eastleigh), the Provincial Bus Co. Ltd (with headquarters at Hoeford, Fareham), the Wilts & Dorset Bus Co. Ltd (serving Bournemouth, Poole, West Hampshire and South Wiltshire, with headquarters at Poole), and all Hants & Dorset coaching activities passed to 'Shamrock & Rambler' (based in Bournemouth). Thus Hants & Dorset disappeared from the Poole and Bournemouth scene after 63 years.

Ticket System Post-War

During 1947 Hants & Dorset introduced 'Insert Setright' ticket machines at Bournemouth depot. The 'Insert Setright' could be well described as a halfway house; bell punch type tickets without fare stage or value printed on them were inserted into a slot in the machine, the machine printing the relevant information onto the ticket, and also recording the value on inbuilt counters. The new machine appeared on the Bournemouth-Sandbanks service, and other routes into Poole operated by Bournemouth-based crews.

'Speed Setright' machines were introduced into Poole and Parkstone depots during 1948/9. These machines were an improved version of the 'Insert Setright'-issued tickets from a paper reel printing all the details upon issue of any class of ticket up to 19s. 11½d. and recording all transactions on inbuilt counters, the revenue being shown in halfpence and shillings. As with the 'Setright', a simple punch was fitted to the machine to cancel tickets. In its day it was top of the range, and vastly simplified the waybill system, and as the reel of paper had no value until converted into a ticket the conductor only had to guard the revenue in his cash bag.

The 'Speed Setright' also had a front slot which allowed insert type, weekly and other special tickets to be issued. Special mention must be made of the Circular Journey Tickets issued between 1960 and 1968, the selected stopping-off points being printed on the insert tickets six of which included Poole in their itinerary, also Sandbanks Ferry where passengers had to be accounted for to the ferry company. Pre-war no-value numbered ferry tickets torn out of a booklet were issued to every passenger making the crossing, in 1946 a set of four insert tickets, adult and child, single and return, were introduced. Later a new issue was produced for the 'Speed Setright'. This procedure was abandoned by 1979 when the ferry company received payment at an agreed rate.

In 1953/4 Bournemouth Corporation replaced the Bell Punch system with the 'Ultimate', an ideal machine for the quick issue of limited value tickets as then used on municipal services. These machines were replaced by 'Speed Setrights' during 1968, although the Bournemouth Corporation Bell Punch tickets remained in use on Hants & Dorset services until the end of December 1970, after which date Bournemouth Corporation were paid directly a proportion for passengers carried within the corporation area. Indeed Hants & Dorset could well have been the last Tilling/NBC company to issue Bell Punch tickets!

On Hants & Dorset the 'Insert Setright' machines had gradually been phased out, in 1968 several 'Almex' machines were in use at both Poole and Bournemouth depots. However the trusty 'Speed Setright' survived, converted to decimal currency in 1971, it remained in use until replaced by the 'Wayfarer II', a machine using microchip technology. Whereas previous ticket machines had been issued to conductors/drivers and taken from bus to bus, the 'Wayfarer' was fitted to the vehicle, the driver inserting his personal cassette to operate the machine. At the end of his shift the driver inserted the cassette in the depot machine which transferred a record of all transactions that had taken place.

Hants & Dorset had assisted with the development of the 'Wayfarer' which was fitted to a Poole-based Bristol VRT during 1982, to be followed by several

No. S517 (GW6279), one of three 1932 vintage AEC Regent H27/25RO Tilling-bodied vehicles loaned from Brighton Hove & District in 1945 and purchased in August 1947. Photographed loading at the bus lay by at Constitution Hill, Upper Parkstone on 12th August, 1947. *Below* a rear view of No. S517 clearly showing the detail of the open staircase whilst unloading at Bournemouth bus station. The vehicle had just been painted in Hants & Dorset livery, although fleet names were never added. No. S517 was disposed of the following April.

(Both) A.B. Cross

others. Following the break-up of the original company in 1983, Hampshire Bus gradually converted to the system, and in January 1988 Poole depot and the remainder of the new Wilts & Dorset followed. The age of the computerised ticket had arrived.

The Post-War Fleet

The war years had caused a shortage of vehicles as bus production ceased for a considerable time, and like most companies Hants & Dorset come through the war with its pre-war fleet, two substantial batches of Bristol 'K' types delivered in 1939/40 greatly assisting the situation. When vehicles again became available they were not necessarily of either chassis or body type preferred by the company, and the utility bodywork quickly showed up its faults. Fortunately the well maintained pre-war fleet was in the main to see the company through those difficult years, assisted by the rebuilding of bodies and the rebodying of older vehicles.

Although a trickle of new vehicles started to appear after the war, such was the shortage that a few vintage specimens survived for several years, including three AEC Regents with Tilling H27/25R0 bodies. These were hired from Brighton Hove & District in 1945 and purchased in August 1947 when they were painted in green livery. They never carried Hants & Dorset fleet names. Numbered S517, S519 and S521 they survived until 1948-1949, at least one operating Poole-Bournemouth routes, their Highbridge bodies and open staircases a memory of 20 years earlier.

Also looking the worse for wear were the Leyland LT5As used on the Sandbanks ferry service. Several had body rebuilds towards the end of the war, but their life was limited. B102, still in wartime grey during the summer of 1948, did not operate another season. The Leylands were replaced by a selection of 1938-1940 Beadle B34F bodied Bristol L types, which had received body rebuilds and subsequently had their rear ends cut away for ferry work. These were:

TS 666	731		TS 701	748	A
TS 672	734	A	TS 702	749	B
TS 680	738		TS 704	751	
TS 688	742	A	TS 707	754	B
TS 690	743	A	TS 708	755	C

A Upon rebuilding, 734/42/3/8 had rear destination blind boxes fitted low down in place of the boot doors.
B Rebodied 1951 with 1947 Beadle B32R bodies off 1930 Leyland LT1 chassis.
C Rebodied 1954 with 1949 ECW B35R body off L5G TS 664 (730).

Two of these vehicles deserve special mention, TS 701 had an experimental Gohin-Poulenc gas producer unit fitted in the boot during 1939, whilst the final duty for No. 749 in its rebodied form was as a crew rest room during the reconstruction of Bournemouth bus station during 1957, although she was later converted into a recovery vehicle.

Bristol K5G, TD 771 (1096) FRU 11, stands at Bournemouth bus station having just arrived with service No. 8 from Upper Parkstone on 17th June, 1948. The Duple L27/28R wartime utility body is fitted to this 1942 chassis. It had just been rebuilt by Reading Coachworks, of Portsmouth, rectifying some of the faults of the austerity design. In February 1954 the 1938 Brush body formerly on vehicle No. 1024 was fitted. Disposed of in October 1959, No. 1096 worked with Sindall (contractor) of Cambridge until 1961.   *A.B. Cross*

Bristol K6A TD 775 (1109) of 1945 awaits to depart from Bournemouth bus station for Parkstone Depot on 12th June, 1948. The utility Strachan L27/28R body is shown to its full effect, note the number box fitted as an afterthought. It is hoped the passengers are sitting comfortably as the wartime wooden slatted seats were not replaced until the following September. In June 1952 the chassis formed the basis for an open-top rebuild using salvaged parts from both the original body and old Brush bodies.   *A.B. Cross*

Commencing with new double-decks delivered in 1946, the standard Tilling livery of green with a cream band above the lower saloon windows, and another below the upper deck windows, became standard, but gone were the well-known cream roofs.

The Spring of 1949 saw six AEC Regent IIIs with Northern Counties L27/26R bodies join the fleet, a diverted order from Western SMT, allocated to Bournemouth, and principally employed on long distance services, they frequently appeared on the Lilliput (14) and put in the odd appearance on Bournemouth-Poole services. These vehicles remained in the area until withdrawn in September 1963.

A new fleet numbering system was introduced on 1st January, 1950. The original system, where only even numbers had been used up to 1939 and lower numbers reused up until 1936, was replaced, and the 20 year-old use of class prefix letters discontinued. The new method consisted of a number only system, blocks of numbers being allocated to different classes of vehicle, and cast metal number plates replaced the previous use of transfers.

The prototype Bristol LDX6B Lodekka LHY 949 (Bristol Tramways No.LC 5000) appeared in the Poole area during the early spring of 1951 mainly working on the No. 4 route. Hants & Dorset ceased purchasing lowbridge double-deckers during 1951, and that November No. 1299 - the first Bristol KSW6B ECW H32/28R highbridge-type double-deck joined the fleet. By April 1952 the batch of 23 had been delivered (Nos. 1299-1321, KRU 965-987), and these were mainly employed on the Poole-Bournemouth routes where no low bridges impeded their passage. The highbridge bodies also allowed an extra five seats on the upper deck, and with the central gangway saved all the anti-social problems of the lowbridge type with its four abreast seating and sunken gangway to inflict banged heads on departing lower deck passengers.

Two further batches of highbridge deckers joined the fleet between June 1952 and May 1953 (Nos 1322-1336, LRU 51-65), and again many were allocated to the Poole-Bournemouth routes. Two vehicles, Nos. 1325 and 1329, were for a time fitted with exhaust brakes. Despite Lodekkas entering the fleet the 'Poole Highbridgers' (as they were known) served well, the first was withdrawn in 1969, and the last in 1974, having spent the majority of their lives on the Poole-Bournemouth routes as thoroughly reliable vehicles. The Bristol 'K' was not known as the 'Engineer's Bus' for nothing!

The first Lodekka in the Hants & Dorset fleet was No. 1337, LRU 67, delivered in April 1953. A pre-production model (chassis No. 100,003) it had several detail differences compared with later production models, the most noticeable being the wide slats in the radiator grill. The vehicle also appeared in official Bristol commercial vehicle publicity material. Apart from visits to Wilts & Dorset and Southern Vectis for demonstration purposes when new, it was allocated to Poole for the majority of its life. The introduction of the Lodekka was the answer to a busman's and passengers' prayer, the internal layout of a Highbridge with the external dimensions of a Lowbridge. At last passengers could board and alight with ease. When further Lodekkas arrived they replaced the Lowbridge K6As on the Lower Parkstone routes, whilst the Highbridgers and 'K' types mainly worked the Upper Parkstone routes.

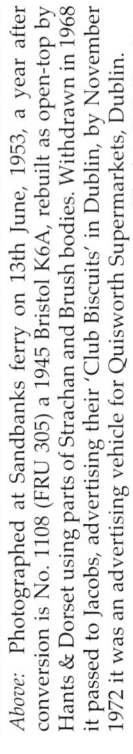

Above: Photographed at Sandbanks ferry on 13th June, 1953, a year after conversion is No. 1108 (FRU 305) a 1945 Bristol K6A, rebuilt as open-top by Hants & Dorset using parts of Strachan and Brush bodies. Withdrawn in 1968 it passed to Jacobs, advertising their 'Club Biscuits' in Dublin, by November 1972 it was an advertising vehicle for Quisworth Supermarkets, Dublin.

The late R.B. Gossling

Top right: No. 1035 (ERU 586) a 1939 Bristol K5G originally numbered TD 710 and fitted with an ECW L27/26R body. Rebodied in 1954 by ECW with a CO32/28R 8 ft wide Highbridge convertible body. Photographed with the roof fitted and in cream livery at Kingland Crescent bus station working the 32 service to Sandbanks.

The late R.B. Gossling

Right: No. 1086 (FLJ 538) a 1940 Bristol K5G had an ECW CO32/28R 8 ft wide body fitted from Fareham garage in 1960 it struck a low railway bridge severely damaging the upper deck, after which it became a permanent open-top. Photographed at Poole in green livery it stands alongside the Hants & Dorset offices in Kingland Crescent bus station in July 1961.

P. Davies

Open-Toppers

No.	1950 No.	Reg No.	Chassis	Built	Original body	To Open-top	WD	Body Notes	Notes
A580	1005	CRU 701	Leyland TD4	3/37	Brush L27/26R	4/52	9/52	Body to 1112, 2/53	3
TD 778	1112	FRU 309	Bristol K6A	7/45	Strachan L27/28R	2/53	9/67	Body Ex 1005, 2/53	3
TD 772	1106	FRU 303	Bristol K6A	10/44	Strachan L27/28R	5/52	8/64		3 10 12
TD 773	1107	FRU 304	Bristol K6A	11/44	Strachan L27/28R	5/52	8/64		3 10 12
TD 774	1108	FRU 305	Bristol K6A	3/45	Strachan L27/28R	5/52	6/68		3 7
TD 775	1109	FRU 306	Bristol K6A	3/45	Strachan L27/28R	6/52	6/68		3
TD 776	1110	FRU 307	Bristol K6A	4/45	Strachan L27/28R	6/52	6/69		3
TD 777	1111	FRU 308	Bristol K6A	5/45	Strachan L27/28R	6/52	8/69		3
TD 634	1020	BTR 310	Bristol K5G	4/38	Brush L28/26R	4/53	9/57	Body to 1137, 1/58	2 3
TD 616	1011	BTR 301	Bristol K5G	4/38	Brush L28/26R	5/53	10/57	Body to 1143, 6/57	3A
TD 618	1012	BTR 302	Bristol K5G	4/38	Brush L28/26R	5/53	10/57	Body to 1128 9/57	3A 4
TD 632	1019	BTR 309	Bristol K5G	4/38	BrushL28/26R	5/53	9/57	Body to 1126, 11/57	3A
TD 644	1025	JT 9353	Bristol K5G	7/38	Brush L28/26R	5/53	9/57	Body to 1121, 1/58	3A
TD 620	1013	BTR 303	Bristol K5G	4/38	Brush L28/26R	4/54	8/63		6 9 11
TD 710	1035	ERU 586	Bristol K5G	4/39	ECW L27/26R	4/54	12/62		6 9
TD 726	1051	ERU 602	Bristol K5G	3/39	ECW L27/26R	5/54	12/62		6 9
TD 758	1083	FLJ 535	Bristol K5G	5/40	ECW L27/26R	4/54	12/62		6 9
TD 761	1086	FLJ 538	Bristol K5G	5/40	ECW L27/26R	4/54	9/64		1 5 6
TD 709	1034	ERU 262	Bristol K5G	1/39	ECW L27/28R	6/54	12/62		6 9
TD 858	1143	GLJ 986	Bristol K5G	2/48	ECW L27/28R	6/57	1970	Body Ex 1011, 6/57	3A
TD 794	1128	GLJ 971	Bristol K5G	10/47	ECW L27/28R	9/57	1970	Body Ex 1012, 9/57	3A 8
TD 792	1126	GLJ 969	Bristol K5G	10/47	ECW L27/28R	11/57	8/64	Body Ex 1019, 11/57	3A 10
TD 787	1121	GLJ 964	Bristol K5G	8/47	ECW L27/28R	1/58	1970	Body Ex 1025, 1/58	3A
TD 852	1137	GLJ 980	Bristol K5G	11/47	ECW L27/28R	1/58	1970	Body Ex 1020, 1/58	3A

Notes

1 Stolen from garage and struck railway bridge, converted to permanent open-top in July 1960.

2 Tour of Austria 1970.

3 3A The open-top bodies were constructed in Hants & Dorset's own workshops with full fronts, utilizing some parts, including lower deck floors and seats from the original Strachan and Brush bodies. Vehicles in note 3 are of six bay construction, while those in 3A were of five bay construction. All were 59 seaters (31/28) as open-toppers except 1005/1112 which was a 57 seater (31/26).

4 First Bristol chassis purchased by company.

5 To Southern Vectis 11/64 as No 908. Exported to Holland 1975.

6 Convertible Open body built by ECW CO32/28R 8ft wide.

7 Preserved Transport Museum of Ireland, Castle Ruddery.

8 Preserved BPTA.

9 To Higgs (dealer) Barnsley, scrap 1/64.

10 To Southern Vectis 11/64 as Nos. 909/10/1. Sold to dealer 1973 exported to USA 9/73.

11 Never worked in Poole/Bournemouth area as open-topper, (Fareham & Southampton) but included for completeness.

12 Nos. 1106 and 1107 were converted to K5G in 4/51 and 2/50 respectively.

E282 (RU 9491). This 1929 Leyland TD1 was rebodied in May 1946 with a Beadle L26/26R body, the original radiator being replaced by one of the 'Cov-Rad' type. Photographed in North Street, Poole during June 1948, renumbered 917 in the December 1949 renumbering scheme it was withdrawn the following month. *A.B. Cross*

Standing at Kingland Crescent on 1st June, 1953, Bristol K6A No. 1179, (HLJ 36) is a typical example of the Bristol, ECW double-decker of the post-war period. New in December 1948 as No. TD 887 it was delivered direct from ECW to London Transport where on loan it worked from Upton Park depot until March 1950. Serving Hants & Dorset for 16 years, No. 1179 was withdrawn in August 1966. *The late R.B. Gossling*

As already stated the rebuilding of existing bodies and fitting new ones to older vehicles had kept the fleet strength up in the years following the war. When it was decided to operate open-top buses on suitable services during the summer months, the rebuilding technique was again applied. The home-built bodies were unique, each one slightly different. Known to staff as the 'Banana Boats' and remembered for what could be described as 'excessive body movement', they gave a good account of themselves. In preservation 1111 carried out a tour of Austria during 1970, in the process climbing the 5,000 ft Felbertauern Pass, a little more strenuous than the climb out of Branksome Chine!

As over a period of time a majority of these vehicles operated from both Poole and Bournemouth depots they are worthy of a full description. The bodies were constructed from the best parts of older bodies available. The first vehicle converted was Leyland TD4, 1005, using much of the existing Brush body in the reconstruction, but there appears to have been difficulties in using the Leyland chassis. Following the 1952 season the body was fitted to Bristol 'K', 1112, and in subsequent conversions 'K' type chassis were used, and when the older chassis were due for replacement the bodies were transferred to post-war ones. Twelve open-top bodies were provided by this method with a further six convertible bodies supplied by ECW, this allowing the use of the vehicle during the winter months. As the changes were complex the basic conversion history is laid out in the table on page 157.

Although a number of wartime utility vehicles had been reconstructed into the open-tops, one batch remained untouched, the Guy Arab I supplied in 1942-1943. One of these 1102 (CD 955) DCR 866, new in April 1943, was allocated to Poole towards the end of 1954 during its last months with Hants & Dorset. One of four fitted with a Roe body, although rebuilt by Portsmouth Aviation in February 1950, it was a reminder of times past and was withdrawn in the February 1956.

Towards the late 1950s many older vehicles were withdrawn. In September 1957 Poole depot had an allocation of 60 vehicles all with Bristol chassis, except one. Of the double-deck vehicles 15 were of pre-war or wartime construction, all of which had either been rebuilt or given exchange bodies by the company. The body exchange system allowed the chassis to be off the road for the minimum amount of time, a completed body being fitted when required. Others had received new bodies from ECW - including 1033, a 1938 Bristol 'K' that had been rebodied in March 1954 with an ECW H32/28R body which was 8 ft wide.

Likewise the convertible open-tops, 1034, 1035, 1051 & 1083 also had 8 ft bodies fitted to their 7 ft 6 in. chassis, whilst 1051 with a new convertible open top body could see its old body still at work on the chassis of 1089!

The one non-Bristol in the single-deck fleet, No. 564 a Bedford OB with a Beadle B27F body, was to depart at the end of 1957 to become a mobile shop in Coventry. The other 10 vehicles all had Bristol chassis, the oldest three dating from 1940 having been rebodied by ECW, whilst two coaches, 653 and 657, were fitted with Dutfield C30F bodies and 649 had its Beadle C31F rebuilt by the company; it had been in bus livery since 1953.

Parkstone at the same period had 20 operational vehicles, all double-decks, 17 of which were Highbridgers, one Lodekka, and two K-type lowbridge vehicles

Hants & Dorset purchased nine Guy Arab I chassis with utility bodies in 1942/3, these spending a majority of their time at Southampton, Eastleigh, and Winchester depots, although there is unsubstantiated evidence that several worked in the Poole-Bournemouth area when new. In December 1954 two were transferred to Bournemouth and Poole depots. No. 1102 ((DCR 866), a Roe-bodied example rebuilt by Portsmouth Aviation Coachworks in 1950, was photographed at Poole bus station in 1955. *R.H.G. Simpson*

The precursor, No. 1068 (APR 423) a Bristol K5G of 1940 with an ECW L27/26R body originally numbered TD 743. Following the rebuilding of the bodywork by Hants & Dorset in February 1953 the vehicle was fitted with experimental Cave-Browne-Cave heating equipment and operated from Southampton depot. The later installation of a supercharger involved the fitting of a 'Lodekka' type grille, which remained until the end. Photographed at Parkstone depot towards the end of its life, when mainly employed on a works contract to Fawley, the regular driver being Ron Quincey. *A.B. Cross*

Bristol K5G No. 1095 (FLJ 978) awaits to depart from Kingland Crescent on 1st June, 1953 with the No. 2 service to Bournemouth. Delivered in April 1942 as No. TD 770 the Strachan L27/28R body was of semi-utility design, rebuilt by Reading's of Portsmouth in April 1947. No. 1095 passed to Thames Valley in March 1960 as No. 475, being withdrawn in November 1964.   *The late R.B. Gossling*

No. 1092 (FLJ 544) seen loading at Kingland Crescent displays the results of a Hants & Dorset body swap. New in July 1940 as TD 767 the original ECW L27/28R body was replaced in November 1955 by the 1939, L27/26R ECW, body off vehicle 1037. Extensively rebuilt particularly around the windows, the original high type radiator was retained.   *P. Yeomans*

AEC Regent III No. 1214 with Northern Counties L27/26R bodywork stands at Bournemouth bus station on 18th July, 1953. The vehicle's blind shows route No. 6 (Bournemouth-Sandbanks). Delivered in May 1949 as No. 967, a batch of six vehicles diverted from an order for Western SMT. The entire batch was withdrawn in September 1963 and sold for breaking up the following January.   *The late R.B. Gossling*

During the reconstruction of Bournemouth bus station, most Poole services departed from a temporary terminal point in Avenue Road, Bournemouth. Whilst bus crews discuss the state of affairs, Highbridger No. 1320 waits to depart with a No. 23 for Wallisdown Estate via Ashley Road and Trinidad Estate, in the background No. 1305 stands ready with service No. 4 to Poole.
The late R.B. Gossling

Two classic views of Poole Highbridgers in July 1968. No. 1320 (KRU 986) new in March 1952, withdrawn in 1969. The clean lines of the ECW body, the sun-visor above the windscreen, an additional fitting to many Hants & Dorset vehicles, and the advert for 'Radiograms' date the photograph. Although the new bus station is complete, houses still occupy the present site of Poole Arts Centre in Kingland Road. *Below:* A rear three-quarter view of 1317 (KRU 983) departing from the partly completed new bus station. To the left one of the home built open-toppers, whilst an FLF Lodekka is parked up on the right.   *(Both) P. Davies*

Pure 1950s nostalgia, complete with Bedford CA van, Parkstone-based Highbridger No. 1312 (KRU 978) heads out of Poole up Longfleet Road towards its home depot. New in February 1952, renumbered 1375 in September 1971, the vehicle was one of the last four surviving Highbridgers being withdrawn during 1974. *The late R.B. Gossling*

No. 1021 (BTR 311) stands outside Towngate Street garage, Poole. New in July 1938 as TD 636 with a Brush L28/26R body, this Bristol K5G was rebodied by ECW in 1949 with a L27/28R body of five bay construction. Passing to United Welsh as No. 1021 in March 1960, it returned to Hants & Dorset in the October before going to Costain (contractor) at Westfield, Fife. Alongside is No. 656 (HRU 454), a 1948 Bristol L6B with a Dutfield C30F body, repainted in bus livery in March 1957. *P. Yeomans*

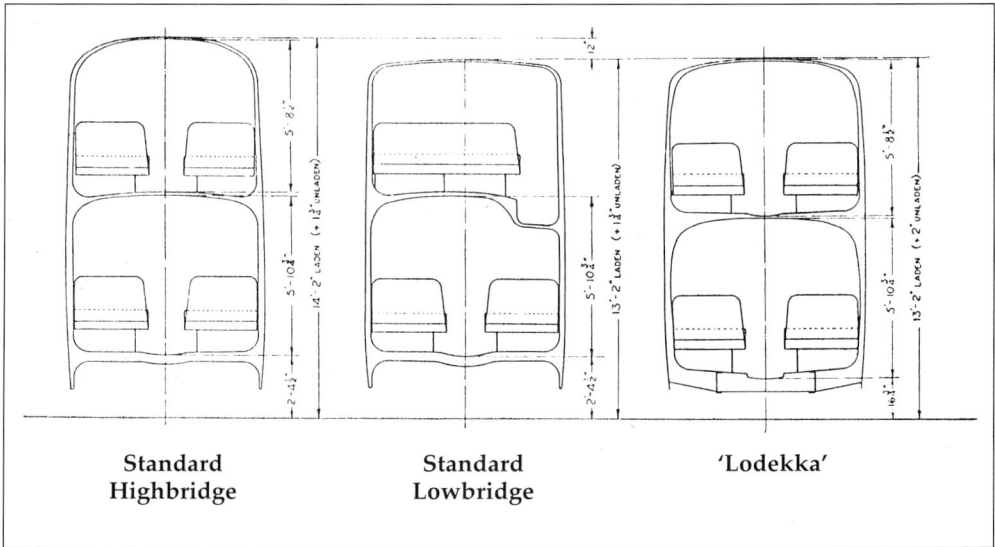

Standard Highbridge	Standard Lowbridge	'Lodekka'

Hants & Dorset's first Lodekka No. 1337 (LRU 67) leaving Poole bus station. Note the full length radiator grille as fitted to early models. Although a Lodekka, the near side upper deck roof corner has still taken a battering from overhanging trees. The houses in the left background have now disappeared, much of the site now being occupied by Poole Arts Centre.   *A. Waller Collection*

one of which - No.1068, APR 423 - was of historical note. Previously allocated to Southampton, the original 1940 body had been rebuilt by Hants & Dorset in February 1953. It was also fitted with the Cave-Browne-Cave heating and ventilating system, which was then being developed at Southampton University. A Southampton Corporation Guy also undertook the experiments, these being the first buses so fitted. It later became standard on Bristol ECW double-decks, but 1068 was the first Tilling Group vehicle and the only lowbridge so fitted. When a supercharger was experimentally fitted in 1955 a Lodekka-style bonnet and grill were added, thus making Parkstone's oldest resident easily distinguishable.

Poole Depot Allocation, 1st September, 1957

Orig. No.	No.	Reg No.	Chassis	Type	Built	Notes
Single-Decks						
983	564	JEL 278	Bed.OB	B27F	1949	(B27F 11/52)
TC 814	649	GRU 858	L5G	C31F	1947	(L5G 1/56
TC 824	653	HRU 451	L6B	C30F	1948	
TC 828	657	HRU 455	L6B	C30F	1948	
TS 806	760	FLJ 433	L5G	B35R	1940	R/B ECW 3/49
TS 808	762	FLJ 435	L5G	B35R	1940	R/B ECW 4/49
TS 810	764	FLJ 437	L5G	B35R	1940	R/B ECW 5/49
TS 816	765	GLJ 994	L5G	B35R	1947	
TS 819	768	GLJ 997	L5G	B35R	1948	
	793	NRU 6	LS5G	B43D	1953	
	794	NRU 7	LS5G	B43D	1953	
Double-Decks						
TD 660	1033	JT 9361	K5G	H32/28R	1938	R/B ECW 3/54
TD 709	1034	ERU 262	K5G	CO32/28R	1939	R/B ECW 6/54
TD 710	1035	ERU 586	K5G	CO32/28R	1939	R/B ECW 4/54
TD 726	1051	ERU 602	K5G	CO32/28R	1939	R/B ECW 5/54
TD 744	1069	APR 424	K5G	L27/26R	1940	R/B Ex 1085, 10/54
TD 748	1073	APR 428	K5G	L27/26R	1940	Rebuilt 6/53
TD 752	1077	APR 432	K5G	L27/26R	1940	R/B Ex 1045, 2/55
TD 758	1083	FLJ 535	K5G	CO32/28R	1940	R/B ECW 4/54
TD 764	1089	FLJ 541	K5G	L27/26R	1940	R/B Ex 1051. 4/54
TD 765	1090	FLJ 542	K5G	L27/26R	1940	Rebuilt 1/52
TD 766	1091	FLJ 543	K5G	L27/26R	1940	R/B Ex 1053, 5/54
TD 767	1092	FLJ 544	K5G	L27/26R	1940	R/B Ex 1037, 11/55
TD 768	1093	FLJ 976	K5G	L27/26R	1942	R/B Ex 1087, 2/54
TD 769	1094	FLJ 977	K5G	L27/26R	1942	R/B Ex 1086, 9/53
TD 770	1095	FLJ 978	K5G	L28/26R	1942	R/B Ex 1030, 1/54
TD 796	1130	GLJ 973	K5G	L27/28R	1947	
TD 857	1142	GLJ 985	K5G	L27/28R	1948	
TD 865	1157	GLJ 993	K6A	L27/28R	1948	
TD 876	1168	HLJ 25	K6A	L27/28R	1948	
TD 877	1169	HLJ 26	K6A	L27/28R	1948	
TD 878	1170	HLJ 27	K6A	L27/28R	1948	
TD 879	1171	HLJ 28	K6A	L27/28R	1948	
TD 880	1172	HLJ 29	K6A	L27/28R	1948	
TD 881	1173	HLJ 30	K6A	L27/28R	1948	
TD 882	1174	HLJ 31	K6A	L27/28R	1948	
TD 883	1175	HLJ 32	K6A	L27/28R	1948	
TD 884	1176	HLJ 33	K6A	L27/28R	1948	
TD 885	1177	HLJ 34	K6A	L27/28R	1948	
TD 887	1179	HLJ 36	K6A	L27/28R	1948	
TD 898	1190	HRU 846	K6A	L27/28R	1949	

Orig. No.	No.	Reg No.	Chassis	Type	Built	Notes
Double-Decks						
TD 911	1203	HRU 859	K6A	L27/28R	1949	
TD 912	1204	HRU 860	K6A	L27/28R	1949	
TD 913	1205	HRU 861	K6A	L27/28R	1949	
TD 914	1206	HRU 862	K6A	L27/28R	1949	
	1225	JEL 244	K6A	L27/28R	1949	
	1313	KRU 979	KSW6B	H32/28R	1952	
	1314	KRU 980	KSW6B	H32/28R	1952	
	1315	KRU 981	KSW6B	H32/28R	1952	
	1319	KRU 985	KSW6B	H32/28R	1952	
	1320	KRU 986	KSW6B	H32/28R	1952	
	1321	KRU 987	KSW6B	H32/28R	1952	
	1322	LRU 51	KSW6B	H32/28R	1952	
	1325	LRU 54	KSW6G	H32/28R	1952	
	1336	LRU 65	KSW6G	H32/28R	1953	
	1337	LRU 67	LD6B	H33/25R	1953	
	1339	LRU 69	LD6B	H33/25R	1954	
	1370	SRU 983	LD6B	H33/27R	1956	
	1371	SRU 984	LD6G	H33/27R	1956	
	1384	SRU 997	LD6B	H33/27R	1957	
	1385	SRU 998	LD6B	H33/27R	1957	

Notes
1033 Was the last Brush-bodied bus delivered to the company in July 1938, (one Utility 1101 excepted).
1095 Rebodied with Brush L28/26R body, others received ECW bodies from donor vehicles.
1337 First Lodekka purchased by Hants & Dorset.

Parkstone Depot Allocation, 1st September, 1957

Orig. No.	No.	Reg No.	Chassis	Type	Built	Notes
Double-Decks						
TD 743	1068	APR 423	K5G	L27/26R	1940	1
TD 873	1165	HLJ 22	K6A	L27/28R	1948	
	1299	KRU 965	KSW6B	H32/28R	1951	2
	1300	KRU 966	KSW6B	H32/28R	1951	
	1301	KRU 967	KSW6B	H32/28R	1951	
	1303	KRU 969	KSW6B	H32/28R	1951	
	1304	KRU 970	KSW6B	H32/28R	1951	
	1305	KRU 971	KSW6B	H32/28R	1951	
	1306	KRU 972	KSW6B	H32/28R	1951	
	1307	KRU 973	KSW6B	H32/28R	1952	
	1308	KRU 974	KSW6B	H32/28R	1952	
	1309	KRU 975	KSW6B	H32/28R	1952	
	1310	KRU 976	KSW6B	H32/28R	1952	
	1311	KRU 977	KSW6B	H32/28R	1952	
	1312	KRU 978	KSW6B	H32/28R	1952	
	1316	KRU 982	KSW6B	H32/28R	1952	
	1317	KRU 983	KSW6B	H32/28R	1952	
	1318	KRU 984	KSW6B	H32/28R	1952	
	1329	LRU 58	KSW6G	H32/28R	1952	
	1338	LRU 68	LD6B	H33/25R	1954	
Single-Decks						
TS 670	733	BOW 166	L5G	B32R	1938	3

Notes
1. Fitted with Cave-Browne-Cave heating/ventilating system.
2. First post-war Highbridge in Poole area.
3. Driver training vehicle, with 1947 Beadle body fitted in 1951.

The requirement to have enough saloons with cut-away bodywork for the Sandbanks ferry had always been a case of modifying an elderly vehicle This method was updated between 1960-1962 when eighteen 1949-50 Bristol L6A and L6G coaches with Portsmouth Aviation bodies had their chassis lengthened to 30ft and new ECW FB39F bodies fitted. Of the 18 vehicles, 14 eventually had cut-away rear ends.

The first 30 ft-long double-decks to work in Poole arrived in November 1961. These Bristol FL6B, ECW H37/33RD vehicles were put to work on the Poole-Bournemouth routes. They had driver-operated electric jack-knife doors on the rear platform, and like a flashback to the past, cord-operated bells on both decks. No. 1406 UEL 727 a 30 ft-long Bristol LDL6G new in November 1957 was allocated to Bournemouth during the summer of 1958 and worked route 6 to Sandbanks.

Poole Depot Allocation, 1st September 1963

No.	Reg No.	Chassis	Type	Built	Notes
Double-Decks					
1116	FRU 827	K5G	L53R	1946	
1121	GLJ 964	K5G	OT59R	1947	3
1123	GLJ 966	K5G	L55R	1947	
1126	GLJ 969	K5G	OT 59R	1947	3
1129	GLJ 972	K5G	L55R	1947	
1130	GLJ 973	K5G	L55R	1947	
1152	GLJ 988	K6A	L55R	1948	4
1153	GLJ 989	K6A	L55R	1948	
1155	GLJ 991	K6A	L55R	1948	
1156	GLJ 992	K6A	L55R	1948	
1157	GLJ 993	K6A	L55R	1948	
1158	HLJ 15	K6A	L55R	1948	
1159	HLJ 16	K6A	L55R	1948	
1161	HLJ 18	K6A	L55R	1948	
1162	HLJ 19	K6A	L55R	1948	
1169	HLJ 26	K6A	L55R	1948	GD
1170	HLJ 27	K6A	L55R	1948	GD
1171	HLJ 28	K6A	L55R	1948	
1174	HLJ 31	K6A	L55R	1948	BK
1176	HLJ 33	K6A	L55R	1948	BK
1177	HLJ 34	K6A	L55R	1948	BK
1178	HLJ 35	K6A	L55R	1948	BK
1179	HLJ 36	K6A	L55R	1948	U
1183	HLJ 40	K6A	L55R	1949	U
1187	HLJ 44	K6A	L55R	1949	MA
1190	HRU 846	K6A	L55R	1949	U
1191	HRU 847	K6A	L55R	1949	U
1192	HRU 848	K6A	L55R	1949	4
1203	HRU 859	K6A	L55R	1949	AV
1204	HRU 860	K6A	L55R	1949	AV
1205	HRU 861	K6A	L55R	1949	AV
1206	HRU 862	K6A	L55R	1949	4
1208	HRU 864	K6A	L55R	1949	
1225	JEL 244	K6A	L55R	1949	
1299	KRU 965	KSW6B	H60R	1951	
1300	KRU 966	KSW6B	H60R	1951	
1301	KRU 967	KSW6B	H60R	1951	
1303	KRU 969	KSW6B	H60R	1951	
1304	KRU 970	KSW6B	H60R	1951	
1305	KRU 971	KSW6B	H60R	1951	
1306	KRU 972	KSW6B	H60R	1951	
1307	KRU 973	KSW6B	H60R	1952	

No.	Reg No.	Chassis	Type	Built	Notes
Double-Decks					
1308	KRU 974	KWW6B	H60R	1952	
1309	KRU 975	KSW6B	H60R	1952	
1310	KRU 976	KSW6B	H60R	1952	
1311	KRU 977	KSW6B	H60R	1952	
1312	KRU 978	KSW6B	H60R	1952	
1313	KRU 979	KSW6B	H60R	1952	
1314	KRU 980	KSW6B	H60R	1952	
1315	KRU 981	KSW6B	H60R	1952	
1316	KRU 982	KSW6B	H60R	1952	
1317	KRU 983	KSW6B	H60R	1952	
1318	KRU 984	KSW6B	H60R	1952	
1319	KRU 985	KSW6B	H60R	1952	
1320	KRU 986	KSW6B	H60R	1952	
1321	KRU 987	KSW6B	H60R	1952	
1322	LRU 51	KSW6B	H60R	1952	
1323	LRU 52	KSW6B	H60R	1952	
1325	LRU 54	KSW6G	H60R	1952	
1326	LRU 55	KSW6G	H60R	1952	
1328	LRU 57	KSW6G	H60R	1952	
1329	LRU 58	KSW6G	H60R	1952	
1336	LRU 65	KSW6G	H60R	1953	
1338	LRU 68	LD6B	H58R	1954	
1384	SRU 997	LD6G	H60R	1957	5
1385	SRU 998	LD6B	H60R	1957	
1394	UEL 715	LD6G	H60R	1958	
1395	UEL 716	LD6G	H60R	1957	
1465	4388 LJ	FL6B	H70RD	1961	
1466	4389 LJ	FL6B	H70RD	1961	
1467	4390 LJ	FL6B	H70RD	1961	
1468	4391 LJ	FL6B	H70RD	1961	
1475	7675 LJ	FS6B	H60RD	1962	
1477	7677 LJ	FS6B	H60RD	1962	
1478	7678 LJ	FS6B	H60RD	1962	
1479	7679 LJ	FS6B	H60RD	1963	
1480	7680 LJ	FS6B	H60RD	1963	1
1487	7687 LJ	FL6G	H70RD	1962	
Single-Decks					
675	KEL 403	LL6B	FB39F	1950	
752	ERU 516	L5G	B35R	1939	
767	GLJ 996	L5G	B35R	1948	
782	KRU 988	LL6B	FB39F	1951	4
784	KRU 990	LL5G	FB39F	1952	
793	NRU 6	LS5G	B43F	1953	
794	NRU 7	LS5G	B43F	1953	
814	2716 EL	MW5G	B43F	1959	2
Coaches					
854	SRU 968	LS6G	C39F	1956	
855	SRU 969	LS6G	C39F	1956	

Notes
1. Allocated to Wareham outstation.
2. Allocated to Bere Regis outstation.
3. Both open-top vehicles were officially designated as 'Traffic Spares'.
4. Vehicles designated as 'Engineers Spares'.
5. To LD6G in 8/61.

Buses loaned to London Transport, AV=Hounslow, BK=Barking, GD=Godstone, MA=Amersham, U=Upton Park.

No. 677 (KEL 405) aboard the Sandbanks ferry. New in August 1950 as a Bristol L6G coach with a Portsmouth Aviation C28F body, in 1961 the chassis was lengthened and a new ECW FB39F body was fitted, in June 1962 the rear panels were cut away for ferry working. The scene aboard the ferry is full of nostalgia, the adverts for cafes and attractions of the 1960s and the cars of the period. Only the bus remains, sold out of service in 1971 for preservation and 30 years later still appearing at rallies in immaculate condition. *PM Photography*

Bristol LS6G No. 861 leaves the Sandbanks ferry in June 1968. One of the last batch of LS vehicles supplied to the company in February 1957, it was a coach until August 1967 when converted for OMB operation, the coach seats remaining minus head rests. Renumbered 1792 in September 1971 and withdrawn during 1974. *P. Davies*

By late 1964 the company had obtained an all 'Bristol' fleet, with 86 buses allocated to Poole, whilst neighbouring Bournemouth had 121.

In February 1965 the first front-entrance double-decks entered service at Poole on Poole-Bournemouth routes, these Bristol FLF6B and FLF6G ECW H38/32F being numbered 1516-1527. Their appearance at Poole allowed three of the FL6B models, 1465-1467 and two of the FS6G, 1511-1512, to be transferred away. During 1967 the company purchased its last new half-cab buses with a final batch of Bristol FLF6L ECW H38/32F Lodekkas, this batch being unusual in that they were fitted with four-speed semi-automatic gearboxes. Various members of the group were employed at times in the Poole-Bournemouth area.

Owing to delivery problems from Bristol Commercial Vehicles during 1968, Hants & Dorset purchased 10 Bedford VAM 70, Willowbrook B40D saloons, Nos. 3001-3010. During 1970 they had their front skirts modified to allow use on the Sandbanks Ferry, replacing the earlier Bristol LL6A and LL6B vehicles on the service.

Both the Hants & Dorset and Wilts & Dorset fleets were renumbered on 5th September, 1971, Wilts & Dorset vehicles taking numbers below 999, and Hants & Dorset vehicles numbers above, the basic system being:

1001-1099 = coaches	1401-1498 = LD Lodekkas
1101-1168 = Bristol FS Lodekkas	1501-1515 = Bedford VAM saloons
1201-1274 = FL & FLF Lodekkas	1521 upwards Bristol LH saloons
1299 LDL Lodekka	1603 upwards Bristol RELL saloons
1301 upwards intended for Bristol VRT	1701 upwards intended for Ley/Nats.
1338-1399 = Bristol KS & KSW	1761-1799 = Bristol LS saloons*
	1801-1860= Bristol saloons*
	1901 upwards other vehicles

* including coaches converted to bus duties

At the end of 1972 the 3000 series was opened for new and acquired vehicles.

The first rear-engined double-decks joined the fleet in 1971, six Daimler Fleetline CRG6LX, Roe H43/31Fs, a diverted order from the Gosport & Fareham Company, their fleet numbers were the first to be issued under the 1971 renumbering scheme. Nos. 1901-1904, VRU 124J-127J, entered service on 18th July on service No. 1 (Bournemouth-Poole via Penn Hill, one-man operated), and on service No. 2 in the evenings and Sundays (also one-man operated). Brought in to replace the last of the 'Poole Highbridgers', they were later joined by Nos. 1905-1906, VRU 128J-129J.

The loss of the Wilts & Dorset fleet-name was a severe blow to the employees of that company, in what was reputed to be a generous gesture on the part of Hants & Dorset management it was decided that the future livery of the combined fleet would be NBC Poppy Red! The first vehicles to arrive in the new livery at the end of 1972 were the company's first Bristol VRTs. One of these entered service at Poole in December 1972 numbered 1304, CRU 304L, for two weeks before being transferred to Basingstoke as No. 3304.

The problem of vehicles suitable for the Sandbanks ferry arose again in 1974, this time a batch of 10 new Bristol LH6L, ECW B43F saloons Nos. 3530-3539, ORU 530M-539M, were modified at the front before entering service.

Bristol FLF6B No. 1519 (CLJ 870C) heads past Park Gates East with service 31 to Westbourne, via Lilliput, Canford Cliffs, and Branksome Chime, knowledge denied to potential passengers owing to the lack of a 'via' blind. New in May 1965 and photographed not long after, note the old road layout outside Poole Municipal buildings, the now obsolete traffic signs and old type 'Keep Left' bollards, also the policeman on point duty. *G. Thorogood Collection*

Underneath the arches, Lodekka No. 1391 (UEL 712) passes along Surrey Road in June 1968 heading towards Bournemouth on the No. 8 service. The arch in the foreground carried the railway from Gas Works Junction around to Bournemouth West Junction and into Bournemouth West. The viaduct in the background carries the line between Gas Works Junction and Branksome and on to Poole and Weymouth. *P. Davies*

Once a coach No. 862 (UEL 736), a Bristol LS6G C39F of 1957, was converted for use as a 37-seat one man operated bus in June 1967, although retaining coach seats. Photographed at Poole awaiting the next duty on 20th July, 1971, the vehicle was renumbered 1793 in the December, withdrawn and sold to Cowley (Dealer) the following May.   *D.M. Habgood*

The end of the road for two faithful servants, Bristol KS6B No. 1270 (KEL 713) a 1950 Lowbridge, with Highbridger No. 1299 (KRU 965) behind, languish at Poole depot on 20th July, 1971, both vehicles being sold to Cowley (Dealer) the following May.   *D.M. Habgood*

The former Parkstone depot when in use as the Western Area repair works was often the last resting place of vehicles before disposal. These Lowbridge and Highbridge Bristols await their fate.   *G. Thorogood Collection*

No. 3008 (MRU 71F) a 1968 Bedford VAM70 with Willowbrook B40D body pulls off the Sandbanks ferry, the front and rear panels of these vehicles being altered in 1970 to allow ferry working. To the right of this scene the famous TV *Candid Camera* spoof took place where custom officers ask boat passengers returning from a trip to Brownsea Island 'if they had anything to declare'.   *PM Photography*

A desperate shortage of vehicles within the company during 1974 resulted in hiring from various sources, Poole having the loan of five Bournemouth Corporation Weymann H37/25Ds, Leyland PD3s Nos. 150-3 & 155, 8150 EL-8153 EL, 8155 EL, during June, July and September, whilst Western National (Devon General) Weymann H33/26R AEC Regent V, Nos. 943/7/8, 943/7/8 HTT, arrived in September and stayed until the year's end. Second-hand vehicles acquired from other companies also appeared, some of those operating in the Poole area including former Maidstone & District Leyland Atlanteans, MCCW H44/31F of 1960 vintage. By mid-1975, 3995/6, 528/32 HKJ, had moved to Basingstoke. Towards the end of 1974 three Bristol VRTs, 3313-3315, GLJ 465N-GLJ 467N, were delivered to Poole, alleviating many of the past problems. Also sent to Poole and Bournemouth were the four former King Alfred Leyland Atlanteans with Roe H43/31F bodies, Nos. 2301-2304, HOR 589E-592E, 2302 and 2304 being allocated to Poole.

During 1975 some of the early Bristol Lodekkas were being withdrawn-including 1401 (1337) the company's first of the type. At the same time two second-hand Bristol FSF6B H34/26F Lodekkas were put to work at Poole. Numbered 3480-3481, WNJ 39/40, they had originally been Brighton Hove & District 39-40, and later Southdown 2039-2040.

By 1970 the veteran open-toppers operating the Bournemouth-Sandbanks route had faded from sight except for one vehicle based at Poole. To stimulate trade on the Sandbanks route four former Brighton Hove & District convertible open-top Lodekkas, OPN 801-803 and RPN 9, were acquired from Southdown for the 1976 season. Renumbered 3482-3485, but retaining their NBC leaf green livery, they were an added attraction and continued into the 1977 season, after which 3483-3485 were disposed of, 3482 being retained as a tree-lopper and renumbered 9086.

September 1976 saw Fleetline 1904, the last double-deck in Tilling Green livery, repainted in Poppy Red, and shortly after two former Wilts & Dorset Bristol FLF Lodekkas, 208 and 213, EMR 289D, EMR 294D, were transferred to Poole. Later in 1977, 209 and 210, EMR 290D, EMR 291D, were sent from Basingstoke in exchange for Bristol VRTs 3315 and 3322. As with other companies, Hants & Dorset celebrated the Queen's Silver Jubilee in 1977 with 'Silver Jubilee' buses. Two VRTs 3307 and 3311 were based at Poole for a time, both appearing in an overall dark silver livery with blue waist and cant rails and a suitable inscription in gold and blue on the lower deck panelling, the fleet name being placed above the entrance in small red capitals. No. 3307 was sponsored by Kennedys, the builders' merchants, and 3311 by Beales department store. At the end of 1977 new VRTs entered service at Poole displacing earlier models 3334-3337. For the 1978 season a batch of Bristol VRT ECW H43/31F with detachable tops were ordered, but their stay was short, for in 1979 they were exchanged for conventional VRTs from Southern Vectis. As Hants & Dorset fleet numbers 3414-3419, UDL 671S-676S, allocated to Poole they remained in their NBC green livery for a considerable time.

Daimler Fleetline No. 1904 (VRU 127J) with Roe H43/31F body operating between Bournemouth and Poole on 20th July, 1971, two days after vehicles Nos. 1901-1904 entered service. They were the first rear-engined and one man operated double-decks in the Hants & Dorset fleet, a diverted delivery from the Gosport & Fareham company.   *D.M. Habgood*

No. 3996 (532 HKJ) one of several second-hand 1960 Leyland Atlantean MCCW H44/33F vehicles purchased from Maidstone & District Motor Services in March 1973. Photographed shortly after entering service at Poole at April 1974 in NBC poppy red livery, although the 'double arrow' is missing ahead of the fleetname.   *D.M. Habgood*

Later Open-Toppers

No.	Reg No.	Chassis	Built	Body	Acquired	WD	Notes
3482	OPN 801	Bristol LDS6B	1959	ECW CO33/27R	3/76	12/77	2 3 4
3483	OPN 802	Bristol LDS6B	1959	ECW CO33/27R	3/76	1977	2 4
3484	OPN 803	Bristol LDS6B	1959	ECW CO33/27R	3/76	12/77	2
3485	RPN 9	Bristol FS6B	1960	ECW CO33/27R	3/76	1977	2
3374	UFX 855S	Bristol VRT	1977	ECW CO43/31F		1979	1 5
3375	UFX 856S	Bristol VRT	1977	ECW CO43/31F		1979	1 5
3376	UFX 857S	Bristol VRT	1977	ECW CO43/31F		1979	1 5
3377	UFX 858S	Bristol VRT	1977	ECW CO43/31F		1979	1 5
3378	UFX 859S	Bristol VRT	1977	ECW CO43/31F		1979	1 5
3379	UFX 860S	Bristol VRT	1977	ECW CO43/31F		1979	1 5

Notes
1. To Southern Vectis as Nos. 705-710.
2. Ex Brighton Hove & District Nos. 1, 2, 3 & 9, ex Southdown Nos. 201-203 & 209.
3. To tree-lopper in 11/78.
4. Hired from Southdown July-October 1975.
5. The only occasion the roofs were removed whilst with Hants & Dorset was for the 1978 Derby.

New VRTs 3400, 3402-3406, 3412, BFX 568T, 570T-574T, 665T, which arrived in Poole during 1979, allowed the disposal of the former King Alfred Leyland Atlanteans Nos. 2301-2304 to the Bristol Omnibus Company who converted them for open-top operation. Although the movement in general was towards total one-man operation, several full crew buses remained, and early in the year No. 1211, 7686 LJ - a 1962 Bristol FL6G - was the last rear-entrance double-deck allocated to Poole. This vehicle was to play an important part in the final day of crew-operated buses from Poole and Bournemouth depots on Saturday 29th November, 1980, when 1211 departed from Bournemouth with the last service 133 via Wimborne to Poole, arriving back in Poole at three minutes past midnight. Whilst 1210, 7685 LJ, departed on service 132 from Poole to Bournemouth via Wimborne, and thus became the last bus to use the surviving section of Bournemouth bus station.

The closure of Bournemouth depot put extra work upon Poole, and at the end of 1980 the veteran Poole breakdown vehicle No. 9083, ERU 513 - a rebuilt Bristol L5G of 1939 vintage, was replaced by No. 9097, a converted Bristol LH6L formerly No. 3528, NLJ 528M. A further batch of new VRTs 3449-3456, KRU 849W-856W were delivered to Poole. The company, having disposed of many of their earlier Bristol LH models, purchased 42 second-hand from Bristol Omnibus Company in November and December 1981. Of these, 10 had their front ends modified to use the Sandbanks Ferry, and again (as with previous second-hand purchases), some commenced service in their previous owner's green livery.

Until late 1982 the fleet was classic NBC, consisting mainly of Bristol VRT double-decks, Bristol RE, Bristol LH and Leyland National single-decks. However the need to replace older vehicles and increase capacity gave rise to the purchase of unusual vehicles. In July a former London Transport DMS 1196, THM 696M, was loaned by Essex dealer 'Ensign Bus' for evaluation in the Poole-Bournemouth area and carried the temporary fleet No. 1907. This particular vehicle later passed to Maidstone & District as No. 5023. However, later the first batch of Fleetlines supplied by Ensign, having had their centre entrance removed to increase the seating capacity to 76, entered service early in 1983. Based at Poole Nos. 1907-1916 were to all intents and purposes the last vehicles supplied to the depot by Hants & Dorset.

Leyland Atlantean Roe H43/33F No. 2304 (HOR 592E), new in 1967 to 'King Alfred' of Winchester, acquired by Hants & Dorset in April 1973 and equipped for one man operation on Poole-Bournemouth services is seen at Poole bus station on 7th September, 1975, in NBC red livery. In the background work has commenced on construction of Poole Arts Centre.   *G.R. Mills*

Open-top No. 3485 (RPN 9) new in 1960 to Brighton Hove & District as No. 9, and later Southdown as No. 209, awaits to depart for Sandbanks from the temporary bus stops at the Triangle on 26th July, 1976, the day after the Bournemouth bus station fire. Note the almost ironic advert for a well-known antiseptic cream ideal for burns and other ailments!   *B.L. Jackson*

No. 3819 (REU 322S) one of the former Bristol Omnibus Company Bristol LH6L vehicles purchased during 1981 waits at Sandbanks before returning to Poole. Note the 'South Wessex' sticker, a branding for local buses following the Market Analysis Project (MAP) in the area.

A. Kennedy

The time honoured custom of converting a former passenger chassis into breakdown vehicle. 1939 Bristol L5G TS 702 (ERU 513) commenced life with a Beadle B34F body, this being replaced by a B32R body by the same builder in June 1951. Renumbered 749 in December 1949 and withdrawn in March 1957 for temporary use as a crew room during the reconstruction of Bournemouth bus station, before conversion into a recovery vehicle based at Poole.

D.M. Habgood

Freight Rover Sherpa with a Carlyle B18F body, D509 NDA. New in 1986 to Yorkshire Rider as No. 1909 before passing to Blue & White and working in the Poole-Bournemouth area where it was photographed in Westover Road, Bournemouth during 1995.   *C.G. Roberts*

Verwood Transport Routemaster NMY 655E waits to depart from Serpentine Road, Poole in May 1988. Not only was a half-cab bus in service a rarity by that time it also had an interesting history. New in 1967 to British European Airways as No. 55 it operated between the West London Air Terminal in Cromwell Road and Heathrow Airport towing a luggage trailer. Later operated by London Transport as RMA 58 before joining Verwood Transport.   *B.L. Jackson*

Chapter Nine

Wilts & Dorset Bus Company Ltd

The management of the new company was initially based at The House of Travel, Oxford Road, Bournemouth, before moving to Towngate House in Poole, the vehicles receiving the Wilts & Dorset fleet name, and it was business as usual in the Poole area. One of the principal reasons for the splitting up of the component companies of the NBC was the Government's long-term plan to sell them, the smaller units making this a more viable proposition.

The 1985 Transport Act came into force on 26th October, 1986, from which date bus services were freed from the Road Service Licensing system which had originated with the Road Traffic Act of 1930 and were therefore now open to competition. Under de-regulation those services which operators considered unprofitable to operate were in many cases not registered as 'commercial' with the Traffic Commissioners and were withdrawn, but such services if considered socially necessary by local authorities could be subsidised by seeking tenders from operators for their provision. The immediate effect was to cause little change to the networks of Bournemouth Transport and Wilts & Dorset. The results of this legislation were unpredictable, as in parts of the country very little happened, whilst in others competition became aggressive to the point of being hazardous and unsafe. Fortunately affairs never reached that point in the Poole area, but the next two years were to see many changes as existing and new operators changed tactics.

One new service was the Hospital Express Service operated by Mr George Pearson whose base was at West Howe. This service was operated by two single-deck vehicles and set out to link all the hospitals in the conurbation. As at April 1987 the service ran on Mondays to Fridays from Poole (Serpentine Lane) via Longfleet Road, Sea View, Alderney (Post Office for Hospital), Alder Road Parade, Surrey Road, Queen's Road, Bourne Avenue, Royal National Hospital, Central Station, Ashley Road, Haviland Road, Castle Lane, Iford and Fairmile to Christchurch (Bargates). This operation ceased in September 1987 due to lack of support and the delay in the opening of the new Bournemouth District Hospital - a major traffic objective - was also given as a reason for withdrawal. Verwood Transport introduced its Service 102 on Mondays to Fridays between (Poole Serpentine Road) and Bournemouth Square - this really being an extension of its Verwood to Poole service - but it was later withdrawn.

A new bus service started on Easter Monday (30th April, 1987) when another new operator - 'Poole Bay Services' - commenced operations with Service 200 (Daily) Boscombe Pier - Poole Quay via Boscombe, Lansdowne, Old Christchurch Road, Bournemouth Pier, Square, Westbourne, Upper Parkstone, Ashley Cross, Park Gates, Longfleet Road. This operator also opened some routes in Bournemouth. The buses used were three ex-Plymouth Citybus double-deckers still painted in Plymouth red and cream livery, although other vehicles were later added to the fleet. On 29th June, 1987 a further service, No.

Poole Bay Services Leyland Atlantean, MCO 250H, loads at Poole Quay before departing for Boscombe on 3rd May, 1987. This Park Royal H47/32D vehicle was new to Plymouth Citybus (Plymouth Corporation) in 1970 as No. 250, in whose livery it remained. *L. Ronan*

Poole Bay Services Bristol RE, EHU 383K, near Compton Acres *en route* to Boscombe on 25th July, 1988. The vehicle had been acquired from Badger-Vectis in the April, apart from red being added to the existing green and yellow livery little else has changed, the Badger-Vectis fleet number 54 and the original Badgerline number 1286 are still in position above the off side headlight. *L. Ronan*

203 linking Bournemouth with Hamworthy and Rockley Sands was introduced. From 18th October, 1987 'Poole Bay Services' 200 was re-numbered 50 and from 30th November, 1987 it was extended from Boscombe via Southbourne to Christchurch. Service 52 Boscombe - Poole via Bournemouth and Compton Acres operated during the Summer of 1988. This operator ceased trading (after giving the statutory 42 days' notice) on 25th November, 1988. At the close of business the fleet consisted of two ex-Plymouth Leyland 'Atlantean' double-deckers and four Bristol RE single-deckers.

The sale of the constituent companies of the NBC had commenced in July 1986. There was competition for the purchase of Wilts & Dorset, the three important bids came from 'Badgerline' (the former Bristol Omnibus Company), Alan Rolls, the Wilts & Dorset General Manager, together with the Isle of Wight-based Southern Vectis, and the third from within Wilts & Dorset management, consisting of Douglas Smith the non-executive Chairman, Hugh Malone Managing and Finance Director, Andrew Bryce Operations Director, and Rodney Luxton Engineering Director. The sealed bid of the latter was accepted and on 24th June, 1987 Wilts & Dorset was purchased by its management from within the National Bus Company, making that company the 36th to be disposed of, and the halfway point in the liquidation of the NBC.

No sooner had the new company been formed than serious competition arose in Poole with the appearance of Badgerline (originally registered as Quayshelf 175 Ltd of 85 The Ridgeway, St Albans, Herts, but later the legal address became 8 Southernhay West, Exeter, Devon). This company was a joint venture involving Badgerline and Southern Vectis, both of whom had competed with the management of Wilts & Dorset to buy that company from NBC. The company applied for an Operators Licence under the title 'Poole Pandas' but this title does not seem to have been used on buses or publicity, as the licence was issued in the name of Quayshelf Ltd. The company's fleet consisted of 15 yellow and green single-deck and double-deck buses, mostly Bristol VRTs and REs, drafted in from the parent companies and based at 'Yellow Buses' (Bournemouth Transport) Mallard Road, Bournemouth depot. A feature of this operation was that conductors were employed on their vehicles. This operation was launched at a short ceremony held at 10 am on 4th September, 1987 at the Arndale Centre (Dolphin Square), Poole, where Badgerline Iveco minibus No. 50 had been on display. Actress Barbara Windsor and the Mayor of Poole cut a ribbon, followed by the actress making a short tour on an open-top bus (owned by 'Roman City' - another Badgerline subsidiary) to Bournemouth and back. On 5th September free rides were offered on the operator's Services 1, 2, 3, 6, 7 and 8, and Badgerline services officially commenced on 6th/7th September, 1987, these being:

1   Wimborne (Peak Hours)-Broadstone (Broadway)-Bournemouth via Waterloo
     Estate, Poole, Upper Parkstone
2   Mudeford-Christchurch-Wessex Way-Bournemouth-Upper Parkstone-Poole-
     Turlin Moor
2A   Poole Station-Upton (Moorland Way) via Hamworthy, Turlin Moor
3   ('Minilink') Poole Station-Bourne Estate (Gussage Road) via Lower Parkstone,
     Upper Parkstone, Rossmore

This weekend welcomes the introduction of a BIG new bus service

6 NEW Badgerline SERVICES AROUND POOLE
CHRISTCHURCH AND BOURNEMOUTH

Badgerline – Introducing the best travel service for town and around.

🦡 Pleasant and professional staff to provide a friendly and courteous service – welcome back the conductor on our 'big bus' services.

🦡 Eye catching in bright Badgerline colours.

🦡 Frequent service – every 10 minutes during the day on main routes.

BIG BUS SERVICE

Service 1
Broadstone to Poole and Bournemouth. Extended to Wimborne at peak hours.

Service 2/2A
Turlin Moor to Poole, Bournemouth, Christchurch and Mudeford.

Service 7/8
Canford Heath to Poole

MINI LINK SERVICES

Service 3 Bourne Estate to Poole
Service 6 Burton to Christchurch
Service 9 Wimborne to Poole

Fast, frequent and convenient

Information ☎ Bournemouth 536189

Big travel bargains from Badgerline

HALF FARE
for Children and OAP's

Come and Ride FREE
Launch Preview
This Saturday 5th September between 9am and 6pm you could travel free.

Service	
1	Poole to Broadstone
2	Christchurch to Mudeford
2	Poole to Turlin Moor

Service	
3	Bourne Estate to Poole
6	Christchurch to Burton
7/8	Poole to Canford Heath

The freedom of Poole for just £4.50

POOLE Badgercard

Travelling regularly around Poole. A Poole Badgercard means Big Savings.

For seven days unlimited travel on Badgerline Big Bus and MINI LINK services in the Poole area.

Available from Badgerline Agents

Plus Holders of a valid Poole Badgercard can travel to Bournemouth for only 10p single fare (pay on the bus).

Day Returns Save in off-peak

FARE CARDS

If you travel regularly between two points, a Badgerline Fare Card could mean savings of up to **40%**

Available from Badgerline Agents

See BARBARA WINDSOR who will "Carry On" and perform the official launch ceremony at The Arndale Centre (Dolphin Square) Poole at 11.30am on Friday 4th September 1987. She will then take a short tour of the town and to Bournemouth and back by open top bus (see leaflet for details).

SERVICE 1/9 — WIMBORNE · MERLEY ESTATE
SERVICE 7/8 — BROADSTONE · CANFORD HEATH
SERVICE 2A — HILLBOURNE · WATERLOO ESTATE · CHEEKMOOR · UPTON · HAMWORTHY · TURLIN MOOR · POOLE
SERVICE 3 — BOURNE ESTATE · ROSSMORE · UPPER PARKSTONE · LOWER PARKSTONE · BRANKSOME · OAKDALE · STANLEY GREEN · FOXHOLES ESTATE
SERVICE 2 — MUDEFORD · PUREWELL · CHRISTCHURCH · BURTON · BLACKWATER · FAIRMILE
SERVICE 6

POOLE BAY · BOURNEMOUTH · WESTBOURNE

Badgerline

New Badgerline Bus Service and MINI LINKS commence 6th and 7th September 1987

7   Poole Station-Foxholes Estate-Canford Heath-Stanley Green-Poole Station
8   Poole Station-Stanley Green-Canford Heath-Foxholes Estate-Poole Station
9   ('Minilink') Poole Station-Wimborne via Oakdale, Broadstone

Service 6 ran from Christchurch to Burton.

The Poole terminus of the operation was Serpentine Road adjacent to Poole railway station.

With the arrival of Badgerline on the local bus scene there were no less than six operators competing for bus passengers in the area. An indication of the effect of this competition was, for example, the Canford Heath Estate which had a bus to Poole every half-hour, suddenly finding that there were six Badgerline and 12 Wilts & Dorset buses to Poole every hour. With this vast increase in the bus service in Poole, residents in the Upton, Hamworthy and Canford Heath areas complained about the buses being a nuisance. At Parkstone there was a continuous procession of buses as the various operators, all desperate to obtain their share of the traffic, plied between the centres of Poole and Bournemouth, whilst there were complaints from residents in the Wallisdown and West Howe areas who felt that they had not benefited!

A further incursion took place in October with 'Shamrock & Rambler' who had started a network of services in Bournemouth late in 1986 under the title 'Charlie's Cars'. Sold by the National Bus Company to 'Drawlane' on 3rd July, 1987, this operator, who had not hitherto operated in Poole, started to run into Poole from Bournemouth from 19th October, 1987. The services were:

C   Hampshire Centre (Castle Lane)-Poole via Muscliff, Moordown, Winton, Bournemouth, Penn Hill, Lower Parkstone
F   Somerford-Poole via Purewell, Christchurch, Tuckton, Iford, Bournemouth, Upper Parkstone
K   Hampshire Centre (Castle Lane)-Poole via Kinson, West Howe, Wallisdown, Bourne Estate, Upper Parkstone, Lower Parkstone

Wilts & Dorset responded vigorously to this competition firstly by increasing the frequency of many services combined with the hiring and purchase of vehicles as a stop-gap until the introduction of its first 'Skipper' services on 13th September, 1987. 'The King's Singers' (who were performing at the Poole Proms) gave the service a musical send off at the launch of the services at Poole Bus Station. Passengers who were holders of 'Poole Proms' tickets could claim a free journey on the new services. The launch of a new fleet of 25 MCW Metrorider buses took place on 7th December, 1987.

Competition from Wilts & Dorset proved to be too strong for both Badgerline and Charlie's Cars. Badgerline suddenly withdrew from the Poole area on 26th March, 1988 without giving the statutory 42 days' notice, at a time when the fleet had risen to 32 vehicles. This was in spite of publicity given to new Spring services due to commence on 14th March, 1988. The Charlie's Cars operation ceased on 3rd December, 1988.

Two other operations worthy of mention are Maybury's of Cranborne and 'Blue & White'. Maybury's started their Service 194 (Bournemouth - Poole via

Serpentine Road, Poole, during the Badger-Vectis operation. Bristol RE No. 55 (EHU 390K) stands to the fore, a Fiat mini-bus behind.   *C.G. Roberts*

Bristol VRT No. 71 (PPH 464R) heads a line up followed by Badgerline Ford Transit Mini-bus No. 4486, (C486 BFB) and Verwood Transport Routemaster NMY 648E, originally British European Airways No. 48, later London Transport No. RMA 11.   *L. Ronan*

Photographed on a wet 30th December, 1987 in Serpentine Road is Badger-Vectis Daimler Fleetline No. 72 (BNE 737N). Apart from a service number this former Great Manchester PTE vehicle can only offer a picture of a badger on the destination blind. *D.M. Habgood*

In years past the names Shamrock & Rambler and Charlie's Cars were synonymous with the best in coach travel, by 1987 Charlie's Cars was a fleet name used by Shamrock & Rambler on its ill-fated mini bus operation in the Poole-Bournemouth area. Leyland 'Sherpa' minibus D218 DLJ stands at the Avenue Road bus stop, Bournemouth, it was at this site on 7th May, 1908 where tram No. 72 left the rails and plunged into the gardens in the background. *C.G. Roberts*

Upton) on 11th March, 1991, this service running on school days only, and it was withdrawn after 6th November, 1992. Another venture of Maybury's was the 'Rockley Rag Top' which ran from Rockley Park to Sandbanks Ferry via Poole, Lilliput, and Compton Acres for the Summer Season of 1992, commencing 1st July. Blue & White buses appeared with another new service on 6th April, 1992, this being operated with minibuses by Mr Pearson (already mentioned). This service ('Route 16') ran from Kinson to Bournemouth Square via Wallisdown, Alder Road, Upper Parkstone, Branksome and Westbourne. Both operators later ceased operations.

A sting in the tail came to Bournemouth Corporation when Bournemouth Heritage Transport Services (BHT), who were closely associated with the then Bournemouth Passenger Transport Association (BPTA) and who for the past few years had operated a few sightseeing heritage tours, in 1993 suddenly commenced a set of commercial services within the Borough of Bournemouth using former London Transport Routemasters under the fleet name 'Routemaster Bournemouth' This action put Bournemouth Corporation in the position Wilts & Dorset had been previously with Badger-Vectis. Ironically amongst the vehicles purchased to combat the Routemasters were five former Wilts & Dorset Fleetlines! However, the sight of green and cream Routemasters was short lived, Bournemouth Heritage Transport going into voluntary liquidation during August 1994.

Originally BHT had considered renaming itself 'Hants & Dorset Omnibus', but following an objection from Wilts & Dorset the idea was dropped. With the original Hants & Dorset Motor Services Ltd name having been struck from the register, Wilts and Dorset seized the opportunity and registered a new company 'Hants & Dorset Motor Services Ltd', having acquired the Blandford-based Damory Coaches in May 1993. The following month the new acquisition became Hants & Dorset Motor Services Ltd, trading as Damory Coaches, with a registered office at Towngate House 2-8 Parkstone Road, Poole, Dorset, a subsidiary of Wilts & Dorset Bus Company Ltd. The expansion of Damory operations in recent years has created a situation where vehicles are out-stationed at Poole garage, resulting in Hants & Dorset vehicles again operating out of Poole!

Apart from several services operated into Poole by Bournemouth Corporation, who since 1982 have traded under the fleet name of 'Yellow Bus' - and from October 1986 as a result of the 1985 Transport Act operated as a private limited liability company, 'Bournemouth Transport Limited'- Wilts & Dorset are now the sole provider of services in the Poole area. By careful management, judicious alterations to timetables and services together with high quality vehicles of the latest design, the company has successfully entered the 21st century as one of the few remaining fully independent former NBC companies to have survived.

The Wilts & Dorset Fleet 1983-2001

Following the splitting of the company, the new Wilts & Dorset - having received its share of the divided fleet - turned to more former London Transport Fleetlines for service at Poole. A further 10, plus four Leylands and six Daimlers were acquired in August 1983 allowing older Bristol REs to be withdrawn. Another six were purchased during 1986 and four more in 1987 bringing the total to 30, the latter four, third-hand from South Wales Transport, being required to combat the Badger-Vectis competition.

Former London Transport 'DMS' Fleetlines

No.	Reg No.	Chassis	Chassis No.	Body	Type	Built	Acq.	LT No.	Disp.	Note
1907	OUC 45R	Leyland	7602359	MCW	H44/32F	11/76	12/82	DMS 2045	1993	1
1908	OJD 179R	Leyland	7602922	MCW	H44/32F	12/76	12/82	DMS 2177	1993	2
1909	OJD 191R	Leyland	7603258	MCW	H44/32F	1/77	12/82	DMS 2191		
1910	OJD 193R	Leyland	7603269	MCW	H44/32F	1/77	12/82	DMS 2193		
1911	OJD 217R	Leyland	7603767	MCW	H44/32F	7/77	12/82	DMS 2217		
1912	OJD 190R	Leyland	7603257	MCW	H44/32F	1/77	12/82	DMS 2190	1993	3
1913	OJD 225R	Leyland	7603998	MCW	H44/32F	5/77	12/82	DMS 2225	1993	4
1914	OJD 230R	Leyland	7604086	MCW	H44/32F	6/77	12/82	DMS 2230		
1915	OJD 231R	Leyland	7604139	MCW	H44/32F	6/77	12/82	DMS 2231	1993	5
1916	OJD 242R	Leyland	7604608	MCW	H44/32F	7/77	12/82	DMS 2242	1992	6
1927	KUC 223P	Daimler	68531	MCW	H44/32F	2/76	8/83	DMS 1223	1990	7
1928	KUC 239P	Daimler	68581	MCW	H44/32F	2/76	8/83	DMS 1239		
1929	KUC 964P	Daimler	68521	MCW	H44/32F	1/76	8/83	DMS 1964		
1930	KJD 16P	Leyland	7601494	MCW	H44/32F	7/76	8/83	DMS 2016	1991	
1931	KJD 18P	Leyland	7601496	MCW	H44/32F	7/76	8/83	DMS 2018	1990	7
1932	KJD 14P	Leyland	7601492	MCW	H44/32F	7/76	8/83	DMS 2014		
1933	KUC 231P	Daimler	68560	MCW	H44/32F	2/76	8/83	DMS 1231	1986	8
1934	KUC 240P	Daimler	68583	MCW	H44/32F	2/76	8/83	DMS 1240	1991	
1935	KUC 951P	Daimler	68501	MCW	H44/32F	12/75	8/83	DMS 1951	1991	
1936	OUC 26R	Leyland	7601629	MCW	H44/32F	9/76	8/83	DMS 2026		
1937	KUC 127P	Daimler	68398	P.Royal	H44/33F	8/75	1986	DMS 1127	1991	
1938	KUC 135P	Daimler	68418	P.Royal	H44/33F	9/75	1986	DMS 1135		
1939	KUC 150P	Daimler	68461	P.Royal	H44/33F	10/75	1986	DMS 1150		
1940	KUC 172P	Daimler	68562	P.Royal	H44/33F	11/75	1986	DMS 1172		
1941	KUC 178P	Daimler	68577	P.Royal	H44/33F	11/75	1986	DMS 1178		
1942	KUC 969P	Leyland	7600199	MCW	H44/32F	5/76	1986	DMS 1969	1991	
1943	KUC 902P	Daimler	68419	MCW	H44/32F	9/75	9/87	DMS 1902	1991	9
1944	KUC 924P	Daimler	68466	MCW	H44/32F	11/75	9/87	DMS 1924		10
1945	KUC 935P	Daimler	68481	MCW	H44/32F	12/75	9/87	DMS 1935	1992	11
1946	KUC 956P	Daimler	68507	MCW	H44/32F	12/75	9/87	DMS 1956		12

Notes
1. To Bournemouth Corporation (White Bus Fleet) as No. 530.
2. To Bournemouth Corporation (White Bus Fleet) as No. 532.
3. Renumbered as W&D No. 4912. To Bournemouth Corporation (White Bus Fleet) as No. 531.
4. Renumbered as W&D No. 4913. To Bournemouth Corporation (White Bus Fleet) as No. 533.
5. Renumbered as W&D No. 4915. To Bournemouth Corporation (White Bus Fleet) as No. 534.
6. Renumbered as W&D No. 4916. To Maybury, Cranborne.
7. To North (Dealer).
8. Withdrawn owing to accident damage.
9. Acquired from South Wales Transport. SWT No. 852.
10. Acquired from South Wales Transport. SWT No. 853.
11. Acquired from South Wales Transport. SWT No. 854. To Maybury of Cranborne, became 'Rag Top'.
12. Acquired from South Wales Transport. SWT No. 855.

Bristol VRT NOB 417E stands at Serpentine Road, Poole on 16th February, 1990. New in 1973 to West Midlands PTE as No. 4417, this Met-Cam H43/32F vehicle passed to Cooke of Newport IOW, before joining the fleet of Maybury of Cranborne. *L. Ronan*

The Rockley Rag Top, Daimler Fleetline, MCW 044/32F, KUC 935P, waits for passengers at Poole Quay on 20th August, 1992. Operated by Maybury's of Cranborne the vehicle feels at home, before sale and conversion to open-top was No. 1945 in the Wilts & Dorset fleet, previous to which it had been No. 854 with South Wales Transport, and originally DMS 1935 with London Transport. *B.L. Jackson*

It is a credit to all concerned that the operation of buses across the Sandbanks ferry has always run smoothly. The two outstanding events both featured Bristol LH vehicles. On 24th October, 1984 the 5.45 pm Swanage-Bournemouth service was aboard the ferry during a gale when one of the guide chains snapped with the ferry in mid-channel and the ferry was unable to move. A tug and Poole lifeboat were summoned, the ferry passengers being rescued by the tug and taken to Poole Quay and the vessel with the vehicles aboard was later towed to safety.

The acquisition of further Fleetlines and Leyland Nationals had allowed the fleet of Bristol REs to be reduced: by the latter part of 1984 only six remained at Poole, B45D Nos. 627, CRU 137L; 1635, TRU 127J; 1639, UEL 559J; 1640, UEL 560J; 1641, UEL 561J; and DP5OF, 1649, XLJ 724K. Their final day of regular service was Saturday 25th October, 1986, after which they went into store - but they were yet to have their swansong. Late 1985 saw the withdrawal of the first Fleetlines as No. 1906 was taken out of service, to be followed by No. 1903 early in 1986, and Nos. 1901-1902 had moved to Swanage whilst Leyland Fleetline No. 1915 was withdrawn following accident damage.

The second ferry incident involving an LH occurred on 1st March, 1986, when No. 3848, YAE 520V, went to board the ferry with the 6.50 pm Swanage-Bournemouth service. Owing to tidal problems, which had created a sand dune on the approach ramp the wheels of the vehicle sank and caused the drain tap on the air tank to snap off after striking the ferry ramp, causing the brakes to lock on. Leaving the bus on the approach ramp the ferry departed for Sandbanks, but upon return the incoming tide partly engulfed the bus slewing it sideways across the ramp. The ferry had to stay in position to prevent the vehicle from being swept into the navigational channel. After several recovery attempts Royal Marine divers from Hamworthy were called in, managing to secure a cable to the almost submerged vehicle. By the time it was recovered at 1 pm the following day the tidal currents had caused severe damage, seat cushions being washed up along the coast as far away as Christchurch! The vehicle was a complete write-off.

The activities of Badger-Vectis in September 1987 required Wilts & Dorset to draft vehicles from other depots into Poole and withdrawn vehicles from storage were re-licensed, including Fleetlines Nos. 1901/2 and Bristol REs Nos. 627/30, 1626/39. A variety of second-hand vehicles were also purchased and whilst these were being prepared for service, 15 vehicles, a mixture of Bristol VRT and Leyland Nationals, were hired from South Wales Transport, several of which were in the new South Wales livery of light green and lime. Of the acquired vehicles the most interesting were the 15 former West Midland PTE Bristol VRTs. Having passed to Martins (dealers) of Middlewich, 10 were hired to Crosville in December 1986 for service in Liverpool, retaining their blue and cream livery but with 'Crosville' fleetnames and fleet numbers HVG 960-HVG 969 applied. Owing to their lack of power steering they were blacked by the union, and following protracted strikes Liverpool depot was closed in March 1987 and the vehicles returned to Martins.

Over the years thousands of buses have made the short crossing at the entrance to Poole harbour aboard the Sandbanks ferry. This Bristol LH holds the record for the longest voyage, sailing the length of the harbour on 25th October, 1984. Trapped aboard the ferry following the chain failure the previous evening, assisted by the tug *Pullwell Delta* the ferry and bus arrive at Hamworthy Quay. *Wilts & Dorset Bus Company*

Bristol RELL6G No. 1629 (UEL 559J) fitted with an ECW B45D body. The Bristol chassis, ECW body and Gardner engine was an ideal combination providing a vehicle that was reliable, well liked by crews and served the company well for many years. *D.M. Habgood*

Acquired Vehicles 1987

Ex West Midlands PTE, Bristol VRT, MCW H43/33F

W&D No.	Reg. No.	WMPTE No.	Built	W&D No.	Reg. No.	WMPTE No.	Built
3461	GOG 636N	4636	1974	3469	JOV 711P	4711	1975
3462	GOG 649N	4649	1975	3470	JOV 712P	4712	1975
3463	GOG 654N	4654	1975	3471	JOV 719P	4719	1975
3464	GOG 671N	4671	1975	3472	JOV 720P	4720	1975
3465	GOG 673N	4673	1975	3473	JOV 723P	4723	1975
3466	GOG 682N	4682	1975	3474	JOV 724P	4724	1975
3467	JOV 688P	4688	1975	3475	NOB 402M	4402	1974
3468	JOV 708P	4708	1975				

Ex West Yorkshire PTE, Leyland Olympian, Roe H47/29F

W&D No.	Reg. No.	WYPTE No.	Built	W&D No.	Reg. No.	WYPTE No.	Built
3908	UWW 12X	5012	1982	3911	CUB 70Y	5070	1983*
3909	UWW 17X	5017	1982	3912	EWY 80Y	5080	1983*
3910	CUB 67Y	5067	1983*	* Later converted to convertible open-top.			

Commentators have remarked that Wilts & Dorset were late on the scene with the purchase of mini-buses; they certainly were not burdened with having a fleet of first generation 16-seat vehicles, which were little more than converted vans! Thus when the requirement came they were able to purchase purpose built vehicles. A fleet of 23-seat MCW Metroriders was ordered, one being on display at the Bus & Coach Show held at the NEC Birmingham, Wilts & Dorset having been involved in the design work with MCW. Twenty-five of these vehicles were allocated to Poole and delivered between October and December 1987, further Metroriders being added to the fleet during 1988 and 1989.

The urge to employ open-tops on the Sandbanks route again came to the fore in 1987 when two Leyland Olympians Nos. 3906-7, A989-90 XAF purchased from 'North Devon' the previous year were converted into convertible open-tops. The suspension was also modified to be adjustable to lift the body as the vehicle boarded or left the ferry, thus becoming the first two double-decks to operate a through service. This event was marked at a ceremony at Sandbanks attended by the Mayors of Poole and Swanage and the Chairman of Purbeck District Council. It was also an opportunity to launch the new livery of the recently privatised company, the drab Poppy Red of the former NBC being replaced by a bright smart new livery of masons red, black and white. A further open-top was added to the fleet by accident, when Lymington based VRT No. 3351, OEL 232P, had the top deck damaged by a falling tree during the Great Gale of October 1987. It was reconstructed as a permanent open-top, often seen around Poole during the winter with a canvas cover over the top deck, and being used as a single decker!

Following the acquisition of Verwood Transport in February 1989 VRT No. 3384, URU 691S, was repainted in the Verwood two-tone blue and gold livery complete with Verwood fleet names and mainly employed to operate former Verwood services. No. 3384 was no stranger to unusual liveries, when new it had appeared in all-over advertising livery for J. Hill, followed by Poole Pottery, and then National Travelworld. Other Poole buses carried advertising liveries over the years, including Bristol LH6L No. 3822, REU 328S, which in light blue livery with advertising operated the 'Poole Quay shuttle' service between 1985-1987.

Above: Purchased to counteract Badger-Vectis activities former West Midlands PTE Bristol VRTs Nos. 4719 (JOU 719P) and 4682 (GOG 682N) at Poole depot on 15th August, 1987 awaiting repainting before entering service with Wilts & Dorset as fleets numbers 3471 and 3466. *Below:* No. 3468 (JDV 708P) former West Midlands PTE Bristol VRT No. 4708 resplendent in the New Wilts & Dorset livery heads along Longfleet Road, Poole on 23rd February, 1990, note the cost of petrol at that date.   *(Both) L. Ronan*

South Wales Transport Leyland National No. 811 (AWN 811V) on hire to Wilts & Dorset during November 1987 waits to depart from Poole bus station with a service to Turlin Moor.

B.L. Jackson

No. 3911 (CUB 70Y) at Poole Quay on 14th May, 1997. One of five Leyland Olympians purchased from West Yorkshire PTE in 1987 to overcome the Badger-Vectis opposition. No. 3911, 3912 and 4910 were later converted to convertible open-top.   *L. Ronan*

The Poole Quay Shuttle, which operated between 1985 and 1987 had a dedicated overall advertising livery bus allocated. Former Bristol Omnibus Bristol LH6L 3822 (REU 328S) stands at Poole bus station on 20th March, 1987.   *L. Ronan*

Leyland Fleetline No. 1916 (OJD 242R) heads away from Poole bus station with a service for Wimborne. New to London Transport as No. DMS 2242 in 1977, it passed to Hants & Dorset in 1982 and subsequently the Wilts & Dorset fleet. Later renumbered 4916 it went to Maybury of Cranborne in 1992.   *L. Ronan*

The end of 1990 saw the withdrawal of the former West Midland PTE VRTs and approximately half the former London Transport DMSs, others being placed in the reserve fleet or reduced to low mileage duties. Replacements were in the form of further second-hand vehicles, firstly a batch of six Olympians with Roe H43/29F bodies from Country Bus & Coach (formerly London Country North East), numbered 3914-3916, 3918-3920, A144 DPE, A145 DPE, A156 FPG, A158 FPG, A160 FPG, in the Wilts & Dorset fleet and allocated to Poole, and early the following year three Olympians with Roe H43/31F bodies were purchased from Stevensons of Utoxeter, numbered 4924-4926, TTT 172X-TTT 174X; they had been new in 1982 to Plymouth Corporation (Citybus).

Very few Leyland Nationals have ever been allocated to Poole and the arrival of new vehicles saw their departure when in April 1993 DAF double-deckers arrived. These were powered by the DAF RS200L turbocharged transversely-mounted diesel engines, fitted with Optare 'Spectra' H49/29F bodies constructed on the Alusuisse system. They featured seats with Holdsworth moquette of a design unique to Wilts & Dorset, the interiors being designed to assist elderly, disabled and partly-sighted passengers with large diameter textured handrails, coloured bell pushes, non-slip floor coverings, and high visibility step nosings. Also introduced in September were some DAF 'Delta' single-deckers with Optare 48-seat front entrance bodies with the same interior specification as the Spectras.

At the end of 1994 Poole had an allocation of 91 vehicles, the April 1995 allocation of 83 clearly demonstrating the changing fleet.

Poole Allocation April 1995

MCW Metro Rider B23F, 1987
2301-2340, E452 MEL-E491 MEL

MCW Metro Rider B23F, 1989
2354-2359, F354 URU-F359 URU
2370, F370 URU

Optare B31F, 1993
2528-2530, K528 UJT-K530 UJT

Optare B31F, 1995
2538-2541, M538 LEL- M541 LEL

DAF Optare H48/29F, 1993
3101-3103, K101 VLJ-K102 VLJ
3117-3118, L117 ALJ-L118 ALJ

DAF Optare H48/29F, 1994
3121-3125, L121 ELJ-L125 ELJ

DAF Optare H48/29F, 1995
3140-3143, M140 KRU-M143 KRU

Bristol VRT/ECW O43/31F, 1976
3351, OEL 232P

Bristol VRT/ECW H43/31F, 1979
4405, BFX 573T   4407, BFX 574T
4412, BFX 665T

Bristol VRT/ECW H43/31F, 1980
4437, GEL 687V
4450-4451, KRU 850W-KRU 851W
4455, KRU 855W

DAF Optare B48F, 1993
3501-3502, L501 AJT-L502 AJT

Bristol LH6L/ECW B43F, 1980
3849, AFB 585V

Leyland Atlantean/Roe CO47/29F
4910, CUB 67Y   3911, CUB 70Y
3912, EWW 80Y

Leyland Atlantean/Roe H47/29F, 1982
4913, UWW 16X

Leyland Atlantean/Roe H43/29F
3914-3915, A144 DPE-A145 DPE   1983
3916, A156 FPG   1984
3918-3920, A158 FPG-A160 FPG   1984

Leyland Atlantean/East Lancs H43/31F 1982
4924-4925, TTT 172X-TTT 173X
3926, TTT 174X

Bristol VRT 3384 (URU 691S) at Poole bus station on 3rd March, 1995 painted in the two-tone blue livery of Verwood Transport. Following the take-over of the company in February 1989 it was decided to have one vehicle in its livery mainly to operate former Verwood routes.

L. Ronan

MCW Metrorider No. 2323 (1 SAR) new in October 1987 originally registered as E474 MEL. When repainted in advertising livery for S&R Dairies of Poole, the registration was changed to correspond with the advert. Photographed at Poole bus station on 29th January, 1993, No. 2323 was one of the fleet of Metroriders purchased to combat Badger-Vectis operations in the Poole area.

L. Ronan

After a gap of 20 years, crew-operated open-top operation returned to the area with the introduction of Bristol FS6G ECW CO33/27R No. 4001, XSL 288A, on service 152, Summer-only Poole-Sandbanks, in 1997. The vehicle had an interesting history. New in 1961 to Bristol Omnibus Company as No. 8576, 866 NHT, it was based at Weston-super-Mare to operate seafront services. In 1976 the original cream livery was replaced by brown and white, and the name 'Western Pioneer' added. She was withdrawn early in 1981, passing to Stagecoach (Gloagtrotter) Perth, and acquired by Wilts & Dorset in January 1992 from Hampshire Bus. Following refurbishment and painting in a special livery to operate at Swanage in conjunction with the Swanage Railway, in 1997 she was repainted in all-cream livery with red relief and carrying old style Wilts & Dorset fleet names as fleet No. 4001 and operated for two seasons to Sandbanks until sold in October 1999 to Dewer of Cockenzie for sight-seeing tours in the Edinburgh area.

Further second-hand vehicles entered the fleet in January 1998 when four DAF SB200 Ikarus B49F single-decks were acquired from Wall's of Manchester, Nos. 3507-3510, N10 WAL, N12 WAL, N15 WAL, N16 WAL. At the same time six DAF NCB H47/30F Palatine bodied double-decks were also purchased from Wall's and one the following year from 'A Bus' of Bristol, Nos. 3418-3153, M17 WAL, M20 WAL, N13 WAL, N14 WAL, and No. 3157, M645 KCP. These vehicles had their suspension modified to suit the Sandbanks ferry and to date five have been adapted as convertible open-toppers. Although several are allocated to Swanage they are very much part of the Sandbanks ferry scene.

Poole depot has also seen other second-hand vehicles, including Metro Riders from Trent, Grimsby & Cleethorpes, and other companies, although their stay has been short. After reconditioning they have moved to other depots within the company.

The Optare 'Solo' B30F midibuses first appeared in 1998. Wilts & Dorset was responsible for close liaison with Optare in the designing of these buses which have very low entrance steps, no interior steps and are designed to make the use of these vehicles easier for those with baby buggies, shopping trolleys and wheelchairs. Fitted with catalytic converters they are also environmentally friendly. The first vehicle delivered to Poole was No. 2602, R602 NFX, and with others was placed on the Poole bus station-Canford Heath services 155,156 and 157, a civic launch for the service being held on 20th May, 1998. On a later date a special launching ceremony took place at the Two Riversmeet Leisure Centre, Christchurch, when the buses were introduced on routes into that town. These vehicles are now to be found throughout the Wilts & Dorset network

In the early summer of 2000 the first low floor wheelchair-accessible Optare Spectras H50/28F entered service at Poole. An updated version of the previous model, these vehicles have the lowest entrance step of any double-deck in this country. During May 2000 four Optare Excel B43F single-decks Nos. 3601-3604, W601 PLJ-W604 PLJ, arrived at Poole.

Sadly in the early hours of Monday 13th November, 2000 an arsonist started a fire in the bus parking area at the rear of Poole bus station. The fire broke out in Optare Spectra double-deck No. 3121 (L121 ELJ) other vehicles also being destroyed, Optare Solo B30F No. 2650 (T650 AJT), Daf Ikarus B49F No. 3508

The Bristol VRT has been a faithful servant to many companies, Wilts & Dorset being no exception, including No. 4451 (KRU 851W) originally numbered 3451 seen here. This 21 year-old vehicle is now in the low mileage fleet, mainly employed on schools and works journeys. *B.L. Jackson*

For two seasons crew-operated open-top services returned to Sandbanks. Bristol FS6G 4001 (XSL 288A) waits to depart with service 152 for Poole on 29th August 1997. Having commenced life at Weston-super-Mare as *Western Pioneer* operating seafront services, and between 1992-1996 as *Nellie* running in conjunction with the Swanage Railwaythe vehicle is now with Scottish owners and has given 40 years service. *J.D. Ward*

Entering Poole bus station on 15th September, 1998 is No. 3509 (N15 WAL) a Daf Ikarus B49F vehicle new in 1996 to Wall of Manchester and acquired by Wilts & Dorset in January 1998. Sister vehicle No. 3508 was destroyed in the fire of November 2000.   *L. Ronan*

No. 3907 (A990 XAF) one of two Leyland Olympians purchased from North Devon in 1986, and converted to convertible open-top the following year, demonstrates its special suspension as it draws off the Sandbanks ferry on 29th July, 1999.   *J.D. Ward*

The scene at Poole following the fire of 13th November, 2000. Extreme left is damaged Bristol VRT 4423 (ELJ 215V) followed by Optare Spectra No. 3121 (L121 ELJ), Leyland coach A106 EPA of Levers; Daf Ikarus No. 3508 (N12 WAL), and coach B205 REL of Levers.   *Chris Harris*

No. 2664 (V664 DFX) one of the Optare Solos dedicated to the Canford Heath service arriving at Poole bus station in June 2001. Fitted with a low entrance and no interior steps they are ideal for the elderly and people with shopping trolleys, baby buggies and wheelchair users.   *B.L. Jackson*

(N12 WAL). Three coaches were also lost, Tiger Laser No. 3205, Tiger Plaxton No. 7042 (both on loan from associated company Levers Coaches of Fovant), and Leyland Leopard No. 9079. One other bus damaged was Bristol VR No. 4423 (ELJ 215V) but this was later repaired. However, thanks to the prompt action of some staff in removing buses to safety, the damage was minimised. Vehicles from other depots were sent to Poole and two additional Olympians, Nos. 214 and 222, BBW 214Y and CUD 222Y, both with two doors were hired from the Oxford Bus Company as extra services were required owing to the closure of the Sandbanks ferry for refit. Two further Optare Solos, Nos. 2687-2689, X678 XJT- X689 XJT, arrived in December as replacements.

By early 2001, all the early 23-seat Metroliners, having served the company well from 1987 onwards, had been withdrawn from service. Three further Optare Spectras H50/27F double-decks, 3169-3171, Y169 FEL-Y171 FEL, arrived at Poole in March 2001. As the company enters the new century, these vehicles clearly demonstrate the advances made in public transport since the first trams rumbled through the streets of Poole a century before.

Like all bus companies there is a constant need to update the fleet, the two chassis-builders that in turn were the backbone of both the old Hants & Dorset and Wilts & Dorset companies, Leyland and Bristol, have ceased production, their remaining numbers declining in the present fleet. Today the Optare is the mainstay of the fleet, Wilts & Dorset being the largest operator of Spectras in the country, and indeed the world!

Ironically, it has been announced that the Leyland Olympians are destined not to last long, proving expensive to operate as they get older, as a result the refurbished Bristol VRTs could remain in service for the next five years. To celebrate the tramway centenary, VRT No. 4422, ELJ 214V is being repainted in the blue and white tram livery, like the tram a reliable vehicle 100 years after its predecessor.

Poole Allocation May 2001

Optare Metro Rider B31F, 1993
2533, K533 UJT

Optare Metro Rider B31F, 1996
2542, N542 UFX. 2546-2547, N546 UFX-N547 UFX,
2370, F370 URU

Optare Solo B30F, 1998
2601-2613, R601 NFX-R613 NFX

Optare Solo B30F, 1999
2636-2649, T636 AJT-T649 AJT
2651-2670, V650 DFX-V670 DFX
2673-2676, V673 FEL-V676 FEL

Optare Solo B30F, 2000
2687-2688, X687 XJT-X688 XJT

Optare Spectra H48/29F, 1993
3101, K101 VLJ, 3118, L118 ALJ

Optare Spectra H48/29F, 1994
3122-3124, L122 ELJ-L124 ELJ

Optare Spectra H48/29F, 1995
3142-3144, M142 KRU-M144 KRU
3146, M146 KRU

DAF NCB Palatine H47/30F, 1995
Ex Wall, Manchester, 1995
3149, M18 WAL (Notes 5, 6)

Optare Spectra H50/28F, 2000
3165-3166, W165 RFX-W166 RFX

Optare Spectra H50/27F, 2001
3169-3171, Y169 FEL-Y171 FEL

Optare Delta B48F, 1993
3502-3503, L502 AJT-L503 AJT

*DAF Ikarus B49F *1995, 1996*
Ex Wall, Manchester, 1998
3507, N10 WAL*. 3509-3910, N15 WAL-N16 WAL

Optare Excel B43F
3601-3604, W601 PLJ-W604 PLJ

Poole Allocation May 2001 (continued)

No.	Reg No.	Chassis	Body	Type	Built	Acq.	Notes
4404	BFX 572T	Bristol VRT	ECW	H43/31F	3/79	3/79	
4407	BFX 575T	Bristol VRT	ECW	H43/31R	3/79	3/79	
4417	UDL 674S	Bristol VRT	ECW	H43/31R	5/78	4/79	1
4422	ELJ 214V	Bristol VRT	ECW	H43/31F	12/79	12/79	
4423	ELJ 215V	Bristol VRT	ECW	H43/31F	1/80	1/80	
4426	ELJ 218V	Bristol VRT	ECW	H43/31F	1/80	1/80	
4427	ELJ 219V	Bristol VRT	ECW	H43/31F	1/80	1/80	
4429	GEL 679V	Bristol VRT	ECW	H43/31F	2/80	2/80	
4437	GEL 687V	Bristol VRT	ECW	H43/31F	4/80	4/80	
4449	KRU 849W	Bristol VRT	ECW	H43/31F	11/80	11/80	
4450	KRU 850W	Bristol VRT	ECW	H43/31F	11/80	11/80	
4451	KRU 851W	Bristol VRT	ECW	H43/31F	12/80	12/80	4
4908	UWW 12X	Olympian	Roe	CO47/29F	3/82	6/87	2(a) 5 6
4912	EWW 80Y	Olympian	Roe	CO47/29F	3/83	6/87	2(b) 5 6
4920	A160 FPG	Olympian	Roe	H43/29F	6/84	6/90	3

Notes
1. Ex Southern Vectis No. 674.
2. Ex West Yorkshire PTE Nos. (a) 5012, (b) 5080.
3. Ex London Country Bus No. R60.
4. Permanent open-top.
5. Convertible open-top.
6. Suspension converted to operate Sandbanks ferry.

Service 147 is considered to be the oldest motorised established Stage Carriage route in the Country having started in September 1899 running from County Gates to Canford Cliffs. Today commencing from Gervis Place, Bournemouth, it is routed via Canford Cliffs Parade, Compton Acres, Lower Parkstone, and Park Gates East to Poole bus station. Although a vastly different scene from when the service was inaugurated, it has, like the old tram route from Poole to Christchurch, survived. Today the latter is still the main bus artery for the area, a century after the opening of the Poole & District tramway.

Optare Spectra H50/27F No. 3169 (Y169 FEL) was the latest acquisition to the Wilts & Dorset fleet when photographed in June 2001.   *B.L. Jackson*

Appendix One

Bere Regis & District Double-Deckers

It is impossible to detail the many vehicles used by Bere Regis & District on the Poole route over the years, however, the double-decks deserve recording because of their special interest.

Reg No.	Chassis	Chassis No.	Body	Type	Body No.	Built	Acquired	Sold
AFM 518	Leyland TD4c	10227	Massey	H28/24R	5952	5/36	3/46	12/58
AFM 519	Leyland TD4c	10228	Massey	H28/24R	5953	5/36	2/46	1/57
YG 710	Leyland TD2	1552	Leyland	H27/24R†		1932	2/48	12/52
CXX 289*	AEC Regent	06614536	LTPB	H30/26R		1936	1954	
DGX 288*	AEC Regent	06614686	LTPB	H30/26R		1936	1954	
BLH 793*	AEC Regent	06614976	LTPB	H30/26R			5/54	
FCG 526	Leyland PD1	460632	NCB	L29/26R		6/47	6/49	1960
FCG 527	Leyland PD1	460634	NCB	L29/26R		6/47	6/49	1960

Notes
* To date no photographic evidence of these vehicles being employed on the Poole service has appeared but vehicles included for completeness.
† At some stage rebodied as a C32R coach by Bere Regis & District.

Previous Owner
AFM 518 Chester Corporation No. 27.
AFM 519 Chester Corporation No. 28.
YG 710 Ripponden & District No. 10, 1934 to Halifax Joint Omnibus Committee No. 148. 7/36 to Western Scottish Motor Traction. 1948 to Bere Regis & District.
CXX 289 London Transport No. STL 1594.
DGX 286 London Transport No. STL 1744.
BLH 793 London Transport No. STL 737.
FCG 526 Hants & Sussex No. LD 55.
FCG 527 Hants & Sussex No. LD 56.

Disposal
AFM 518 Scrapped.
AFM 519 To Bere Regis AFC, later chicken shed at Bere Regis.
CXX 289 Scrapped by Bere Regis & District.
DGX 286 Scrapped by Bere Regis & District.
BLH 793 Scrapped by Bere Regis & District.
FCG 526 To Silentnight Barnoldswick, scrapped 10/64.
FCG 527 Scrapped by Bere Regis & District at Dorchester 11/60.

AFM 519 was a 1936 Leyland TD4c with a Massey H28/24R body, surviving with Bere Regis until scrapped in January 1957. *V. Jeffery Collection*

Almost a reflection on the early days of Hants & Dorset in Poole, this Leyland TD2 with Leyland L27/24R body was vintage when photographed at Kingland Road in June 1948. New in 1932 to Ripponden & District Motor Services as No. 10, two years later it passed with stage carriage services to Halifax Joint Omnibus Committee as No. 148. Sold again in July 1936 to Western Scottish where it remained until withdrawn in 1947, passing through two dealers before joining Bere Regis & District in February 1948. It was later rebodied with a second-hand 31-seat rear entrance coach body, being finally withdrawn in December 1952.   *A.B. Cross*

Waiting to depart from the Kingland Road stop in Poole for Bere Regis FCG 527 is a 1947 Leyland PD1 with a L29/26R NCB body.   *The late R.B. Gossling*

Badger-Vectis Poole Fleet

No.	Reg No.	Chassis	Body	Type	Old Co. No.	Notes
40	PDL 492H	Bristol RE	ECW	B49F	SV 851	
41	PDL 493H	Bristol RE	ECW	B49F	SV 862	
42	YHU 502J	Bristol RE	ECW	B53F	BL 1182	
43	YHY 585J	Bristol RE	ECW	B53F	BL 1205	
44	YHY 586J	Bristol RE	ECW	B53F	BL 1206	
45	YHY 596J	Bristol RE	ECW	B53F	BL 1216	
46	AHT 206J	Bristol RE	ECW	B53F	BL 1222	
47	TDL 566K	Bristol RE	ECW	B49F	SV 866	
48	TDL 567K	Bristol RE	ECW	B49F	SV 867	
49	TDL 565K	Bristol RE	ECW	B49F	SV 865	
50	TDL 568K	Bristol RE	ECW	B49F	SV 868	
51	DAO 294K	Bristol RE	ECW	B53F	BL 1261	7
52	EHU 377K	Bristol RE	ECW	B53F	BL 1276	1
53	EHU 381K	Bristol RE	ECW	B53F	BL 1280	1
54	EHU 383K	Bristol RE	ECW	B53F	BL 1286	1
55	EHU 390K	Bristol RE	ECW	B53F	BL 1296	
56	HHW 916L	Bristol RE	ECW	B53F	BL 1303	
57	HHW 919L	Bristol RE	ECW	B53F	BL 1306	
58	LHT 173L	Bristol RE	ECW	B53F	BL 1319	
59	MHW 285L	Bristol RE	ECW	B53F	BL 1325	1
60	OAE 954M	Bristol RE	ECW	B53F	BL 1332	
61	JEU 508N	Bristol LH6G	Plaxton	C49F	BL 2086	
62	JEU 509N	Bristol LH6G	Plaxton	C49F	BL 2084	
63	E932 KEU	Fiat	Robin Hood	MB19	BL 4932	
64	E937 KEU	Fiat	Robin Hood	MB19	BL 4937	
65	E938 KEU	Fiat	Robin Hood	MB19	BL 4938	
66	E939 KEU	Fiat	Robin Hood	MB19	BL 4939	
67	E940 KEU	Fiat	Robin Hood	MB19	BL 4940	
68	E942 KEU	Fiat	Robin Hood	MB19	BL 4942	
69	E943 LAE	Fiat	Robin Hood	MB19	BL 4943	
70	PPH 470R	Bristol VRT	ECW	H43/1F	BL 6509	
71	PPH 464R	Bristol VRT	ECW	H43/31F	BL 6503	
72	BNE 737N	Daimler F/L	NCB	H43/31F		2 (a)
73	WBN 978L	Leyland Atlantean	Park Royal	H43/32F		2 (b)
74	WBN 965L	Leyland Atlantean	Park Royal	H43/32F		2 (c)
80	FDV 793V	Bristol LHS	ECW	B35F	SV 200	3
81	KDL 204W	Bristol LHS	ECW	DP31F	SV 204	4
	WAE 187T	Bristol LH6L	ECW	B43F	BL 435	5
	AFB 594V	Bristol LH6L	ECW	B43F	BL 463	5
	LHT 170L	Bristol RE	ECW	B53F	BL 1316	6

Notes
1. To Poole Bay Services 4/88.
2. Ex Greater Manchester PTE Nos. (a)7421, (b)7100, (c)7087. Acquired 9/87.
3. On loan from Southern Vectis 10/87-3/88.
4. On loan from Southern Vectis 10/87-3/88. New to WNOC 1980 No. 1563, to Devon General 1/83 as No. 95. To SV 5/86.
5. On loan from Badgerline 3/9/87-24/9/87.
6. On loan from Badgerline 9/87-10/87.
7. New to Cumberland Motor Services No 294.

Acknowledgements

The authors wish to acknowledge the help, assistance and encouragement of many people including Roger Grimley for assistance on the Poole Independents, Peter Roberts for notes on the Rossmore Bus Company, A. Waller for assistance and permission to use material concerning Hants & Dorset tickets, P. Davies for advice and checking the Hants & Dorset vehicle histories, John Gillham provided the excellent route map of Poole & District Tramways, along with a photograph, the staff of Bournemouth and Poole Reference Libraries, the Dorset County Archivist's Office, Public Record Office, (Kew), Hampshire County Records Office, the National Motor Museum, Beaulieu, the National Tramway Museum, Crich, the PSV Circle, Wilts & Dorset Bus Company, and Mr Brian Walter. Acknowledgements are made to the following sources of information (including some official items): *Bus & Coach, Buses* (formerly *Buses Illustrated*), *Modern Transport, Passenger Transport, Tramway & Railway World, Buses Annual, Bournemouth Times, Bournemouth Evening Echo, Poole & Dorset Herald, Mates History of Bournemouth* and *Bus Business*. Various published works have been consulted including, *Hants & Dorset, A History*, Colin Morris; *Bus Operators, Hants & Dorset*, D. Fereday Glenn; *Hants & Dorset Fleet History, Part 1 & 2*, The PSV Circle; *The Tickets of Hants & Dorset Motor Services, Part 1 & 2*, Andrew Waller.

J. Bennett, D.M. Habgood, C. Harris, S. Hursthouse, C. Miles, G.A. Pryer, L. Ronan, and many others who often by supplying a snippet of information have helped to complete this complex history.

The copyright of the various photographers is acknowledged alongside the captions to the photographs. Where other sources have been used they have been acknowledged in the text.

Both authors are former professional busmen who have witnessed the changes in the industry over the years, some good, others open to question and others not so good. Therefore this book is dedicated to the tram and bus crews who over the years have provided essential services to the inhabitants of the Poole area.

C.G. Roberts, Lake, Isle of Wight
B.L. Jackson, Weymouth, Dorset
July 2001

The Wilts & Dorset fleet name as applied to vehicles in todays Wilts & Dorset fleet.

B.L. Jackson